Couchette #9

9A	9D
9B	9E
9C	9F

£20

£20

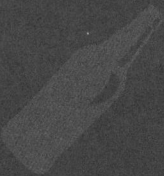

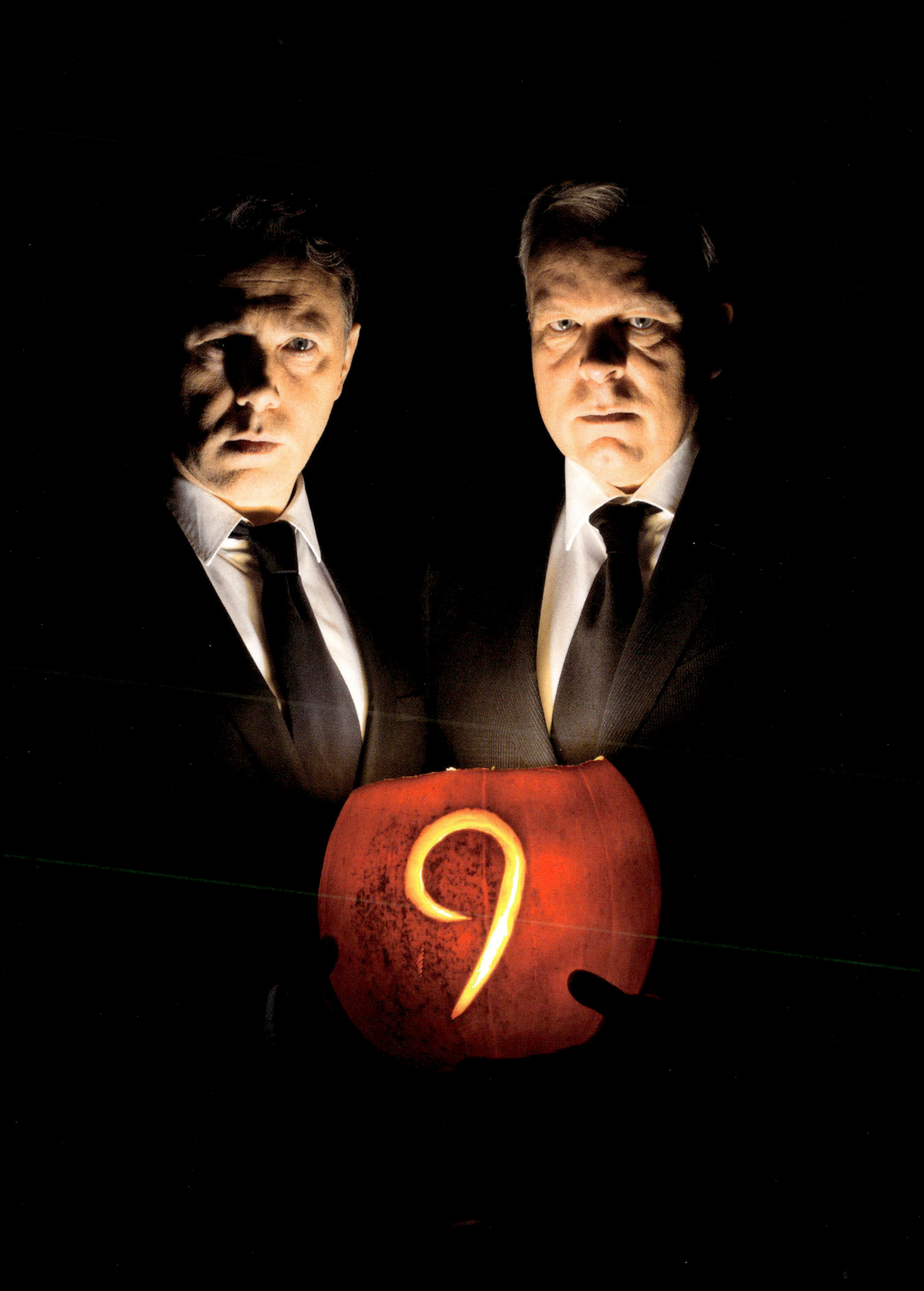

First published in Great Britain in 2021 by Hodder Studio
An Hachette UK company

3

Contributors:

Steve Pemberton
Reece Shearsmith
Adam Tandy
David Kerr
Guillem Morales

Simon Rogers
Christian Henson
Dan Zeff
Graeme Harper
Jim O'Hanlon

Amy Maguire
Matt Lipsey
Yves Barre

A CIP catalogue record for this title is available from the British Library

Hardback 9781529351262
eBook 9781529351248

Interiors designed by Amazing15
Colour Orgination by Alta London UK

Printed and bound in Germany by Mohn Media GmbH

The authorised representative in the EEA is Hachette Ireland,
8 Castlecourt Centre, Dublin 15, D15 XTP3, Ireland (email: info@hbgi.ie)

Hodder & Stoughton policy is to use papers that are natural, renewable and recyclable products and made from wood grown in sustainable forests. The logging and manufacturing processes are expected to conform to the environmental regulations of the country of origin.

Hodder & Stoughton Ltd
Carmelite House
50 Victoria Embankment
London EC4Y 0DZ
www.hodder-studio.com

THE INSIDER'S GUIDE TO

INSIDE NO. 9

BY

MARK SALISBURY

WITH

STEVE PEMBERTON & REECE SHEARSMITH

HODDER *studio*

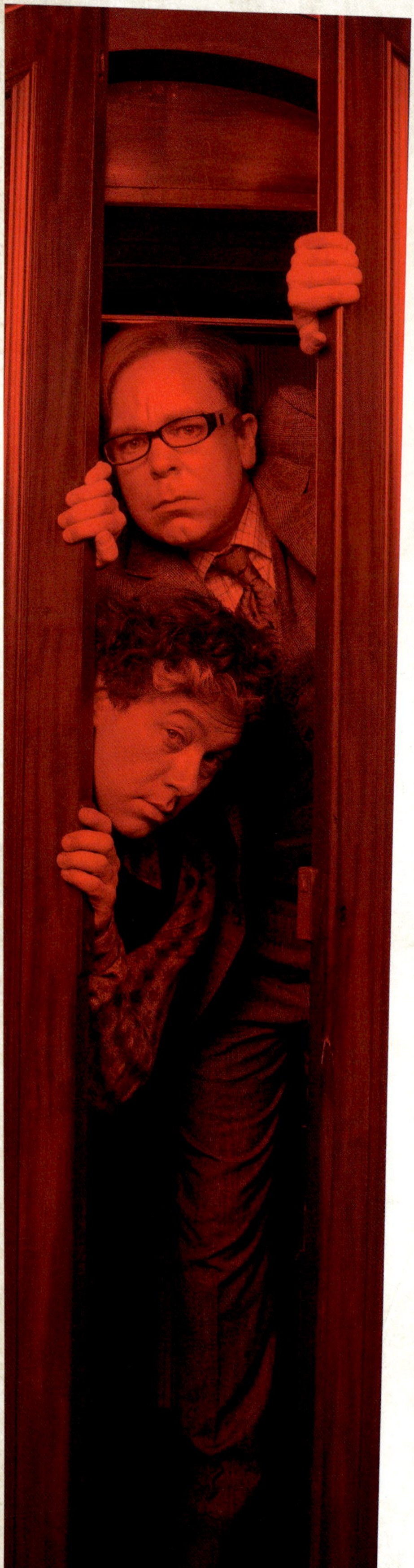
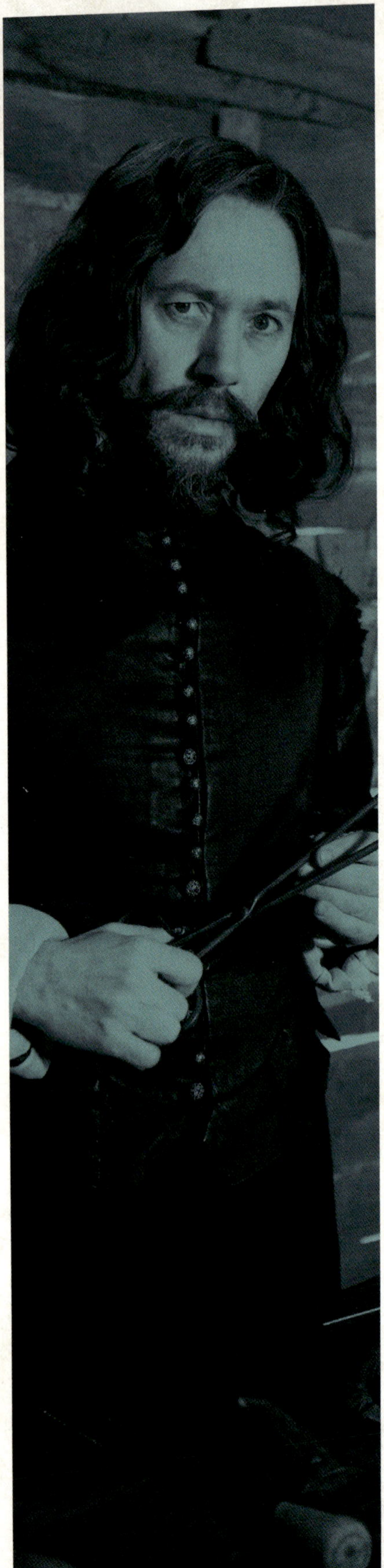
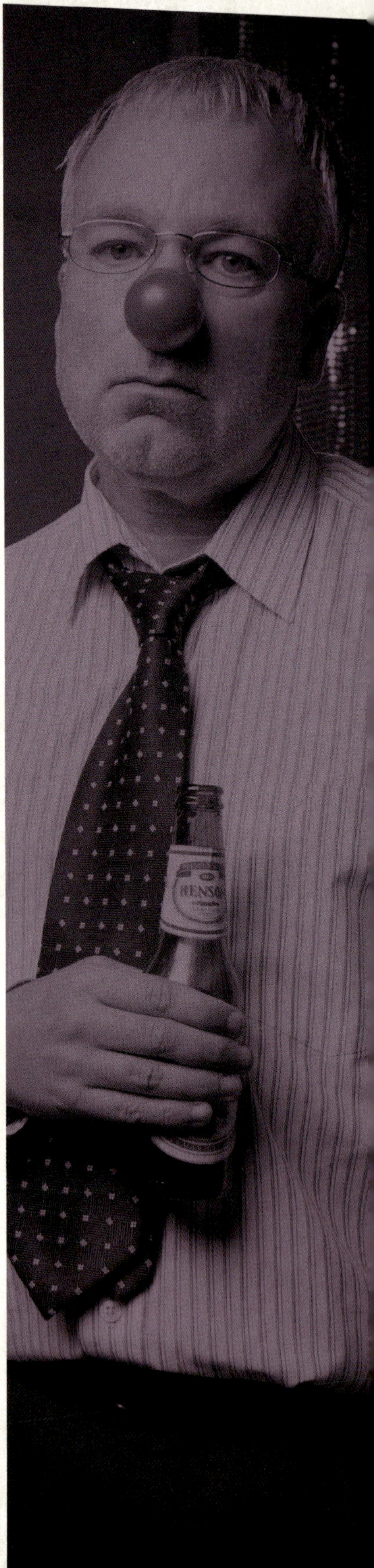

CONTENTS

Introduction....................6

SERIES ONE
'Sardines' 14
'A Quiet Night In' 24
'Tom & Gerri' 30
'Last Gasp' 38
'The Understudy' 44
'The Harrowing' 52

SERIES TWO
'La Couchette' 62
'The 12 Days of Christine' 72
'The Trial of Elizabeth Gadge' 80
'Cold Comfort' 90
'Nana's Party' 96
'Séance Time' 102

SERIES THREE
'The Devil of Christmas' 112
'The Bill' 122
'The Riddle of the Sphinx' 130
'Empty Orchestra' 136
'Diddle Diddle Dumpling' 142
'Private View' 148

SERIES FOUR
'Zanzibar' 156
'Bernie Clifton's Dressing Room' 164
'Once Removed' 170
'To Have and To Hold' 178
'And the Winner Is . . .' 186
'Tempting Fate' 192

Halloween Special: 'Dead Line' 198

SERIES FIVE
'The Referee's a W***er' 212
'Death Be Not Proud' 220
'Love's Great Adventure' 230
'Misdirection' 236
'Thinking Out Loud' 244
'The Stakeout' 250

Introduction

It was the morning of 7 September 2011 and Reece Shearsmith and Steve Pemberton were in a quandary. The pair had already started to formulate plans for a third series of their cult BBC Two dark comedy *Psychoville*, but were unsure whether the channel had any interest in continuing with it.

That afternoon they were scheduled to meet with Janice Hadlow, the controller of BBC Two, with the show's future on the line. 'They didn't say they wanted a third series,' recalls Reece, 'so we ended up going in to talk about the next thing, not knowing whether it was going to be *Psychoville 3* or whether they would say, "Oh, we don't want that any more." So, quickly, in the morning, we said to each other, "What shall we say if they say they don't want it?"'

'The feeling we had was they were looking for "big and funny",' says Steve. 'This was the quote we'd got from our agent. They're not necessarily looking for "more dark". But we were keen *Psychoville* wasn't a show that was cancelled. Equally, we didn't want to give up on *Psychoville*, if it had a chance.'

As soon as Hadlow started speaking, Shearsmith knew *Psychoville* was over. 'Because the first sentence was, "So guys, what's next?" And it was done and dusted in that moment,' he reveals. 'She didn't mean, "What's next for *Psychoville*?" She meant, "What's next?" Which was an amazing thing, because it propelled us into the next project with the BBC. So it was good we had something to come back with, even if it was just a vague idea.'

During the first series of *Psychoville*, the show's executive producer Jon Plowman had asked them to come up with an additional seventh episode, something cheaper, with no more than two or three characters, to sit in the middle of the run. It's what's known as a 'bottle episode' in the trade. They took Plowman's parameters as a challenge and set to work, with the remarkable 'Maureen and David' the result. While massively indebted to Alfred Hitchcock's 1948 psychological thriller *Rope*, itself based on a play by Patrick Hamilton, this now celebrated episode of *Psychoville* began (and ended) with a murder, was set entirely in one room, and, just like *Rope*, was purportedly shot in a single, unbroken take. (In actuality, it was two, as the camera dolly wouldn't hold its charge.) 'It was a challenge to write. And we had one day to rehearse and two days to film,' notes Reece. 'But everyone got very excited when, within three days, we had a whole half hour filmed and finished.'

For Shearsmith and Pemberton, 'Maureen and David' proved pivotal. 'I'm so glad we did it, because it gave us that discipline,' says Steve. 'And thank goodness we didn't have enough money, and budgets were tight, because if we hadn't had that experience of writing that episode, we wouldn't have gone in and pitched more of the same. So our next project grew organically from *Psychoville*, which is what was lovely, because *Psychoville* grew organically out of *The League of Gentlemen*.'

'That [episode] propelled us to think we could do a series of those type of things, where it's one set or one story. We wanted to do a *Tales of the Unexpected*-type series,' concurs Reece. 'And we had it in the back of our minds to say that when they asked, "What's next?" Then Janice said, "Have

NUMBER FIVE

52

No. 5

52

55

5

WELCOME

you read the works of Saki?" And we were like, "Yes." Although we hadn't. But her ears pricked up at the idea of these dark, little tales.'

'It wasn't very formulated, but we said, "We could call it *Happy Endings,* and they could be self-contained stories,"' continues Steve, who mentioned two ideas they had that might spark the basis of a story. 'I remembered a girl I'd seen on *Swap Shop* who collected air in jars from wherever she'd been, which eventually became "Last Gasp". And we'd seen two people on the tube once who were dressed identically, husband and wife, and they silently did this mime of getting an apple out. I think Janice was aware it hadn't been done in a long time, this idea of self-contained short stories, so the result of that meeting was they said, "Go away and write two episodes." Kudos to Janice Hadlow; she saw the potential. And to Jon Plowman for getting us in that meeting and saying, "Shall we commission two?" We'd delivered *The League of Gentlemen* and *Psychoville* by this stage, so they trusted us to get on with it.'

ABOVE: Reece and Steve toyed with a few different numbers and names before settling on *Inside No. 9.* Here, a sketch in one of Steve's notebooks shows an earlier iteration: *Number 5.*

ABOVE: A page from producer Adam Tandy's notebook shows doodles and ideas for the opening credits.

Television anthology series such as *Tales of the Unexpected, Thriller, Beasts, Armchair Theatre* and *Hammer House of Horror* are often mentioned as having inspired *Inside No. 9*. Yet as far as Pemberton and Shearsmith are concerned, their two biggest influences were Alan Bennett's series of dramatic monologues, *Talking Heads,* and the BBC's flagship single-drama series, *Play for Today,* which ran from 1970 to 1984. 'That's the one I remember really loving,' says Steve of the latter. 'The stuff by Mike Leigh, Alan Bennett and Jack Rosenthal was a major influence.'

Nowadays, anthologies are on every television channel or streaming service. Back in 2011, there were none. Neither the first series of Ryan Murphy and Brad Falchuk's *American Horror Story* nor Charlie Brooker's *Black Mirror,* a technology-based anthology with which *Inside No. 9* is often erroneously compared, had yet to air. Despite the influence and legacy of American anthology shows such as *The Twilight Zone, The Outer Limits* and *Alfred Hitchcock Presents...,* as well as the aforementioned *Tales of the Unexpected, Thriller, Armchair Theatre* and *Beasts,* the perceived wisdom among television executives had long been that audiences weren't interested in anthologies. 'We were told all through *League* and *Psychoville,* "No one wants to watch a thing where you've got to start again at the beginning the following week,"' sighs Reece. '"You'll lose your audience. No one has the intention to return if you're not invested in the characters." That was the given for many years. And so to suddenly have an anthology show was great.'

Still, the pair had other commitments that prevented them from starting immediately. Pemberton was filming his ITV series *Whitechapel*, then both men were due to star in West End theatre productions — Pemberton in Oliver Goldsmith's *She Stoops to Conquer* and Shearsmith in Alan Ayckbourn's *Absent Friends* — meaning they couldn't start writing until spring 2012. Not that the pair had very much of anything in mind beyond their two embryonic notions. 'We've never been ones for doing pitches. Very often commissioners want to see two sides of A4, to show what the idea is,' reflects Steve. 'That's the most awful thing to do, I think, because as you're working, things occur to you and it changes and you grow with the idea. We are very fortunate we were trusted to go away and write two scripts. But it was by no means a *fait accompli* they would give us a commission for a series.'

The first episode they wrote would eventually become series two's 'Nana's Party', while the second, 'Tom & Gerri', was based on a play that was written while they were on the dole in the nineties. 'One was a lot darker, the other more sitcom-friendly, and the note came back that Janice loved the darker story, and loved what we'd done with the family party, and did we want to spin that off into its own sitcom?' says Steve. 'Suddenly we were being offered two series. At one time we would have gone, "Yeah and yeah." But the point of writing a self-contained story is you can bring it to an end, whereas a sitcom has to restart every week and we really didn't want to do that. We wanted you to not know where it was going, and not know if the characters were going to live or die. So we put "Nana's Party" to one side to focus on these single stories. That's when it was commissioned as six and we had to come up with five more.'

But once again, the boys were busy with other commitments. 'We wrote quite sporadically and when we could,' says Steve. 'I was going to do [ITV sitcom] *Benidorm* in the summer and started on the "Last Gasp" idea while Reece worked on "The Harrowing". So we developed those separately, but came together to write. One was Gothic horror and the other completely suburban, so we started to get excited about the contrasts we were developing.'

'The constraints were: once you enter a place you never leave it,' states Reece. 'That's a restrictive way to work, but we were aware it was only six. We were also aware of trying to do a funny one, which is where "A Quiet Night In" came from. So it was about getting the six right. That was the next thing, and there was time to do that.'

They ditched the working title *Happy Endings* when they realised there was a death in every

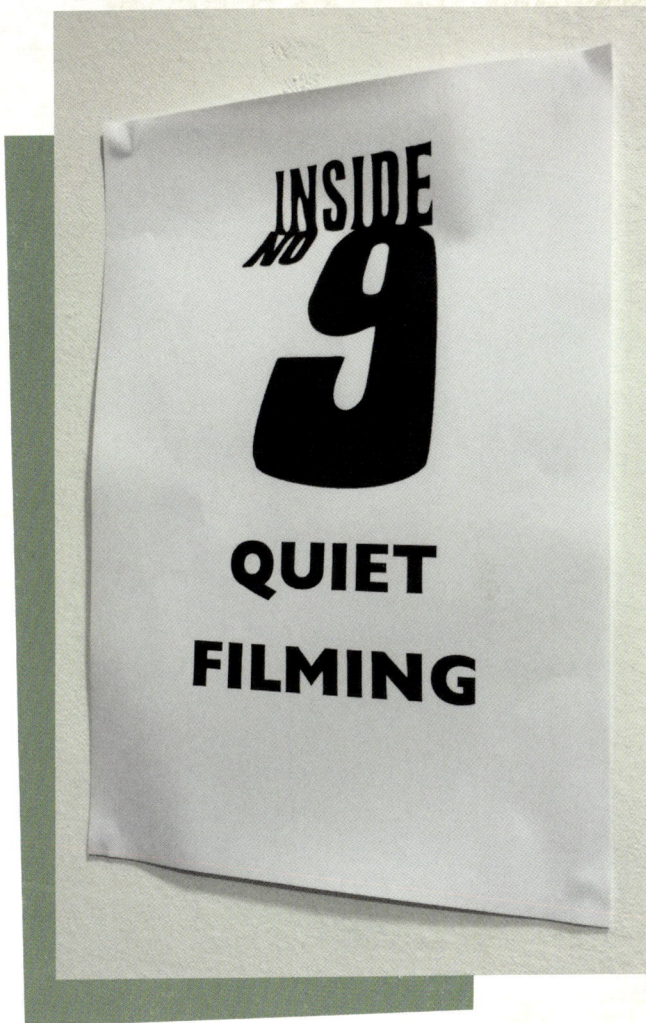

episode, and focused in on finding the right title and a way of tying them all together. Eventually, they hit upon the idea of a number as the link.

Then the question became: which number?

'It was born out of sitting there going, *No. 1*? No. *No. 2*? No. *No. 3*? No,' recalls Reece. 'We called it *No. 9*. Then *Inside No. 9*.'

'It was the alliteration,' says Steve.

With *Psychoville* producer Justin Davies having left the BBC for pastures new, Jon Plowman asked Adam Tandy to step in and produce *Inside No. 9* for him. A hugely experienced film and television producer who had worked on *The Thick of It*, *Come Fly with Me* and *Detectorists*, Tandy had also been a production executive on the first series of *The League of Gentlemen* and would go on to become a key creative component of the new show. 'Jon had a schedule clash and didn't have anybody to produce *Inside No. 9*, which might have been called *Happy Endings* or *Curtains* at that point,' recalls Tandy. 'He asked whether I'd be prepared to produce the first three episodes. The first three were going to be hived off because Reece and Steve had some availability issues, so we knew we had to shoot three first, then shoot another three the following summer. And I thought, "That'll fit in very nicely at the end of *The Thick of It*." I was very pleased to do it.

'Reading the scripts, you realised this was going to be a quality production and needed a lot of care to make it right,' Tandy continues. 'I felt it was important, given the range of the things they were trying to tackle, that you couldn't have a house style. Very early on I said, "The house style is there is no house style." So the main thing I wanted to make sure was, whatever we did, each of the episodes felt like its own thing. There is an argument that, if you had all the money in the world, you would get separate directors and separate production teams to make them as singles. But we didn't have that ability, financially. We only had sitcom money, so we had to make it fit into a BBC Two budget. So sets were paired up and cannibalised.'

With the accomplished television director David Kerr – whose credits included Channel 4's hit comedy *Fresh Meat* and the BBC's *That Mitchell and Webb Look* – already on board to helm the entire series, Tandy's first big decision was to choose which three were to be shot from the six scripts Pemberton and Shearsmith had delivered. 'We chose to go with "Tom & Gerri", then "Last Gasp" and, finally, "Sardines". But there were practical reasons for that. Knowing we were going to shoot both "Sardines" and "Tom & Gerri" on sets, we needed something we could shoot on location, and "Last Gasp" has a very ordinary suburban setting. That felt like that could be the middle episode of three.'

ABOVE: The cover of producer Adam Tandy's budget notebook for series five.

RIGHT: Steve and Reece in costume as witchfinders Clarke and Warren in 'The Trial of Elizabeth Gadge', series two.

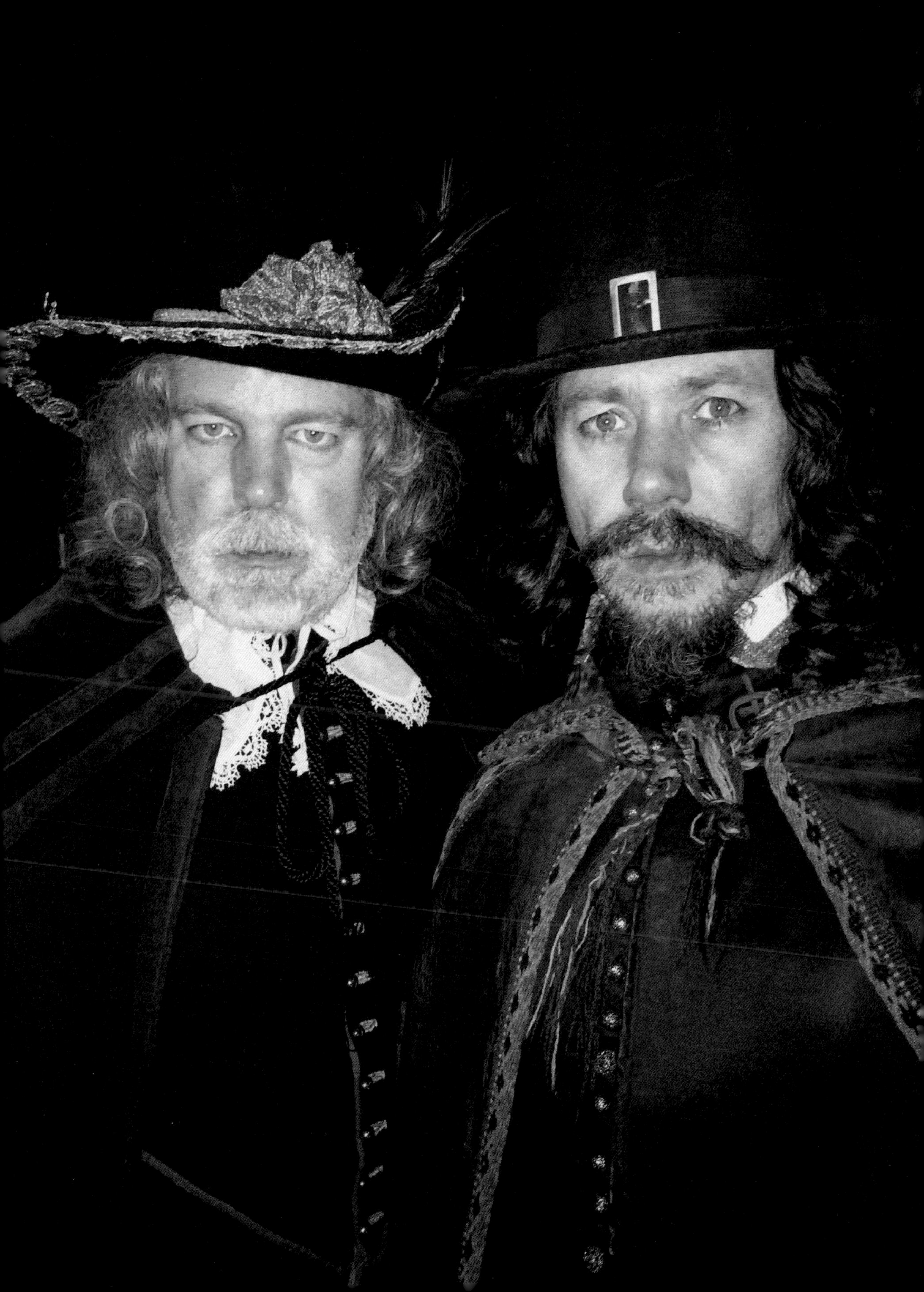

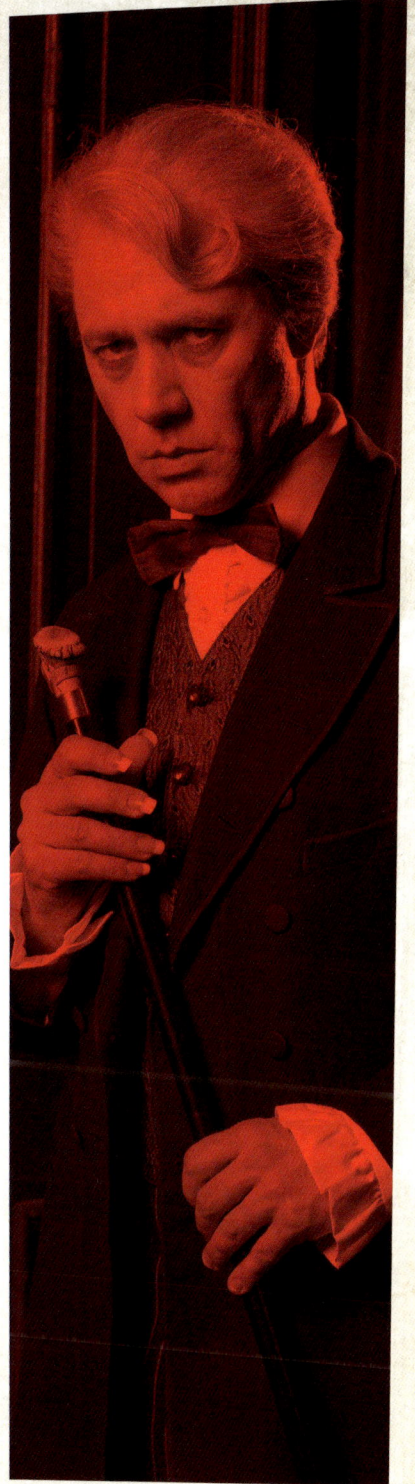

SERIES ONE

KATHERINE PARKINSON

TIM KEY

LUKE PASQUALINO

STEVE PEMBERTON

REECE SHEARSMITH

OPHELIA LOVIBOND

SARDINES

INSIDE NO 9

ANNE REID

JULIAN RHIND-TUTT

ANNA CHANCELLOR

MARC WOOTTON

BEN WILLBOND

TIMOTHY WEST

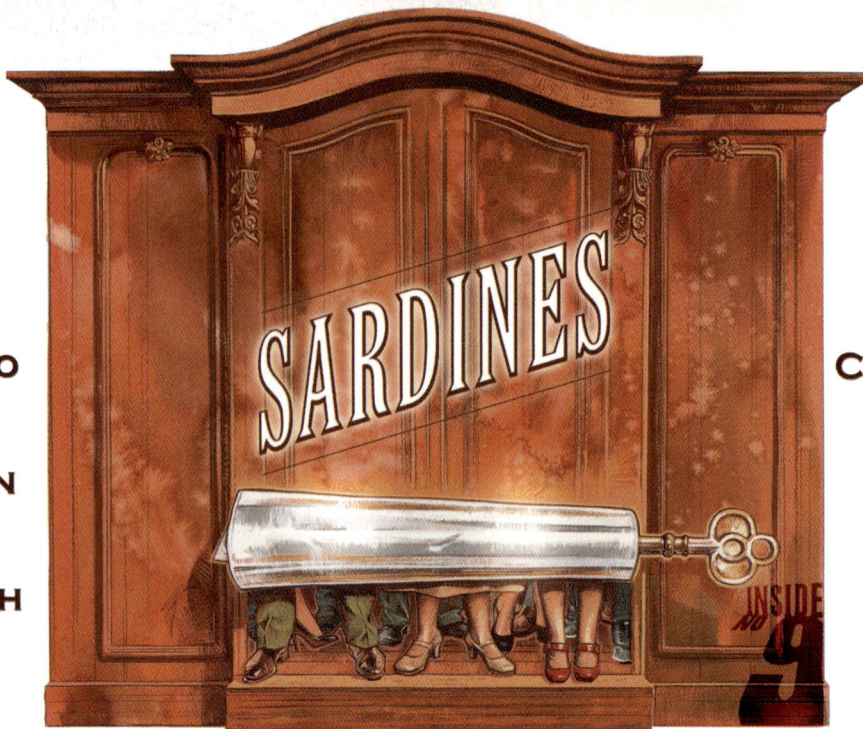

BBC TWO PRESENTS A BBC COMEDY PRODUCTION AN INSIDE NO. 9 FILM "SARDINES" KATHERINE PARKINSON TIM KEY LUKE PASQUALINO STEVE PEMBERTON REECE SHEARSMITH OPHELIA LOVIBOND ANNE REID JULIAN RHIND-TUTT ANNA CHANCELLOR MARC WOOTTON BEN WILLBOND TIMOTHY WEST

BBC TWO

SCREENPLAY BY STEVE PEMBERTON & REECE SHEARSMITH EXECUTIVE PRODUCER JON PLOWMAN PRODUCED BY ADAM TANDY DIRECTED BY DAVID KERR

Sardines

- Series **1**
- Episode **1**
- Directed by **David Kerr**

ABOVE: A unique poster is created for every episode of *Inside No. 9*. The poster for 'Sardines' was designed by Graham Humphreys.

A dark and perversely comic caper culminating in a sting-in-the-tail twist that would become synonymous with the show, 'Sardines' was the perfect opening episode of *Inside No. 9*. Based around a Victorian parlour game that's a variation of hide and seek – a game both Shearsmith and Pemberton had played as children – 'Sardines' was also partly inspired by a large wooden wardrobe that used to be at one end of the room the pair rent as their office. As they were brainstorming potential ideas, they began thinking about an entire family hiding inside the wardrobe and quickly realised it was the perfect hook on which to hang a story.

'We didn't know where it was going; we didn't even have the conceit of what the episode was. But we thought it was going to be fun seeing all these people crammed into the tightest space you could imagine,' begins Steve. 'Sometimes we just have to find the hook that makes us want to write. Then the ending will come. We decided on some kind of family celebration and settled on an engagement party.'

'Sardines' is set mostly inside a spacious walnut wardrobe, in the guest bedroom of a country pile, on the occasion of the engagement of Rebecca (Katherine Parkinson) and Jeremy (Ben Willbond), a celebration attended by assorted family and friends. The episode begins with Rebecca searching the bedroom and its en suite for other guests, opening the wardrobe and finding Ian (Tim Key), a colleague of her fiancé, already inside. As per the rules of the game, Rebecca joins him. Eventually, all the remaining eleven guests are squashed in. But Ian isn't who he says he is. And the game ends with Ian, real name Pip, locking the doors, dousing the wardrobe with lighter fuel, and setting it alight; his revenge for the horrific abuse he suffered as a boy at the hands of Rebecca's father, Andrew (Timothy West).

The game itself provided them with an easy plot structure. 'Often with writing, if you can parcel out how to tell the story, it makes it easier,' notes Reece. 'So the notion of beginning with one person in the wardrobe and another arriving every two minutes was very appealing.'

'The first thing we did was make a list of characters,' continues Steve. 'It said: "Rebecca really wants this game to work. She's the head girl type, holding it all together." "Stinky John, friend from college who smells." We'll then give each character one trait that you can start off with. "Ian, a boring man who bores everyone he's with." We'll give everyone one thing to hit. And that's your first draft. Then you try to make it more complex, so a character who seems very confident and outspoken can have a moment when a very quiet thing happens. We've done that since *League of Gentlemen*, looking to create three-dimensional characters. So Stinky John appears to be this joke, but he's the tragic heart of the whole thing.'

Only once they've completed a first draft will the boys do a 'comedy pass'. 'It's, "What's the funny thing we can inject that gives it the slightly comedic spin?"' says Reece. 'But it is the last thing we worry about, unless we sit down to go, "Let's think of a funny idea," which is crippling in itself.'

Their original draft ended with all twelve characters packed inside and someone saying, 'We're all here. No one's looking for us now.' They sent it to Jon Plowman, whose immediate reaction was: 'Great

ABOVE: Steve and Reece as Carl and Stuart, two of the participants in this ill-fated game of sardines.

setting, great characters, really funny. But it's missing *something*,' and, somewhat surprisingly, pushed them to make it darker. 'Plowman said, "Could they not all burn to death in the end?"' remembers Reece. 'We thought, "This is what you said you didn't want! You wanted a funnier one!" So we went back and very lightly sketched in the horror of this past historical abuse with the dad.'

'If you ask Reece and Steve for something darker, you will get it,' laughs director David Kerr. 'You might regret asking, because they certainly deliver.'

Rereading the script, Reece and Steve discovered it only required minor tweaking to turn it into something altogether more disturbing. Suddenly, a throwaway remark about carbolic soap took on an ominous meaning, and became the catalyst for a story about infidelity, incest and child abuse. 'They talk about Stinky John before we meet him, saying, "Something must have happened to him; he stopped washing." That was already in the script, although we had no sense it was anything to do with abuse. It just took changing the odd line and everything was terribly sinister,' says Steve.

'It suddenly elevated it into something else,' adds Reece. 'And we've found that without this extra element that gives it a graver or bolder meaning, the scripts seem a bit frivolous. Totally serviceable, but they need that extra thing to become a bit meatier.'

'It was very carefully crafted in terms of tone,' notes Tandy. 'It may feel like an Edwardian comedy at times, almost a farce, but there's always that dark undercurrent. Because the whole thing is set in a guest room, which has been used as a box room for people's memories, which is exactly where they don't want to be. They don't want to be in a place that reminds them of that bathroom, where the carbolic soap is.'

'I wanted it to creep up on people,' says Kerr. 'I wanted to lull people into a feeling of watching a light comedy, then spring it on them, almost before they realise it, what's going on beneath that genteel surface. Obviously, it's an old-fashioned game. But I wanted it to feel like a classic gathering, in a very English country house setting, so it's subliminally tapping into all that Agatha Christie-type murder-mystery stuff.'

Heading up the starry ensemble of 'Sardines' was Katherine Parkinson, whose TV credits included *The IT Crowd* and *Doc Martin*. 'Katherine is a remarkable actress,' says Kerr, who directed her in the BBC comedy series *Whites*. 'She's incredibly smart and her instinct for line readings is amazing. But her physical comedy is great. She can also play wounded pride brilliantly, which is important to Rebecca. There's so much vulnerability in that character. And yet she's got this carapace of strength and togetherness.'

ABOVE: As the wardrobe becomes uncomfortably crowded, Reece's acid-tongued Stuart elects to hide under the bed.

Rachel: Oh. Right. So when does the game start?
Rebecca: This is the game, Rachel. We're playing it.

Parkinson was also a massive fan of *The League of Gentlemen* and had written to Pemberton and Shearsmith years earlier to say she would do anything in everything they ever wrote. 'Very often people say that,' laughs Steve. 'But we'd written this tiny character in *Psychoville*, who runs a cryogenic clinic. It was six or seven lines, and Katherine came in and did it, and we were like, "Oh, you meant it then?" So we knew she would get the comedy of it. But you're always looking for people who have dramatic skills as well.'

In contrast, comedian Tim Key, who plays the seemingly tedious Ian, was both a TV novice and a late bit of casting. 'We'd been thinking about someone else who pulled out,' reveals Tandy. 'But once we thought of Tim, it was obvious it was going to be him.'

'We really pushed for him because he wasn't very well known, which was good for the character. We did talk about some more established actors, but I'd loved *Cowards*, the sketch show he was in,' says Steve. 'We knew he'd be perfect as this anonymous character in the corner. But also be very funny. He was a revelation,' adds Reece.

'Don't underestimate how difficult it is to make a character who's meant to be dull, interesting to watch,' insists Kerr. 'It takes a great actor to sustain your interest in someone who's meant to be annoying, and the kind of person you don't really want to be stuck with in a wardrobe. And that's what you see written all over Katherine's character's face. Tim brought all those little details like the breathing, the clearing of his throat, and that sense of space invasion you get from someone who is making your flesh creep. Rebecca was such an uptight character anyway; it felt like a really great dynamic.'

ABOVE: Newly engaged couple Jeremy and Rebecca (Ben Willbond and Katherine Parkinson) are just two of the characters who find their relationship becoming strained during their time hiding in the increasingly cramped wardrobe.

Come the twist, however, Kerr needed the audience (and those remaining in the wardrobe) to forget Ian was even there. 'I shifted the focus on to Rebecca, then Reece and Steve's characters, and all of the other relationships that draw you in, and make you less conscious of his presence, because it was very important he should recede, and literally become part of the furniture.'

Next to enter the wardrobe are Rebecca's uptight brother Carl (Pemberton) and his partner Stuart (Shearsmith). 'You could say my portrayal of Stuart as a really outrageous camp man is a very two-dimensional, first-thought idea,' reflects Reece, 'but I feel we

TOP: To make shooting in such a cramped space possible, production designer Tom Sayer built two wardrobes, one for the interior scenes and one for the shots of characters climbing in and out.

ABOVE: Holes cut in the top of the wardrobe created a dappled light.

write a very believable couple in that wardrobe. There was a line we cut for length, when it got really awful, where Stuart shouts across to Carl at the other end of the wardrobe, "Sorry if I embarrassed you in front of your family." It's a really tender moment between them, and he said, "No. Quite the opposite." Hopefully that's a level of understanding that doesn't leave you thinking they're a very two-dimensional couple.'

Carl and Stu are swiftly followed by Ophelia Lovibond's scatty Rachel, Jeremy's ex, for whom he still carries a torch; Anne Reid's Geraldine, the family's former nanny who thinks she's been invited as a guest when, in fact, they want her to serve drinks; Anna Chancellor and Julian Rhind-Tutt as upper-middle-class couple Mark and Elizabeth; Luke Pasqualino as Rachel's roofer boyfriend Lee; Marc

Wootton as Stinky John; and Ben Willbond as Rebecca's fiancé.

'Reece and Steve know how to write smaller characters very vividly,' says Kerr. 'They know what it takes to make those relatively small-on-the-page parts feel incredibly satisfying for an actor. So we've never had difficulty getting people to come and play them, because they can see, even though the word count might not be massive, that there's a huge opportunity to do something with those characters.'

And, finally, the last to enter is Timothy West's abusive patriarch. West had narrated an Arthur Ransome documentary Kerr had directed years earlier, but, more thrillingly for the boys, he had starred in the classic 'Royal Jelly' episode of *Tales of the Unexpected*.

As the characters squeeze inside the wardrobe, the tension and black comedy continues to mount, with the razor-sharp script wringing every uncomfortable ounce out of the increasingly awkward situation, as siblings bicker and pick over old psychological wounds, lovers engage in passive-aggressive behaviour, and others lower the tone with scatological outbursts or sexual innuendo. 'There is a very acute sense of social observation. Almost like a Martin Parr eye on some of those details,' says Kerr. 'The subtlety of perceptions of class is something Reece and Steve tap into beautifully in the writing, and we tried to cast with an eye to that. They're all slightly heightened, but not to a level of grotesquery that draws you out of the story.'

With Pemberton and Shearsmith's regular costume designer Yves Barre unavailable to work on the first series, Kerr drafted in June Nevin, who had collaborated with him on *Fresh Meat*. 'I loved her use of surprising details, bold colours, and the way she could define characters with costume, and on "Sardines" she came up with some very clearly defined looks that helped you key into characters quickly,' says Kerr. 'There's so much you can read into the dress Rebecca is wearing, almost like a set of curtains and a little gaudy, in that way of the upper-middle class. Or the slightly shiny look Lee has. He could be in a nightclub as easily as he could be at this engagement party. Then you've got the flamboyant Stu, who clearly wants to outrage, so why would he have something understated? Yet with

BELOW LEFT: Elevation sketches of the wardrobe created by production designer Tom Sayer show plans for different angles and removable panels for camera traps.

BELOW: The finished wardrobe, ready for its occupants.

Carl, there's a repressed quality in his buttoned-up suits. Seeing those two side by side, you witness two very different aspects of personality, one declaring, "I'm open, I'm loud, listen to me." The other: "I'm closed, back off, and I'm probably messed up."' Nevin also incorporated smaller, subtler details in the costumes, such as the fish on West's tie. 'She gave us all jewel colours — emeralds, violets and deep reds — so there was a sense that everyone belonged,' says Steve.

As for the wardrobe, Tandy knew it would be difficult to shoot inside a real one. 'You were never going to get all the angles, and you had these shots from within, looking out. But you also have these very long scenes inside with the doors shut.'

The answer was to have production designer Tom Sayer build two wardrobes on a soundstage at Wimbledon Studios, cannibalising parts of the apartment he had built for 'Tom & Gerri', which was filmed first. One was used for all the scenes inside when the doors are shut. A second was for all the comings and goings, as characters step in and out of the wardrobe. The latter was made of French walnut and originally belonged to the French ambassador in London. The art department bought it from eBay, gutted it, removed its back, then extended the depth by eight inches, before giving it a new back. A duplicate was then made of the interior, 'so you weren't matching to the original, you were matching to the thing we bastardised,' says Tandy. This one was a breakaway set, with removable walls to allow Kerr to put his camera inside.

To help light the interior — look closely and you may see a manufacturers' label crediting its construction to the Number Nine Joinery — Kerr had Sayer cut out a series of small ceiling holes. 'In comedy there's a tendency to turn all the lights on because people might not get the joke if they don't see it. I wanted to be much more specific about what people could see at any moment in time,' he explains. 'So I loved the idea of creating these little cracks, where the light could float through.' Kerr was inspired by a scene in *L.A. Confidential* where a character is watching from a wardrobe. 'Similarly there's a moment in *Blue Velvet* where you have a chink of light hitting a character's eyes and it tells you all you need to know.'

'It was a really good call, because it meant, instead of just being in gloom, you could move people very slightly in shot and they would come in and out of light,' says Tandy. 'It required precision acting

ABOVE: From left to right: Lee (Luke Pasqualino), Ian (Tim Key), Rachel (Ophelia Lovibond), Mark (Julian Rhind-Tutt), Geraldine (Anne Reid), Elizabeth (Anna Chancellor) and Rebecca (Katherine Parkinson).

from the cast in terms of their marks. But it absolutely worked in terms of being able to give you composition, with light and shade, within the wardrobe.'

Filming in two wardrobes required much planning, with Kerr and director of photography Stephan Pehrsson having to break down the script to work out which elements were going to be shot on what set. 'Sometimes we would run the action in the main set, then pick it up in the adjoining set,' says Kerr. 'My task was to make those two sets feel seamless, so no one would be aware of the conceit and the trickery. I had faith in not needing to jump outside the wardrobe more than we needed to. And typically, that's when a new character arrives.'

Confinement is, of course, a major component of *Inside No. 9*, but perhaps none more so than 'Sardines'. Kerr chose to shoot with wide-angle lenses, either an 18mm or 21mm, and keep the camera close to the actors' faces. 'Claustrophobic intensity was key. I wanted the audience to feel they could experience that as subjectively as possible, so you felt like you were in the wardrobe with them. Very close eye lines. The characters almost looking at you. So you feel the closeness of the space,' says Kerr. He took inspiration from the 2010 film *Buried*, with Ryan Reynolds. 'That movie sustained all of its running time with him inside a coffin lit by a Zippo, then his phone. I felt that was a good example

ABOVE: Once 'Stinky' John (Marc Wootton) enters the wardrobe, the tension becomes unbearable – as does the smell.

12/2/13 "Sardines" Dubbing notes

music sync
39" shared music.

1'48' creak!   4'37"   5'56"   8'24?   13'53'

2'44"

7'13 add creak on Rebecca.

purring   art creaks getting in

9'55 Rebecca too probed.   Lee/Beth?

10'15 creaks - exit

11'08 wind??

13'55 creaks getting in   13'31

13'31 creaks x (dust?)

13'53 big creak (Ian)
14'18 little creak (Rachel)

14'49 creak (Rebecca)

15'20 crows!
15'45 creaks (PoV)

16'05 creak (Martin to Geraldine)
16'15 crows (Rector to Geraldine)

17'22 creaks (footsteps, Elizabeth)

19'26 burn me (clearer?)

19'42 creaks / footsteps)

20'14 push dialogue (pull music?)

21'40 push back on guitar(s) a toot.

22'15 creaks.

23'41 foley?

24'16 creak too discrete / overlapping creaks

creak level lower generally.

27'00 music lower

22'28 creak in gap.

28'22 push dialogue. (music lower)

of how you could keep the pressure up, without letting it release by having lots of exterior shots.'

'We never wanted to cheat and be outside the wardrobe looking in, so it looks like doors are off,' concurs Reece. 'We wanted to really be in tight with them, so you never felt like you were off the hook.'

Before filming, most productions typically stage a read-through of the script with the cast and crew. This is an opportunity for actors to run the lines and to provide a guestimate of the episode's length. Occasionally there will also be rehearsals for the director and cast to work out action and performance, known as blocking. 'There wasn't an awful lot of blocking to do in this that we couldn't do on the day,' says Tandy, 'so we didn't do a full rehearsal. What we did need to know was whether all twelve people could get into the wardrobe. We'd worked it out, obviously, but thought if people aren't expecting how tight it's going to be, it could be a disaster. And it was fine.'

During the read-through, the episode timed out at twenty-two minutes, seven less than required. Not that anybody was unduly concerned, as so much of the drama and comedy would arise through meaningful looks and glances between the characters. 'Because you can't say a line and move, or move and say a line, you have to do it with your eyes,' says Tandy. 'Obviously if you don't shoot them, you can't put them into the edit, so the looks were included in the schedule as part of the daily coverage. But they all had to be done quickly and specifically, because you can't shoot twelve looks from everybody, at the end. So, in the edit, we put in a sound of someone shifting uncomfortably. In other words, they're reacting *internally*. The other thing we did was spend an entire day in the dub, adding little creaks, as people shift their weight.'

Since 'Sardines' was shot in chronological order, only Parkinson and Key were required for the

ABOVE: Adam Tandy's dubbing notes for this episode show the attention to detail, with every single creak and shuffle adding to the feeling of claustrophobia.

RIGHT, TOP: The cast relaxing between takes.

RIGHT, BOTTOM: Labelled water bottles from the set.

full five days. Some were needed for two; Willbond and West just one. 'Part of the joy of the way it was structured was that every day you'd have somebody new joining the wardrobe, on the set, as well as in the story,' enthuses Kerr. 'The actors loved it, too. It was like, "Oh brilliant. We've got Anna Chancellor coming tomorrow."'

'There was an almost theatre troupe sense of camaraderie,' notes Kerr. 'A lot of the time *Inside No. 9* resembles theatre, sometimes very overtly, and there is that sense of a company coming together to put on a show, on a stage almost, because it's a very contained setting.'

'It was a little circle that started with two chairs, then there was four, then six,' recalls Steve. 'And then on the last day you've got Tim West coming in. There was a great, convivial atmosphere. These actors loved working on it, because you can imagine the anecdotes going round. Everyone wanted to carry on at the end of the week. We've had this experience on almost every episode, where the guest cast come in and want to keep going. So while this one had a very dark subject matter, there was a really nice atmosphere.'

A QUIET NIGHT IN

BBC TWO PRESENTS A BBC COMEDY PRODUCTION AN INSIDE NO. 9 FILM "A QUIET NIGHT IN" STEVE PEMBERTON REECE SHEARSMITH DENIS LAWSON OONA CHAPLIN JOYCE VEHEARY KAYVAN NOVAK SCREENPLAY BY STEVE PEMBERTON & REECE SHEARSMITH EXECUTIVE PRODUCER JON PLOWMAN PRODUCED BY ADAM TANDY DIRECTED BY DAVID KERR

BBC TWO

A Quiet Night In

- Series **1**
- Episode **2**
- Directed by **David Kerr**

Pemberton and Shearsmith had toyed with writing an all-silent episode as far back as series one of *Psychoville*, but decided against it because they had too many jokes. But the itch to tell a mostly dialogue-free story remained strong, even if they weren't sure they could keep it up for an entire episode.

'We didn't put pressure on ourselves that it all had to be non-verbal,' says Steve of the process that eventually led to 'A Quiet Night In'. 'And we didn't want to do a spoof either. It was really the notion of wanting to do something where people *couldn't* speak. So we knew a burglary would be perfect, because the people breaking in have to be quiet. And then, if the couple in the house are having an argument and aren't talking to each other, and there's a domestic who's keeping her head down, we knew we had a set-up where we could do the tropes of silent comedy without it feeling like a pastiche. And the fact is, people *can* speak, it's just we're not with them when they do. That was our rule.'

'Initially we thought, if we can get the first ten minutes that'll be really good,' says Reece. 'We

ABOVE: The stylised poster for this episode was created by Matt Owen.

thought, let's close our eyes, visualise what's happening, and write it down in stage directions. But we managed to get to the end, which was extraordinary. So it was an accidental silent comedy. And, having already written the other five episodes, it was enjoyable not to have to worry about words. A lot of them are wordy, because they're like plays, so it was stretching a muscle we didn't normally use, the all-physical side.'

The script went through various titles – 'Silent Night', 'Silent Assassins' and 'White Noise' among them – before they settled on 'A Quiet Night In'. It was eighteen pages of stage directions with every visual joke and pratfall plotted out in exact detail. 'It was an exercise in building,' notes Steve. 'What's the next thing? How do we complicate it further? How do we keep this threat alive? And can we do it visually? It was all about creating a forward propulsive narrative. The burglars have got an objective – to steal the painting – without being seen. So it was about keeping those two sets of characters [the burglars and the householders] apart. We found it a very creative process and it didn't take us long to write. The hardest part was knowing where to stop, because how do you know you've filled half an hour of time?'

'A Quiet Night In' stars Shearsmith and Pemberton as bumbling balaclava-clad burglars Ray and Eddie, who break into the modernist, open-plan, glass-box home of Gerald (Denis Lawson) and Sabrina (Oona Chaplin) to steal a painting, an almost all-white affair, in a nod to *Art*, Yasmina Reza's satirical play that they and *League* cohort Mark Gatiss appeared in in the West End in 2003.

While the episode harks back to the silent comedies of Buster Keaton, Harold Lloyd and Charlie Chaplin, Ray and Eddie were modelled more on Laurel and Hardy. 'One fat, one thin, both stupid. The classic double act, really,' says Reece, who styled Ray's moustache on Peter Sellers' Inspector Clouseau from *The Pink Panther* films.

'Reece and Steve will quite happily say, "This was our Chuckle Brothers episode,"' laughs David

ABOVE: Steve and Reece play hapless thieves Eddie and Ray in this almost-silent comedy about a house burglary gone wrong.

ABOVE: The episode's risk assessment, drawn up by assistant director Tom Dunbar, includes details about working with dogs, as well as the hazards of crawling and dragging bodies.

Kerr. 'Don't underestimate the comic value in watching two idiots in a serious setting, where the stakes are raised. Even though Reece's character is an idiot, Steve's is *more* of an idiot.'

The silent comedy era was acknowledged, too, by the casting of Oona Chaplin, granddaughter of Charlie, as one half of the argumentative couple. 'I don't think we put two and two together when we cast her,' insists Tandy. 'We'd liked her work in *Game of Thrones*.'

'The Chaplin connection was an absolute plus,' contends Kerr. 'It wasn't the driver, but it was a very useful, secondary kind of connection, because I've always been a huge Chaplin fan. But she was hired because she was the right actress for the role. She was also capable of brilliant comedy, and a superb and non-verbal performance. And you've got to find someone fascinating to watch when they're ostensibly not doing much.' The same can be said of Chaplin's onscreen partner, played by Denis Lawson. 'I'm probably not alone in having Bill Forsyth's *Local Hero* as one of my favourite films,' says Kerr. 'That's probably the first thing I remember Denis in, but I've loved him in so much TV work. He can make things alive and funny, and you never see the joins in his performance.'

Ray and Eddie find their efforts to steal the painting are beset by a series of ever-increasing problems and complications, chief among them the bickering couple, Joyce Veheary's housekeeper, two dogs, chilli peppers, and a supposedly deaf and dumb cleaning supply salesman (Kayvan Novak) who, it transpires, is an assassin and a fellow thief. He utters the episode's sole audible line, in homage to Mel Brooks' *Silent Movie* where the only dialogue is spoken by legendary mime artist Marcel Marceau. Then there's the squeaky, inflatable sex doll, featuring breasts and a large, erect phallus, which Ray encounters while hiding under Gerald and Sabrina's bed. The doll is the second of two sexual curveballs the script throws at Ray, who, just prior, watches Sabrina remove her blonde wig then pee standing up.

'Again it's trying to surprise the audience,' says Kerr, 'because just when they think they've figured out what world they're in, you wrong-foot them. You've been watching what you assume is a cis-gender couple – he's a rich old guy and she's his partner – and you are forced to reassess some of your prejudices or presumptions in that moment when you see what Reece's character sees. I love that. The mechanics of the plot aren't drastically changed, because it's still about a couple of idiots trying to steal a painting. But the sexual dynamics and nature of the relationships are certainly more surprising. Archetypes are useful in comedy; you need a bit of shorthand if you've got limited screen time to engage an audience. But that doesn't mean everything needs to be stereotypes. And that's something Reece and Steve constantly push at.'

While the script wasn't written with a specific house in mind, the action required a large, open-plan interior. White Lodge was a brand-new, modernist home in Oxted, Surrey, that had been used for photo shoots. Kerr, who found it on a locations website, and Shearsmith spent a day on site prior to filming, blocking out scenes, road testing the action, even reworking moments to take advantage of what the house had to offer. 'I went round with David, checking angles, thinking, I'll be able to hide behind there, and Steve can come in from the door there. And where can we hide the body of the maid? Oh, there's a cupboard,' recalls Reece. 'It was amazing to find that place, because geographically it fitted our script.'

Since Tandy had decided that the subject matter of each episode would dictate the style of filming, it made sense that 'A Quiet Night In' should look and feel like a silent movie. 'And silent movies don't really have mid-shots. They have wide shots and close-ups for reactions,' he explains. 'And we thought the slapstick and physical comedy would be best captured in those sizes, rather than conventional comedy framing of two-shots and close-ups.'

'There is a dictum: do things that frighten you. And "A Quiet Night In" was a terrifying prospect at a practical directing level,' admits Kerr, who wondered if an audience would put up with half an hour of TV without any dialogue. 'We've become so reliant on scripted dialogue as our means of story consumption, particularly in comedy.' But, having grown up with the likes of Chaplin, Lloyd and Laurel and Hardy regularly on TV, Kerr knew the territory well. He rewatched Buster Keaton's *The General* and *Sherlock Jr* 'to be reminded of the power of the open frame and playing action in long shot, to be confident that you'd see everything you needed to. What that kind of shooting demands is you work with people who know how to be full-body actors. Thankfully, Reece and Steve are great examples of that. They're very conscious of how their whole body is performing.'

In conjunction with Stephan Pehrsson, Kerr opted to frame proceedings 'in a way that felt similar to the human field of view', filming with either a 28mm or 35mm lens. 'That was our starting point, and most of our shots were framed that way.' But it meant choreographing the action so there was absolutely no slack. 'Very often in comedy, or in drama, there's an A story, a B story, even a C story. So when you get to the edit and are looking to pace things up, you can leave the A story and go to another location or set of characters. In the case of "A Quiet Night In", there's nowhere else to go. This is all there is. And it's playing in long masters.'

Despite airing second, 'A Quiet Night In' was the last episode to be filmed for series one. 'We knew it was experimental, we knew it was high risk, so I took it off my list

of the first three to be shot,' Tandy reveals. 'But the fallout from that meant we were shooting a thing, set entirely at night, in a glass house, in the middle of summer, when it didn't get dark until 9.30. And the dark only stayed with us until about four, so we had very, very short shooting days, and I had to find the money for an extra day's filming. We shot, continually, through the night, for six nights, and we were all punch-drunk by the time we got to the end. And because we were shooting in story order, we did all the big stunts on the final day when we were incredibly tired. So it was a very pressurised shoot.'

On the plus side, it didn't rain once, which, given the amount of windows, would have been a nightmare. There was, however, the problem of reflections, with the crew having to wear all black or cover themselves with black cloth while filming. Even so, some digital work was required to erase the odd reflected camera and crew member in post-production.

Then there was the issue of the two dogs, a yappy Yorkshire terrier and a massive Irish wolfhound, who needed to perform on cue. 'You're entirely at the mercy of what a dog is prepared to give you,' says Kerr, 'and generally the take you'll end up using is the one in which the dog performed rather than the actor.' The dogs do, however, provide two of the episode's best sight gags. The first one

TOP: Left to right: Eddie (Steve Pemberton), Sabrina (Oona Chaplin), Gerald (Denis Lawson) and Ray (Reece Shearsmith).

ABOVE: Kayvan Novak and Steve pose between takes.

occurs when the terrier comes in and starts barking at Eddie. To stop it alerting the house's owners, Eddie lays down a bread trail, leading the terrier outside, only for an enormous wolfhound to come bounding in. 'I'm not sure I understood how funny the little dog/big dog joke was when I read it on the page,' says Tandy. 'But that moment made quite a lot of lists of the year.'

Later, in a final bid to be rid of the noisy terrier, Ray, thinking the door is open, throws it against the glass, stunning it. He then stuffs the lifeless animal inside an umbrella stand and proceeds to stab it with an umbrella, although you're never in doubt the dog's fake. 'Always make sure the dummy dog you throw doesn't look real,' insists Tandy, imparting a time-honoured comedy secret. 'As long as the audience knows it's fake, the more you stab it, the funnier it is.' Not that dogs were much of a laughing matter for Pemberton who, like his character, is allergic to them. 'That's the other thing we discovered,' continues Tandy. 'The whole dog sequence was fraught. Because we couldn't be in a situation where Steve's eyes swelled up and he was unable to work. And so there are quite a lot of shots with the dog where it's actually the trainer doubling for Steve.'

Shearsmith was fine with the canines but pulled a calf muscle while chasing after the maid in order to chloroform her. 'You can see it happen,' he notes. 'I was hobbling for the rest of the shoot.'

With its one line of dialogue, sound and music were more crucial than ever for 'A Quiet Night In'. The boys had scripted that Gerald puts on Rachmaninoff's Piano Concerto No. 2 at the start, with the track acting as the soundtrack to the episode. 'It was literally the longest piece on iTunes,' explains Steve of their choice, although Kerr opted not to play it on set 'because the action had to find its own rhythm that was connected to performance.' Come the edit, however, series editor Joe Randall Cutler

needed to make numerous micro cuts in the track, even varying the speed at times to make it fit the action. 'You don't want to be on the beat because that feels like it's not incidental,' says Tandy. 'It has to feel like the action is driving the music rather than the other way round.'

'I'll always think of "A Quiet Night In" as an amazing challenge and a brilliant opportunity, but it was terrifying,' admits Kerr. 'It was only when I got to the edit and saw the first assembly and saw how well it was working, that I felt like I could breathe again. It was a tense time for me, creatively, and I barely slept that week.'

For Kerr and co., it was worth it. 'A Quiet Night In' was another triumph, a narratively innovative, beautifully choreographed exercise in physical and visual comedy, with a dark heart and a wry twist. 'We knew it was special. We knew it was different. We hoped it would be funny,' says Tandy. 'And so it proved.'

TOM
&
GERRI

REECE SHEARSMITH
GEMMA ARTERTON
STEVE PEMBERTON
CONLETH HILL

BBC TWO PRESENTS A BBC COMEDY PRODUCTION AN INSIDE NO.9 FILM "TOM & GERRI" REECE SHEARSMITH GEMMA ARTERTON STEVE PEMBERTON CONLETH HILL SCREENPLAY BY STEVE PEMBERTON & REECE SHEARSMITH EXECUTIVE PRODUCER JON PLOWMAN PRODUCED BY ADAM TANDY DIRECTED BY DAVID KERR

Tom & Gerri

■ Series **1**
■ Episode **3**
■ Directed by **David Kerr**

The second script written for *Inside No. 9*, and the first filmed, 'Tom & Gerri' began life as a play called *The Honeymoon Period* that Pemberton and Shearsmith penned in the mid-nineties after finishing college near Wakefield, West Yorkshire, where they met. 'Between leaving Bretton Hall and officially starting *The League of Gentlemen* was about five or six years,' Steve recalls. 'No one was hiring us as actors, so we used to fill our time by writing things. We wrote a play about being on the dole and how that saps you of your life energy. It was very different to how "Tom & Gerri" ended up. There was a prototype Pauline [from *The League of Gentlemen*] character. It was a very nineties, unemployment-type play, but it was what we knew. We did a reading of it at The Finborough Arms in Kensington, but never thought about staging it.'

ABOVE: The 'Tom & Gerri' episode poster was created by Rob Treen.

To turn a two-hour play into twenty-nine minutes of television required a lot of pruning, whittling a cast of twenty down to just four, and transforming it into a Harold Pinteresque power struggle between Tom (Shearsmith), a primary school teacher and aspiring writer, and the homeless Migg (Pemberton), whom Tom invites into the flat he shares with his girlfriend Gerri (Gemma Arterton), a struggling actress. Over the course of the story, Migg inveigles himself into Tom's life and home. But nothing is what it seems, with Gerri turning out to be a figment of Tom's grief-stricken mind, and the manipulative Migg, who we've been led to believe isn't real, winding up dead in the bathtub.

'What you think you're watching has become a bit of a theme in *Inside No. 9*. And with this one especially, we had lots of discussions about how much to play it,' notes Reece. 'All the way through, we knew the ending was going to be that Migg wasn't real,' adds Steve. 'And as we got towards it, we thought, it's obvious to us Migg isn't real, and it's probably obvious to the audience, so let's flip that and make Gerri the one who isn't real.'

One of the most provocative and influential British dramatists of the twentieth century, Harold Pinter has long been a major influence on Pemberton and Shearsmith's writing, and with 'Tom & Gerri' they were trying to tap into the hidden menace that imbues much of his work. 'What he calls "the weasel behind the cocktail cabinet",' notes Steve. 'Something you can't see, but which you're aware of. It hangs in the air. And we definitely wanted that in this.'

BELOW: Left to right: Migg (Steve Pemberton), Tom (Reece Shearsmith) and Gerri (Gemma Arterton).

ABOVE: A sketch of the set design for Tom's apartment created by production designer Tom Sayer.

Pinter, too, is evoked in both their performances and line readings. 'We allowed the dialogue to breathe, so it's not perky all the way through,' explains Tandy. 'There are moments where the famous Pinter pause is there for the camera to use. And the camera does drift around the flat and shots do develop. That's the thing David Kerr brought to the episode. He used the camera in a very interesting way, to explore that world. You felt it was very claustrophobic.'

'It starts off tapping into what I suppose we could call middle-class guilt, that feeling many of us who have enough money to live in relative comfort feel when confronted by someone who doesn't have a home of their own and is plainly suffering and possibly hungry,' says Kerr. 'And there's that sense of social obligation you feel when someone's done you a good turn. If you'd lost your wallet and someone has the decency to bring it back, you immediately feel indebted to them, which is what happens with Tom and Migg. It was a very smart set-up because the power dynamic is immediate.'

'Tom & Gerri' (the title has no significance other than being the characters' names; it is not meant to pay homage to either the adversarial cartoon duo Tom and Jerry or seventies sitcom *The Good Life*) is, essentially, a two-hander between Pemberton and Shearsmith. 'Because Reece and Steve have been friends and collaborators for so long, they know each other's rhythm so intimately in terms of speech, of looks,' continues Kerr. 'Take a scene like the one where their characters first meet. It's a masterclass in subtle detail and what's going on between the lines; in the case of Migg, the little looks and sighs and sneaky narrowing of the eyes. As a viewer, you pick up on so much more than is being said. There's a degree of infiltration going on from one character to the other that is magical. And the way Migg is written, he throws out just enough of a tease or a temptation for Tom to be reeled in the next inch, to inveigle himself into his trust. It unfolds in a way that creeps up on you. You're not aware of the balance of power shifting until it has. That's beautiful writing. Then you have Gerri coming in as the corrective to that, trying to shake Tom out of his torpor and make him conscious of what's really going on, how he's being abused by this sinister outsider who's invaded his space.'

As the first episode to be filmed, 'Tom & Gerri' was also the first cast, with former *Bond* star Gemma Arterton signing on to play Gerri. 'I was keen to aim high, although we weren't quite sure what level of actor we'd actually secure,' recalls Kerr. 'And with Gemma, we were like, "Is it worth offering her? Do you think she might go for it?" And she replied pretty quickly.'

'Gemma was a real coup for us,' says Tandy. 'Having her name attached made it a lot easier to open doors for other episodes and started that thing of having access to pretty much any name we'd like. You always felt you could lift up the phone or write an email to the agent of anybody and expect at least a civil reply.'

The episode's fourth character is Stevie (Conleth Hill), a colleague of Tom who pops round to check up on him. 'Stevie comes in at a point where you've spent so long in this contained, intense *ménage à trois* with Tom and Gerri and Migg,' says Kerr. 'On the one hand it's, "Here's a bit of light relief." On the other, he's about to witness something so dark that it completely shakes you out of any assumptions that this was just a little fairy tale. He brings such a warmth and a natural wit to that character. Also, the slight camp charm he's playing is a reassuring beat that wrong-foots the audience before one of the nastiest reveals in the series – and the most shocking.'

While most of the original play had to be jettisoned – 'The only scene that survived entirely is where they're playing Scrabble and they talk about doing the washing-up and Nanette Newman, which probably tells you how old the script was,' says Steve – certain elements remained, reflecting the boys' 'mid-nineties, post-university, no-work lifestyle'. A case in point being the board games Tom and Migg play. 'We used to play *Escape from Colditz* or *Risk*, games that would take forever, because we had nothing to do.'

'Not being able to do anything and having all the time in the world to do it,' remembers Reece. 'There was a lot of sitting in the flat, wrapped in a duvet, no reason to get up, watching *This Morning*, washing-up piling up, and someone finally going, "Right, I'm going to do it!" Just like *Withnail & I.*'

'All of that is so evocative for us,' notes Steve, wistfully.

TOP: The concerned Stevie (Conleth Hill) visits Tom.

ABOVE: Steve as Migg in the bath, captured on the monitor.

Another holdover from both the play and their time on the dole is the answering machine from which Migg deletes Tom's messages. 'We had one in our house in Asmara Road,' says Steve, 'and it became a sort of ritual: "You. Have. No. Messages."' That episode feels more of a period piece than most. Who checks their answerphone messages any more?' The voice on the machine informing Tom his electricity supply is being cut off belongs to Tandy, making the first of his many vocal cameos. 'I've got a limited range, but when the range is voice on phone, that I can handle.'

They decided to make Tom a disgruntled primary school teacher who always dreamed of being a writer for two reasons. Firstly, 'it suited that story', says Steve, 'if someone's got a slight weakness you can play upon, because that's what Migg is doing.' Secondly, because, at the time, both men had daughters at the same primary school and were able to incorporate some of that experience into the episode.

The idea of Gerri starring as a Land Girl in a touring production of *D-Day Doris/Lucy Land Girl* sprang from a BBC Two series called *Theatre of Dreams*. 'We've often gone to documentaries for inspiration, and in this there was an aspiring actress who went to an audition and it goes terribly wrong,' recalls Steve. 'She kept forgetting the lines and talked about doing this Second World War play.' The

TOP: Director David Kerr speaks to Reece as the crew and Gemma Arterton look on.

ABOVE: Left to right: producer Adam Tandy, Reece, Steve and David Kerr review footage.

director of *Lucy Land Girl* is named Ollie, 'who we presume is Ollie Plimsolls of the Legz Akimbo Theatre Company,' says Reece, referring to the character he played in *The League of Gentlemen*. 'That was a nice little nod. We sometimes do that. We tantalise that they're in the same universe. And sometimes they are. Sometimes they're not.'

Gerri is later revealed to be a figment of Tom's imagination. 'All the scenes with Tom and Gerri are quite acrimonious in a way, and quite brittle,' muses Steve. 'There's a sense in which he's having these conversations because he wishes he could have said things differently. Or he's going over old ground because it's torturing him. He's not imagining this blissful life they had together. He's going over things he did wrong. And that makes it more poignant.'

When it came to presenting a character onscreen who isn't real, Tandy says it was imperative to sow the seeds for the eventual reveal from the very beginning. 'If you just pull a rabbit out of a hat at the end, and say, "Ah-ha!" you're not being fair to your audience, because they need to go, "Oh, it was in plain sight all the time, I just didn't notice,"' he explains. 'So I suggested because Gemma's character is a ghost or a figment of his imagination, we never have a shot from her point of view. She's nearly

> **Gerri:** You invite a tramp in off the street and get pissed with him?
>
> **Tom:** He found my wallet. He was being kind.

always in the back of shot rather than the foreground. We rarely go over her shoulder. And her appearance within the frame is always referenced to her relationship with Tom. And so in the scene in the bedroom, she's farther away from the lens than Reece. And that was deliberate, so you didn't become too sympathetic to that character and start to identify with her.'

'You have to approach a film like "Tom & Gerri" so it makes sense in retrospect,' agrees Kerr. This meant never showing Gerri and Migg together in the same frame. 'That was the most important thing, that there wouldn't be a sense of overlap. So those two worlds, although you weren't conscious of it, existed side by side and did not cross.'

'It's very cleverly filmed,' praises Reece, 'and a deliberate choice on David's part to film the scenes where Gerri and Migg never meet, with one door slamming and the other one opening as they come in. It was designed to start to tip that one of them isn't real, presumably Migg. She even says to Tom: "He's in your imagination."'

'That was important for the psychology of the episode,' adds Tandy. 'You have to be conflicted as to who is real and who isn't. And if they'd met, the game is up.'

When it came to the look and feel of 'Tom & Gerri', Kerr took inspiration from a number of cinematic sources, with Joseph Losey's drama *The Servant*, adapted by Pinter, absolutely key. 'You've got a shifting power dynamic between a couple of

characters and roles being reversed, plus there's the way that film used blocking and framing to reinforce those relationships,' he says. 'Also *Don't Look Now*, and director Nicolas Roeg in general, because there's a sense of mental fracturing going on with his characters; and *The Lives of Others* because of its controlled lens choice to emphasise isolation.'

While Pemberton and Shearsmith based Tom and Gerri's flat (first floor, above a Londis) on one in which they lived in Highgate between 1994 and 1995, Kerr's inspirations were mostly cinematic: 'Both Roman Polanski's *The Tenant* and the Coen brothers' *Barton Fink* have this murky, dirty, claustrophobic, nasty vibe and I wanted that to build in this mundane setting.'

The flat was a set, built onstage at Wimbledon Studios. Production designer Tom Sayer had worked with Kerr on *Fresh Meat*, which revolved around a group of friends sharing a house. 'We went to great lengths on that to build the house as a character, and we took that same approach with this,' explains Kerr. 'It was about creating a flat that felt real and mundane, but could lend itself to this stylised mind-melding psychodrama as Tom's mind and his mental health deteriorates. We wanted to find visual corollaries to that. So the green colour, that can be reassuring but also kind of sickly, was really important. And reflective surfaces allowed light to creep through, or to show Migg's face in a slightly broken-up way. Little visual cues that play into a sense of distorted reality.'

OPPOSITE: The mysterious hare in all its glory, painted by Reece Shearsmith.
BELOW: By the end of the episode, as Tom's state of mind unravels, we see a reversal of fortunes as he becomes unkempt and directionless, while Migg has smartened up and found a job.

In a visual nod to *The Servant*, Kerr had Sayer hang a convex mirror, similar to one in Losey's film, by the front door of Tom's flat. 'There's a lot of very clever set dressing which we do not linger on,' says Tandy. 'The notice for Gerri's memorial service and mementos of her life were all over the noticeboard in that flat. We had to edit round it, otherwise it would have given away the fact she was dead. There's a lot of plumbing and exposed pipe work which starts out in quite good order, but, by the time Tom has his breakdown, you can see his environment is pretty scummy.'

Equally important to chart Tom's mental collapse was the sound. 'There's an awful lot of electrical hums and plumbing sounds which have been added,' continues Tandy. 'As his world becomes much more sewer-like, there's a change to the structure of the mix. By the end, when the phone is cut off and he is absolutely at his lowest, it's actually quite impressionistic. Loud fridge hums and air conditioning noises mixed together.'

Kerr's point of reference was the sound the radiator makes in David Lynch's nightmarish feature *Eraserhead*. 'That slightly other-worldly quality was very much in my mind when I was thinking about the boiler as a hellish heartbeat in this,' he explains. 'Or the sound that cigarettes make when they're smoked. Or the hum of traffic that occasionally reminds you, "You're still in the real world here, folks. This could be happening on a high street near you." Because, in many ways, it's a horror film. But like so many *Inside No. 9*s, it's psychological rather than gory, which is made all the more visceral for happening in plain sight, on a high street, in a mundane setting.'

The Hare

In folklore, hares can be goddesses or messengers, or they can be symbols of fertility, tricksters, or witch's familiars. In *Inside No. 9*, however, the hare represents a game played by the boys with the audience - there is a small brass hare ornament that viewers can delight in spotting. It appears in every episode, in some shape, manner or form.

'Because we didn't have anything running through other than the number nine, we thought, for ourselves, and knowing how people like to find Easter eggs in things, let's have one prop or one ornament which is in every location,' explains Steve. 'But we won't make a thing of it. We won't announce it. It won't have any particular significance. So the art department came and said, "We've got this or this." And we chose the hare. You could imagine it in every location, just sitting there.'

'I thought it was a great idea,' says Tandy. 'The fact it was a hare and has trickster connotations may be what, subconsciously, decided them on it, but once we'd chosen it, there was no going back.'

While 'Sardines' was the first episode broadcast, 'Tom & Gerri' was the first to be filmed, so Kerr positioned the hare on a sideboard in the flat, next to a photograph of Tom and Gerri, and had the camera track over. 'It was about placing the hare somewhere where it could be seen, but not where it's the only thing to look at,' he explains. 'And that's always the guiding ethos: you didn't want to get to the edit and think, "Shit, we put the hare in a shot that we've cut." So it needed to be somewhere where it would be seen, but not somewhere where it feels like that's the point of the shot.'

Since then, the hare has been omnipresent, if not always easy to spot, popping up in photographs ('La Couchette', 'Empty Orchestra'), on bookcases, desks and shelves (too many to list), in pieces ('Thinking Out Loud'), as an award, the Hartley ('And the Winner Is ...'), and as a crossword solution ('The Riddle of the Sphinx'). It was even given its own starring role in series four's 'Tempting Fate'. 'We always ensure its presence, because if it's a new director, they sometimes forget,' notes Steve. 'I remember Dan Zeff wasn't as conscious of it. In "The Trial of Elizabeth Gadge", it's incredibly hard to spot.'

It took until 'Last Gasp' aired before the hare was outed by one eagle-eyed viewer on Twitter. 'Someone said, "Has anyone noticed this was also in 'A Quiet Night In'?" Without us saying a word, and with it being fairly background, they found it.'

Last Gasp

STEVE PEMBERTON   SOPHIE THOMPSON

TAMSIN GREIG   ADAM DEACON

Last Gasp

LUCY HUTCHINSON   DAVID BEDELLA

INSIDE NO 9

BBC TWO PRESENTS A BBC COMEDY PRODUCTION AN INSIDE NO. 9 FILM "LAST GASP" STEVE PEMBERTON SOPHIE THOMPSON LUCY HUTCHINSON DAVID BEDELLA TAMSIN GREIG ADAM DEACON SCREENPLAY BY STEVE PEMBERTON & REECE SHEARSMITH EXECUTIVE PRODUCER JON PLOWMAN PRODUCED BY ADAM TANDY DIRECTED BY DAVID KERR

BBC TWO

Last Gasp

- Series **1**
- Episode **4**
- Directed by **David Kerr**

I n the early 1980s, Pemberton watched an item on the BBC's Saturday morning kids' show *Swap Shop* about a young girl who collected jars of air. For some reason, the story stuck in his head and, decades later, when he and Shearsmith were exploring ideas for *Inside No. 9*, 'this memory of a pointless collection' resurfaced. 'Then it became a question of finding a story for it.' Around the same time, there were a number of news stories about people selling memorabilia belonging to the late Michael Jackson for vast sums of money, with items including Jackson's bed, his famed bejewelled glove and even, inexplicably, scraps of his food. Fusing the two ideas together, they hit upon the story of the air inside a balloon being valuable if it belonged to someone who was famous. And the lengths people will go to to keep hold of it.

ABOVE: The 'Last Gasp' episode poster was created by Matt Owen.

'Last Gasp' centres on terminally ill Tamsin (Lucy Hutchinson) whose parents Jan (Sophie Thompson) and Graham (Pemberton) have arranged with the WishmakerUK charity for her favourite singer Frankie J. Parsons (David Bedella) to visit for her ninth birthday. But when Frankie dies shortly after blowing up a purple balloon, the four remaining adults – Graham, Jan, WishmakerUK representative Sally (Tamsin Greig) and Frankie's assistant Si (Adam Deacon) – start to argue over the ownership and value of the balloon, given that it contains what is, essentially, Frankie's dying breath. And when Frankie turns out not to be dead after all, there is even the suggestion that maybe they should kill him.

While ostensibly comedic in tone, 'Last Gasp' shines a black light on celebrity culture and greed. 'It's probably the most satirical of that batch we wrote,' says Steve, 'in that it was underpinned by this idea of what people attach importance to. In the same way that "A Quiet Night In" looks at art, here you're asking, what is this one-pound balloon now worth? Ten thousand? A million? Because of what someone's willing to pay for it. Because it's brushed against celebrity.'

'Also, it exposes the morals of people and how quickly they evuporate, where money is involved,' adds Reece.

'I loved the script when I read it,' says Kerr. 'It was called "Dying Breath" then. In some ways, it's Mike Leigh meets David Lynch, because you've got the kind of characters you might see in a Mike Leigh film, and the dark heart of suburbia you see in *Blue Velvet*, where there's a white picket fence and this horrible nastiness going on behind it. At one level, it's a meditation on the nature of celebrity, and the idea a star owes something to a fan in return for their fandom. It is a moral exploration seen through the eyes of a family who, on the surface, seem typical, but behind this suburban neighbourliness lurks something darker.'

'It's a descent into the nastier side of people's personalities,' agrees Tandy. 'All these people have black hearts. They're all self-serving, apart from the little girl. They're all absolutely horrible. And I

ABOVE: Left to right: Si (Adam Deacon), Sally (Tamsin Greig), Graham (Steve Pemberton) and Jan (Sophie Thompson).

thought it was going to be a joy to cast. I said, "Let's go and find actors you wouldn't normally get to play wicked roles."'

Tamsin Greig, whose comic turns in *Green Wing* and *Black Books* had made her a household name, was top of the list to play Sally. 'What appealed to me about Tamsin, apart from the fact she's brilliantly funny, was there was always a wholesomeness to her characters,' says Kerr. 'She tended to play people who seemed to have an inherent goodness about them. And the fact that someone who brings that wholesomeness and decency is then capable of turning into something utterly monstrous is terrifying, and so the moral depravity of that character comes as a shock.'

Greig is truly convincing as the amoral WishmakerUK representative, delivering every line with a smile, but dead, shark-like eyes. 'She's horrific, Tamsin's character,' insists Steve. 'You can see it when they're talking about how they're going to split the money and she says, "Well, it's unfair for you to get [the daughter's] share, because this is going to be over for her very quickly."'

ABOVE: Tamsin Greig's costume is adjusted between takes.

| Sally: | It's only a balloon, for goodness' sake. |
| Si: | One that contains Mr Parsons' breath. His actual dying breath. |

'It remains my favourite performance in the whole of *Inside No. 9* by a guest artist,' says Tandy. 'I love that Tamsin Greig is so self-servingly evil. And so unknowing as well.'

Tamsin the daughter rather than Tamsin the actress was played by Lucy Hutchinson, who had appeared in *Psychoville*. 'She was terrific. She completely got it,' says Steve. 'Of course, child labour hours affects things. So the mechanics of how we filmed it were quite different to the others. We couldn't do it in story order.'

'Lucy stunned me at how mature she seemed,' says Kerr. 'She understood what the character was doing. She played it in a way that felt unforced, rooted and naturalistic. As a viewer, you lock into her plight, because not only is she dying, but her living days have to be spent with these two grotesque parents who've got such a warped moral outlook.'

Those grotesques are played by Pemberton and Thompson, who had recently starred as husband and wife on stage in *She Stoops to Conquer*. 'Sophie was so funny and brought this musical cadence to some of the lines,' says Kerr. 'She latched on to the potential of Jan and we leaned into that with the big glasses and the wardrobe. They seem like this Mike Leigh-ish couple, a couple of scary suburbanites. I loved watching the way she and Steve connected. I believed them as a couple.' Rounding out the cast was rapper-actor Adam Deacon as Frankie's assistant.

Notably, 'Last Gasp' was the first episode not to feature Shearsmith. 'BBC Two very much wanted Reece and Steve to be in every one,' says Tandy. 'But sometimes they'd written episodes where there weren't two male leads. So you couldn't always do that.'

'It was also born out of not wanting to feel like we always had to be in them,' says Reece. 'It was nice to be behind the camera the entire week, watching it, seeing some great performances.'

When it came to Parsons, the plan, initially, had been to get a real entertainer to play him. Sting and Simon Le Bon were among the names discussed. 'At some point we thought, "Should we get Tom Jones?"' reveals Steve. 'We did approach him and it went quite far down the line. George Michael was also talked about. That would have had added poignancy with what happened.'

'We went around the houses a little bit with a couple of well-known performers,' says Tandy, 'but

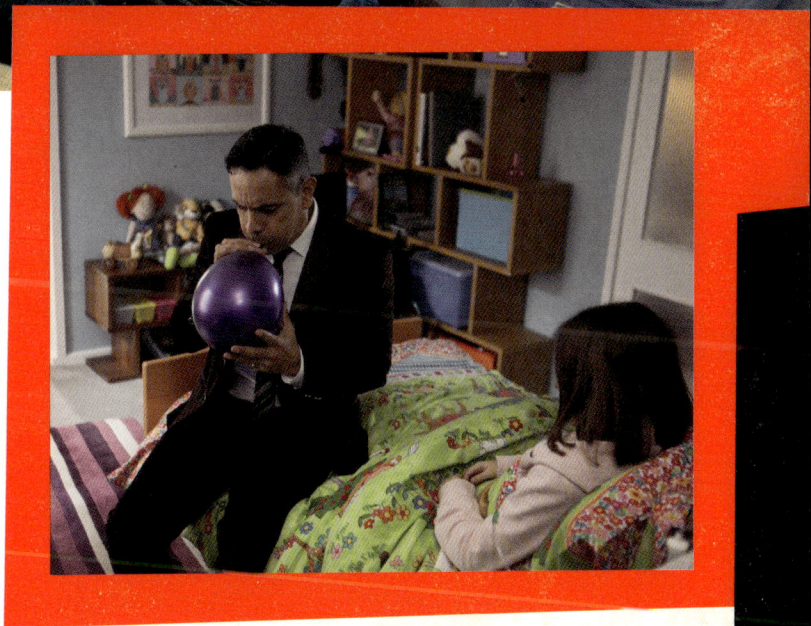

TOP: Filming in progress.

ABOVE: Frankie (David Bedella) makes the ill-fated decision to blow up a balloon for the young Tamsin (Lucy Hutchinson).

ABOVE: Reece didn't appear in this episode, but instead joined the crew behind the camera. Here, he poses with Tamsin Greig and Sophie Thompson.

whoever it was had to "die" in the episode and I think that was a concern. Besides, having a real celebrity in the middle of that very ordinary world would have unbalanced it. Then you've got the issue of clearing the rights to their songs.' And so in parallel with their fantasy casting ideas, they explored other options and, eventually, decided to go with American David Bedella, an Olivier-winning musical theatre performer. 'He had an amazing voice and had recorded the kind of standards Sophie's character would have loved,' continues Tandy. 'We cleared a couple of songs from his LP, but also re-recorded some of the tracks too.'

'He absolutely had that star quality,' says Reece. 'We built the role around him in the end. He was a crooner rather than a pop singer.' The character was named Parsons in homage to their friends Justin and Louise, in whose house Reece and Steve rent the room they use as their office; Justin's father was British comedy legend Nicholas Parsons. For legal reasons, WishmakerUK was a made-up charity, although there are a number of legitimate ones offering exactly the same service to sick children.

Key to the style of 'Last Gasp' was an almost hyperreal suburban aesthetic. 'It had to be naturalistic and rooted in an everyday reality,' says Kerr. 'But I still wanted it to be stylised and heightened. So it's very beige. There's a pastel palette. At the time, I was looking at a lot of Martin Parr's documentary photography. The way he skewers the British middle class, and how clues to character lie in trinkets, knick-knacks, and the choice of soft furnishings. So I was really keen to find a house that felt almost archetypally suburban, like a distillation of all those ideas we have of Disgusted of Tunbridge Wells.'

The production found a 1960s home in Wimbledon to film in, one that required only minimal dressing. 'We brought in some furniture and lots of trinkets and knick-knacks, but the fabric of the house is pretty much as you see it,' continues Kerr. 'And it helps to frame the story in a way that feels archetypical and therefore universal, but is also very identifiable as peculiarly British. There's something disarming about soft furnishings and pastel colours.' Kerr was keen to bring those neutral, pastel colours to the costumes, too. 'It's hard when you want things to be bland on telly,' notes Reece, 'because the temptation is you can't just have a plain blue jumper, you've got to have a little pattern on it. So you fight for a white shirt with the costume people. But that's what normal people wear.'

'It is a slightly washed-out grade partly due to the way we shot it, with all of these very big lights from outside,' says Tandy. 'But it makes their world very drab and grey. The only thing that had any value in the episode is the balloon, for which we chose a very strong, vibrant purple.'

The episode begins and ends with footage shot on Graham's camcorder. Initially, the boys toyed with filming the entire thing on video, like a found footage movie, with the camera recording whoever and whatever came into view in the living room. But they very quickly ditched the idea, deciding that the drawbacks would markedly outweigh the benefits. 'It's also quite a visually uncomfortable aesthetic to sustain,' says Kerr. 'If you're asking your audience to sit through something that's murky and wobbly and blurry, your fear is they're going to reach for the remote. Having a concentrated

dose of it at the front ends up being less a tricksy device and more an insight into Steve's character. It's there to tell you the kind of man he is, the sort that has a camera at the ready to capture these moments. As if they're not real if you haven't filmed them.'

'Last Gasp' climaxes with a literal high, as young Tamsin releases the balloon into the air, thereby preventing any more arguments. It's a bitter-sweet but also uplifting moment, underlined by the choice of Parsons/Bedella singing 'One Day in Your Life' as the closing number. 'Having had such a horrible episode, we wanted to end it with the girl winning, triumphing,' says Steve, who later sold a balloon filled with his breath on eBay for £265, with the proceeds going to charity.

'No one's going to get it,' adds Reece. 'She's letting him go.'

'I loved the conclusion, when nobody wins,' says Kerr. 'All their greed and all of their escalating venality ends with the balloon floating off. To me, that felt like a great way to go out.'

'We got great performances from everybody,' agrees Tandy. 'The only thing I would say is that I think a lot of our hardcore fans don't find that episode rewarding, because it doesn't have much of a twist. It's regularly seen to be one of the ones that's less popular. But I love it. I think the performances alone elevate that episode to something very special.'

'It's filmed very brightly, it could be a sitcom, the characters are quite broad, and yet it's a really nasty episode,' says Reece. 'And it does have a surprisingly hopeful ending which is why people are wrong to dismiss it as a bit sitcom-y and light, because it's quite the opposite. I think because of where it's placed in the series that some do it a disservice. Other people love it. I've read it's some people's favourite.'

ABOVE: As the episode progresses, the characters put all niceties aside and become increasingly desperate for ownership of the balloon containing Frankie's 'dying breath'.

ROSIE
CAVALIERO

STEVE
PEMBERTON

REECE
SHEARSMITH

ROGER
SLOMAN

DI
BOTCHER

LYNDSEY
MARSHAL

JULIA
DAVIS

RICHARD
CORDERY

THE
UNDERSTUDY

BBC TWO PRESENTS A BBC COMEDY PRODUCTION AN INSIDE NO.9 FILM "THE UNDERSTUDY" ROSIE CAVALIERO STEVE PEMBERTON REECE SHEARSMITH ROGER SLOMAN DI BOTCHER LYNDSEY MARSHAL JULIA DAVIS RICHARD CORDERY SCREENPLAY BY STEVE PEMBERTON & REECE SHEARSMITH EXECUTIVE PRODUCER JON PLOWMAN PRODUCED BY ADAM TANDY DIRECTED BY DAVID KERR

The Understudy

- Series **1**
- Episode **5**
- Directed by **David Kerr**

Following 'Last Gasp' was another showbiz episode, with 'The Understudy' set in a world of which Pemberton and Shearsmith have intimate knowledge: London's theatreland. 'It started as one line in a notebook that said, "Chart an actor trying to get up to the leading man from being a small role, mirroring *Macbeth*",' explains Steve, who played Banquo in a production of Shakespeare's tale of ghosts, witches and bloody murder when he was nineteen. 'It was the last one we wrote for this series and we spent ages trying to find our way in.'

Their initial idea revolved around an amateur dramatics group and was to have featured two very familiar faces. 'We talked a lot about *Psychoville*'s Maureen and David as a murderous couple – she was a kind of Lady Macbeth figure – but, ultimately, we felt if *Inside No. 9* was going to be its own

ABOVE: The episode poster for 'The Understudy' was designed by Rob Treen.

show, it was too soon to bring back those characters,' continues Steve. 'So we wrote it as an am-dram company but got about fifteen pages in and stopped.' Partly it was to do with the chosen setting – a community centre – but mainly it was because they had a corker of an opening in mind that didn't fit the am-dram world at all. 'We had this idea of an actor wanting to get home after the show and realising he's got someone coming in to see him. We both knew that feeling of, "I've done two, three hours of a play, and now I've got to talk to these people and answer all their questions about how you remember your lines."'

They abandoned the am-dram backdrop and relocated the idea to a dressing room in London's West End, but the central conceit remained the same. The backstage setting mirrored the themes of *Macbeth* – jealousy and power grabbing – with Jim (Shearsmith), an understudy, taking over from the show's established lead Tony (Pemberton) when he falls off stage, becoming a star as a result. 'We had this great dynamic of an understudy and his girlfriend, Laura, who's also an understudy – she's understudying Lady Macbeth – pushing him,' notes Steve. 'My mum was always saying, "Why don't you push yourself?" As if you're idly not getting jobs because you're not applying yourself.'

But when they got twelve pages into the script they realised if they mirrored *Macbeth* too exactly, everyone would know who the Lady Macbeth character was, so where was the surprise? 'We got to where Tony has his accident and were trying to think of some way he could be out of the picture,' explains Steve. 'We didn't want him to be murdered. We wanted something where it wasn't obvious who'd done it. Or anyone could have done it. And that was tricky, especially because it happens

ABOVE: Left to right: Kirstie (Rosie Cavaliero), Felicity (Julia Davis), Tony (Steve Pemberton), Jim (Reece Shearsmith) and Laura (Lyndsey Marshal).

Does a ghost come to haunt the understudy?

Was he responsible for Main actor's death? Accident? He has to overcome his guilt to assume the role & become a star.

Do we hear new Macbeth (understudy) fight with Macduff over the show relay, but as they fight something obviously goes wrong - the show is stopped & an ambulance called.

(Maybe Cody M jkyhr, as a dresser, is in dressing room listening. She has the sword tip / fake dagger?)

offstage, as it were, so we made him a recovering alcoholic and had someone put vodka in his juice.'

Another moment of inspiration struck when they hit upon the idea of structuring the episode in five acts, just like Shakespeare. 'We've found that you start writing and it's really exhausting to keep the story going, in real time,' says Reece. 'It was a way of breaking it up. So time can have passed. And then when you come into a new scene, you could talk about what's happened in the interim. It solved the issue we had with our first draft, which was that we couldn't get all the action to work in a continuing story.'

ABOVE: A page from one of Steve's notebooks shows the ideas for the episode as they began to sketch it out.

46   The Insider's Guide to Inside No. 9: Series One

As the camera couldn't leave the confines of the dressing room, they found a clever way of bringing the outside world in. 'Every theatre dressing room has a Tannoy with the show on relay, and you can hear everything that's going on onstage,' says Steve. A pair of actors were hired to perform scenes from *Macbeth* in post-production, which were layered in later, along with ghostly, supernatural sounds. 'You're not quite sure what it is,' says Kerr. 'Is it coming through the speaker? Is it something Steve's character, through his mental decline, thinks he's hearing? I wanted to play with that texture in the edit, the sound design and the music as well. Composer Christian Henson deserves all the credit in the world for being so endlessly inventive. Much like Reece and Steve, he doesn't fall back on the same box of tricks. He's constantly pushing himself to find a new idiom for the score.'

When it came to creating the characters, the boys took inspiration and 'characteristics' from a number of fellow actors and crew they've encountered during their time treading the boards. 'Reece and Steve are able to draw on so much of their own lives and experiences and people they've encountered, so it feels truth-filled,' says Kerr. 'I've seen many evocations of the theatrical world which don't quite ring true. And there's not a false note in this. It wasn't just set in a theatre; it was steeped in theatrical lore.'

'You take whatever comes from life as long as it's not identifiable as a whole person,' says Steve. His Tony Warner was 'an Ollie Reed type. A big, boozy, bombastic, larger than life and twice as dreadful leading man,' says Kerr. 'He feels like a very recognisable archetype, but certainly the sort of character we know from British theatre.' Warner's fury at an overrunning act – 'That's two minutes over!' – was based on an actor 'who was obsessed with getting this particular train home', says Steve. 'But that's how these tiny things become magnified. Also that sense: "They won't

BELOW: Steve's character Tony, described by director David Kerr as 'big, boozy [and] bombastic', lectures Julia Davis's stage manager Felicity.

ABOVE: Julia Davis as formidable stage manager Felicity.

have me at the Donmar. I am not their type of actor."'

'That's a direct quote,' adds Reece, whose Jim was drawn from real life, with both men having both understudied and been understudies themselves over the years. 'That sense of someone hovering in the corner, watching your every move is a thing we've experienced – someone being ready to jump into your shoes at a moment's notice. In musical theatre, you can't wait to be off, because you're exhausted. In a play, you'd be mortified to have a night off. So it's hard to get on as an understudy unless something disastrous happens. You're just waiting and hoping the actor will come and watch your understudy run, which was a thing we put in. Some kind actors do. I have not been to one of them.'

'You meet Jim as a struggling actor with some ambition,' notes Kerr. 'At first it seems perfectly reasonable and manageable, but the arc of the story reveals his vaulting ambition. I loved the way the script misdirects the audience into who's pulling the strings, who's really trying to bring about the change in circumstances.' Indeed, the script nudges your suspicions in the direction of Jim's girlfriend Laura, played by Lyndsey Marshal. 'Lyndsey had maybe the hardest role because you have to believe she's the baddie for at least the first half of the show,' says Tandy. 'You think she's Lady Macbeth, egging him on to do this. Whereas she's just pushy.'

It's only right at the end that the true Lady Macbeth of 'The Understudy' is revealed to be Tony's dresser Kirstie. Played by Rosie Cavaliero, Kirstie barely registers for most of the episode. 'I remember Rosie saying when she read it, "Here we go, another one of those in-it-but-not-in-it roles,"' laughs Steve. 'Then once she got to that last scene, where she's this unhinged, almost *Fatal Attraction*-esque character, she was like, "What a fantastic turnaround."'

'It was really important for us to hide the villain in plain sight,' says Tandy. 'It needed to be somebody who makes you think they're just playing the dresser. But we also needed somebody who could do that quiet psychopath thing. She's this mousey thing and then, suddenly, you're astounded at how cold-blooded she is.'

Monstrous, but in an entirely different way, is Julia Davis's stage manager Felicity, a mini-Hitler described in the script as a 'black-clad Australian lesbian'. 'That's got to be drawn from real life. You don't just come up with that,' laughs Tandy.

'The black jumper is definitely a thing,' concurs Reece. 'We did work with one stage manager who did exhibit these eye-rolling tendencies; that sense that, as an actor, you are a child and an inconvenience to their job.'

Davis, creator and star of TV shows *Camping* and *Nighty Night*, was thrilled to be asked to come and play the role. 'She said, "I want really short hair. I want a big padded bum in black jeans and keys hanging down,"' notes Steve. 'She came in with that whole look.'

And finally, there's Roger Sloman and Di Botcher as Bill and Jean, Tony's annoying neighbours who visit him in his room after the show. 'The casting was a joy,' says Kerr. 'Roger, who I adored in *Nuts in May*, is one of the reasons I'm a director. Neither have much screen time, but they land beautifully. You

TOP LEFT: Rosie Cavaliero plays Tony's mouse-like dresser Kirstie, who turns out to be the real 'Lady Macbeth' of the piece.

ABOVE: Steve douses himself in water for Tony's 'sobering up' shower.

feel like you know them and understand the dynamic brilliantly. And they're funny. Again, it feels like social comedy.'

As far back as *The League of Gentlemen*, Pemberton and Shearsmith say they have been warned by producers not to 'write anything too theatrical or about telly or about film because no one knows that world,' says Reece. 'We always manage to. But we've always been slightly cautious.'

'You write what you know, and what they know is performing,' says Tandy, who himself spent five years in stage management. 'So we try to limit the number of showbiz episodes to maybe one a season. It's not a cut-and-dried rule. We had two in the first series. But you don't want to plunder that treasure trove of experience too often. It's a hard note to give, because they write that world really well. And they are some of my personal favourites. This absolutely evokes the seediness of behind-the-scenes in a West End theatre.'

When it came to the dressing room, Tandy considered using a real one, before opting to build it as a set. 'The decision was taken with a slightly heavy heart because of the money it would cost. But we did get exactly what we wanted, which is this very cramped, low-ceilinged, basement feel, which is absolutely what you get with a number one or number two dressing room in the West End. All the Victorian ones have that arrangement because they're close to the stage. You can get bigger rooms, but they're up flights of stairs.'

Together with *Psychoville* production designer Brian Sykes, Kerr made an exhaustive study of dressing rooms, poring over hundreds of photographs, even watching films with a theatrical setting, before creating their own. 'I wanted it to feel subterranean. It's got this patina of sweat, of decades of actors who've been in that space,' says Kerr, who asked Sykes to incorporate skylights into the set so the viewer is aware of the outside world. Colour, too, was crucial, with Sykes painting the walls green. 'Green is an unlucky colour backstage,' says Tandy. 'Some people won't wear green costumes. Theatre folk are very superstitious.' The end result was impressively dingy. 'I remember being delighted it was so authentic, with old pipes and that green that's been painted over a hundred times, and the faded yellowing paint on the door,' says Reece. 'They really got it. They're always shitholes.'

The set was revamped overnight for the episode's fifth and final act that takes place a year later, when a paralysed, wheelchair-bound Tony comes to visit the now-successful Jim in his newly painted room. 'It's a terrible, horrible ending, that last conversation they have together,' says Reece. And yet the scene provoked fits of giggles in both actors on the day.

'We were crying with laughter filming it and that very rarely happens,' says Steve.

'It's such an ostensibly earnest scene they found it difficult to play with a straight face,' remembers Kerr. 'Reece and Steve are so professional in terms of not needing many takes. But there was a lot of corpsing. Unfortunately, when it starts, it's quite tricky to nip it in the bud. Thankfully, we had

ABOVE: Reece in action as understudy Jim.

enough time and got what we needed. And you want to have some fun on the set. It shouldn't all be watching the clock and getting the goods.'

Given that *Macbeth* is Shakespeare's bloodiest play, 'The Understudy' doesn't skip on the red stuff, with Kerr and Stephan Pehrsson aiming for a 'really intense *giallo* colouring, with blood red, obviously, being a key element,' explains the former. 'We also wanted to explore the idea of the mirroring, visually, as a device, so with Brian and Stephan, we worked hard to play with reflections and things seen in half light, building to horror moments like the POV shot towards the curtain with the bloody hand. They're quite intense, *giallo* stabs.'

There are two big horror beats in 'The Understudy'. The first shows blood dripping down the mirror with Reece in front. The second sees blood permeating from the carpet. Both were done practically on set, but neither effect really worked and had to be enhanced in post-production with digital blood. 'It's a very grizzly episode,' reflects Reece. So much so that when series one was released on DVD and Blu-ray, it was given an 18 certificate. 'Because of the blood and guts and the wrist cutting. But you get worse on *EastEnders*.'

ABOVE: Felicity and Laura battle for control.

BBC TWO PRESENTS A BBC COMEDY PRODUCTION AN INSIDE NO. 9 FILM "THE HARROWING" AIMEÉ-FFION EDWARDS HELEN McCRORY REECE SHEARSMITH POPPY RUSH SEAN BUCKLEY SCREENPLAY BY STEVE PEMBERTON & REECE SHEARSMITH EXECUTIVE PRODUCER JON PLOWMAN PRODUCED BY ADAM TANDY DIRECTED BY DAVID KERR

The Harrowing

- Series **1**
- Episode **6**
- Directed by **David Kerr**

Mining for inspiration the rich Gothic horror tradition of Hammer, Amicus, Edgar Allan Poe and *The Addams Family*, as well as the Gospel of Nicodemus, an apocryphal text that describes Jesus's descent into hell, 'The Harrowing' was the first of what has now become the traditional horror series finale. 'We wanted to have a fun half hour that was very Gothic with these mysterious characters,' says Reece. 'It was very much, "Let's do a full-on, all-out horror," because we hadn't done one. Although, increasingly, we've realised the more horrific ones are not set in Dracula's Castle, but in a more domestic setting.'

'It felt like an episode with the stops pulled out,' says Kerr. 'So much of *Inside No. 9* is about claustrophobia and contained settings. This, inherently, felt like it had more scale and a bigger canvas. Of course, you're still dealing with characters trapped in an environment, but it was clearly the most

ABOVE: The episode poster for 'The Harrowing' was designed by Graham Humphreys.

genre episode of the first season, and it had an ambition to touch on movies we've all grown up with. Not just Hammer and Amicus, but also *The Innocents*, *The Haunting*, *The Orphanage*, *The Others* … movies in big spooky houses.'

'The Harrowing' begins with schoolgirl Katy (Aimée-Ffion Edwards) arriving to house-sit for the creepy Moloch siblings, Tabitha and Hector, in their imposing Gothic home, unaware of the horrors in store for her, which include being drugged and possessed by a demon. 'There's a film called *House of the Devil* which has a similar premise,' reflects Reece. 'It's that trope of the vulnerable babysitter. When you go to someone's house you don't know what you're going to get.' The fact the Molochs were paying her £11 per hour for eight hours' work should have set alarm bells ringing for Katy, even before meeting Tabitha (Helen McCrory), a strange, ethereal, vampiric-like woman with white hair, pale skin, long fingernails and hellish taste in art, and her equally weird brother Hector (Shearsmith). The pair were modelled on Madeline and Roderick Usher from Poe's short story 'The Fall of the House of Usher', famously adapted into a 1960 film starring Vincent Price. 'I wasn't trying to do a Vincent Price. But there was definitely an element of him,' says Reece. 'And Tabitha talks about Madeline Usher. That's why they have white hair.'

Casting the late Helen McCrory was a stroke of genius. 'People saw her as "Dame Helen McCrory" and so didn't think she'd want to do something like this,' muses Reece, who starred with her in a production of *As You Like It*. 'But she jumped at the chance. I had to talk her through the part, and she had lots of questions. She took it very seriously and was wildly different in every take.' A consummate theatre actress, McCrory came from a forensic tradition of building a character from the ground up.

ABOVE: The late Helen McCrory as the wonderfully ethereal Tabitha.

ABOVE: This portrait of Hector, painted by Reece, echoes the artwork on the walls in this episode.

'She brought all of that theatrical flourish we wanted for the character,' says Kerr. 'I was thinking Norma Desmond in *Sunset Boulevard*. That sense of someone who'd been shuttered in their chateau for a very long time, not seen a lot of daylight, and out of touch with anything resembling modernity.'

Katy the house-sitter was played by relative newcomer Aimée-Ffion Edwards, who would go on to star with McCrory in the BBC series *Peaky Blinders*. 'When you're trying to find an actress to play a teenager, they've got to look plausibly young. And she did,' says Kerr. 'She had that girl-next-door innocence and natural curiosity. Katy seems to be quite self-possessed, self-assured and sensible, yet is a typical teen who wants to make some money. Subliminally, as a viewer, you expect the rational will triumph over the supernatural, and that her quiet strength will see her through. Ultimately, that helps wrong-foot the audience who think she's probably going to survive this experience.'

The exterior of the Moloch home was a nineteenth-century mansion in Highgate which has since been turned into flats. 'I often go and have a look at it,' says Reece, who lives nearby. 'Although it doesn't look as good as it did. There were a few options, but that was the most *Addams Family*-esque.'

As for the interior, the script required a number of rooms. 'It's not just one set,' sighs Tandy. 'You've got a kitchen, hallway, living room, bedrooms, staircase. How do you find all that in one place, in a way you can shoot it in a week and it's not going to cost an arm and a leg? Ideally we'd have shot it on an enormous soundstage, but we had to go to a location.'

'You think you're being really frugal when you write it's going to be one house,' notes Reece, 'but the state we're in with budgets, it's "You want to go to the bedroom *and* the kitchen? Could it be one or the other? And there's a hallway!"'

Despite the budget issues, Kerr wanted the episode to feel 'properly cinematic. The challenge, always, is trying to do anything at scale. You've got pocket money, and what you're trying to do is a Hollywood-style production number. But it was pretty obvious we weren't going to be building an interior.'

The solution was Langleybury House, a Grade II-listed building in Hertfordshire. A popular filming location, Langleybury had been used for the BBC's 2011 adaptation of *Great Expectations* as well as Oscar Lomax's home in *Psychoville*, a fact that gave Pemberton and Shearsmith some concern, fearing fans would be able to recognise it. Fortunately, they were proved wrong. So much so they would return to shoot both 'Séance Time' and 'The Riddle of the Sphinx'. 'It was pretty dilapidated. But what was wonderful from our point of view was it had this very defining central staircase,' says Kerr, who, during his research, had uncovered an *Addams Family* cartoon with a very similar one. 'It felt the planets were aligning and we were in the right spot for the story. There was a huge number of rooms leading off it, and a sense of rooms beyond rooms. So whatever door you go through, you're not getting out.' Moreover, the staircase allowed for the installation of a stairlift, which, says Kerr, was 'key to the creepiness and the sense of "What on earth is going on up there?" We started to imagine the noise it could make as it moved. That felt really promising, powerful and original. Because although this is dripping with genre tropes, we wanted it to feel fresh.'

Charged with turning Langleybury into the Moloch home was production designer Brian Sykes, who, having worked on *Psychoville*, already knew the place well. 'I think Brian achieved a minor miracle in producing those three episodes – "A Quiet Night In", "The Understudy" and this – which were probably bigger than the first three, for less money.' The budget was so tight, in fact, that Kerr had to choose his camera angles in advance and have Sykes dress the set accordingly. 'There's very little added furniture,' says Tandy. 'The biggest dress is the living room. The kitchen we could only shoot from one angle because we didn't have enough money to dress the other way. The hallway we kept as dark as possible.'

Even the stairlift was a fake. 'We couldn't afford a real one,' says Tandy, who argued it should be cut from the script. 'It's a pulley system and a bit of rail. It's a complete cheat. Luckily, you don't see the whole thing work. You *hear* it. And hear it enough to believe it. But it's no more real than the doors on the Starship *Enterprise*.'

What couldn't really be scrimped on were the Hieronymus Bosch-style paintings that line the walls of the entrance hall and which depict the Harrowing of Hell. 'It was important they should feel as rich and authentic as possible,' says Kerr. The production commissioned two original paintings and hired a couple. The rest were the work of Sykes's art department. 'They were wet when we filmed,' recalls Steve. 'They'd stayed up all night to finish them. That's why some are a bit more abstract.'

'I tried to get the big, main Harrowing one, but they wouldn't let me have it,' laments Reece. 'Because I pilfer everything.'

The script also stipulated the temperature in the house be three degrees below zero for Andras's 'medical reasons'. As the production couldn't afford to refrigerate the set, they added cold breath digitally in post-production, but only had the budget for a few minutes' worth. 'You see it at the beginning

ABOVE LEFT: One of the alarming prosthetic feet that formed part of Andras's costume.

ABOVE RIGHT: Director David Kerr poses with Sean Buckley, fully made-up as the mysterious third Moloch sibling, Andras.

to give a semblance of it,' says Tandy.

The cold also had another significant meaning. 'The ninth circle of hell in Dante's *Inferno* is ice,' explains Steve. 'So that's another number nine we got in.'

Horror, much like comedy, requires a particular set of stylistic tools. 'They're both cinema of sensation, both about creating a specific reaction,' says Kerr. 'On one hand laughter, on the other terror, fear. So you're manipulating an audience's reaction, and working out the best ways to achieve it.' Key to that manipulation was Kerr's use of a 'prowling Steadicam', channelling John Carpenter's seminal shocker *Halloween* with shots designed to explore the house from Katy's point of view. 'David really got the tension of it,' says Reece. 'He embraced the creeping dread and set up a ticking timebomb of: "There's somebody upstairs. Don't go up. There are things wrong with him, but he'll never ring that bell. He's never rung it." ... And then, twenty minutes in, it rings.'

What Katy, and her best friend Shell (Poppy Rush), a goth who joins her for the evening, discover upstairs is even more terrifying and horrific. Bound to a four-poster bed, wearing only a soiled nappy and a dirty gag, is the Moloch's oldest sibling, the emaciated, cloven-footed, milky-eyed Andras (Sean Buckley), who the Molochs claim has been possessed by Castiel, the demon of mischief, for the last fifty years. But Andras's mortal body — sustained by a diet of baby formula and rusks — is failing and the Molochs need a new host to keep Castiel from roaming the Earth. Which is where Katy comes in, served up by Shell, who's in cahoots with the Molochs and desperately wants to be the chosen one but, alas, is 'too fat'. 'It's pretty dark material,' says Kerr, 'but part of the misdirection is being lulled into thinking these people are bonkers eccentrics and can't really be all that bad. They're just slightly deluded, rather than downright evil.'

Andras had originally been scripted as a winged demon but, once again, cost was an issue. 'It was a CGI creature, or at least an actor with CGI add-ons. Jon [Plowman] and I said, "We can't afford CGI, can you rewrite it?"' recalls Tandy. The boys duly obliged, opting to rely on the physicality of a performer augmented with make-up. 'We wanted Andras to have almost a Judderman, creepy quality,' adds Steve in reference to a character in a TV advert for Metz. 'And Sean was absolutely fantastic.'

Buckley, who died in 2016, had worked in physical theatre with Steven Berkoff for many years, 'contorting the body in order to be able to produce a visual representation of emotion,' says Tandy. 'And so him, plus prosthetics, plus a nappy was extraordinary.'

While Kerr examined the Pale Man in *Pan's Labyrinth* for insight, he decided, ultimately, not to go too monstrous with Andras, collaborating with make-up artist Lisa Cavalli-Green and prosthetics designer Kristyan Mallett on a look that involved cloudy contacts, false teeth and deformed feet. 'A lot of his look came from "Sloth" in the bed from *Se7en*,' says Reece. 'I remember giving them lots of photos of him for inspiration.'

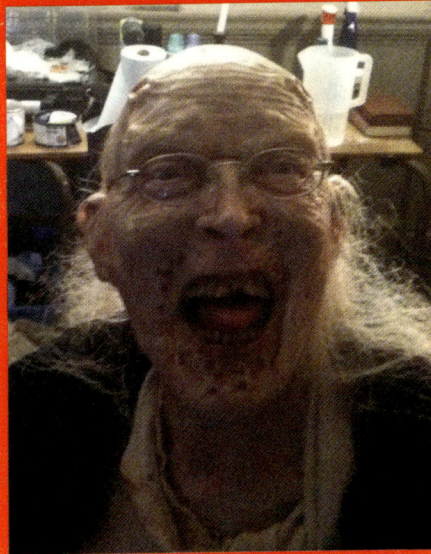

ABOVE: The late Sean Buckley's experience in physical theatre made his performance as Andras all the more unsettling.

Hector:	Begat by the seed of He Who Walks Backwards.
Shell:	Michael Jackson?

'We all felt Andras should sit right on the cusp of being a maltreated human, and someone you think is supernatural,' says Kerr. 'Physically, we wanted to explore prosthetic make-up to see how that could enhance his appearance, but do it in a way that still made you feel that maybe he was just a neglected human.' Kerr worked with Buckley on Andras's movement. 'Dragging his foot, how his noises might work, his laboured breathing. That sense of someone who's been pent-up and chained for a long time. And how that brought a tautness to his physicality, and a repressed energy that was going to find a release. So you have this sleeping dragon awakening.'

And then it was all about not blowing the reveal. 'The thing in a monster movie is, don't show the monster too clearly, too soon. So we play with the sense that there's something beyond the muslin, but not seen clearly,' says Kerr. 'When you have limited resources, you don't attempt the thing you can't quite pull off. So we wanted to make sure what we did, we did well.'

'The great thing about horror is that less is more,' says Tandy. 'So where we put the money was in the detail of those oil paintings and the prosthetics. Those are the bits that really sell the episode. The rest of it was camera work and lighting.'

While Pemberton and Shearsmith had initially hoped Andras's true nature might remain ambiguous, the final shot leaves no doubt that Katy is about to be possessed by a demon, cutting to black as Andras staggers towards her, whispering 'Mischief' through cracked lips.

ABOVE: Shell (Poppy Rush) and Katy (Aimée-Ffion Edwards).

'It was an ending that just stopped,' says Steve. 'All the others had had this twist or a little flourish, and this didn't. And I think that is what made it genuinely unsettling.'

The result was another remarkable episode, switching tone from the comedy-horror of *The Addams Family* to the eccentricity of *House of Usher* before ending on some 'really dark, demonic, nasty stuff,' says Kerr.

Quite how nasty was always a matter of debate, right up until the last day of filming. 'I remember David and I having a quiet conversation on set, working out how far we could go,' reveals Tandy. 'How far could you take the audience before you crossed the line? Given that you'd been in this jolly, comic romp for quite a lot of it, we didn't really have anywhere else to go. So we said, "Let's drive up to the line, but not cross it."'

'The Harrowing' features some of the creepiest music of the series, courtesy of Christian Henson, who has scored every episode of *Inside No. 9*, and who included a decades-old sample of his younger brother going 'Arrrhhh' before his voice broke, as part of the soundscape. 'He has a great array of vintage synthesizers and got them out for this,' says Kerr. 'We talked about Goblin's score for *Suspiria* as a touchstone, and much as the creeping Steadicam I brought into the visual style was a nod to John Carpenter's *Halloween*, Carpenter's scores were something we also talked about. The strange electronica sits very well with the sound design we went for, with the noise of the stairlift and, particularly, the sound of the bell. We tried different bells, and it was very important to play around with the level, so it's just perceptible, initially, but still cuts through. When you're holding back reveals, sound becomes much more important, because you start forming pictures in your head of what you *might* encounter.'

'That is the art of the storytelling,' says Tandy. 'It's there in the script. It's there in the direction. It's there in the acting. You just make sure it's there on the edit. And then the music mix, which is the final moment you can shape emotions. Everybody was at the top of their game for that episode. And it turned out to be a real romp. With that very dark ending. I was so excited to put the button on it, and go, "That's your season finale."'

Inside No. 9 was recommissioned for a second series even before the first had aired. 'We used the first three episodes we filmed – 'Tom & Gerri', 'Sardines' and 'Last Gasp' – as a calling card for casting going forward,' says Tandy. 'But, of course, it also enabled us to deliver them to the BBC and say, "Here's a preview of the series we're making." And it was at that point, they went, "We absolutely want to recommission you."'

'We were delighted because it had never happened to us before,' recalls Steve. 'So that was absolutely joyful knowing that when it went out, not only could you enjoy it, but you knew you had more to do. It was fantastic. But I do remember feeling a certain pressure, given how well the first series had gone. We were like, okay, well, we can't come in now with six ones that are just all right.'

'The bar was high,' notes Reece.

'The bar was *so* high,' continues Steve, 'because the reaction had been really phenomenal. We'd got some of the best reviews and comments we'd ever had. And it's a feeling that has never left us, and it's exhausting, because you almost want one of the series to be less good than the previous, so you've broken the duck. But people were like, "How can they top 'A Quiet Night In'? How can they top 'Sardines'?" So you have that in your mind, and it spurs you on to make sure you've got some strong ideas.'

BELOW: Hector and Tabitha were loosely inspired by Madeline and Roderick Usher from Poe's 'The Fall of the House of Usher'.

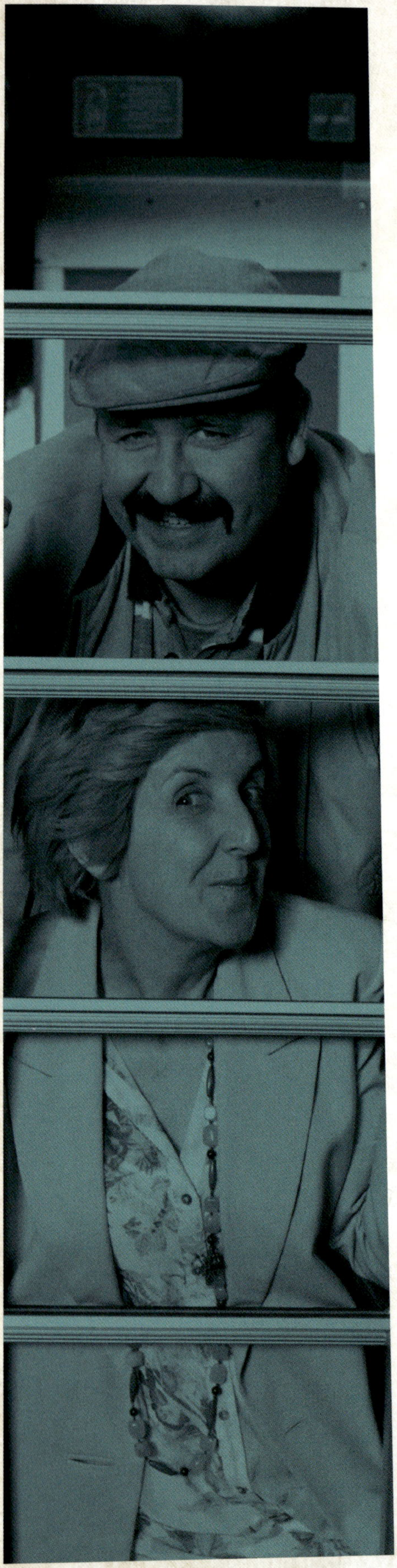
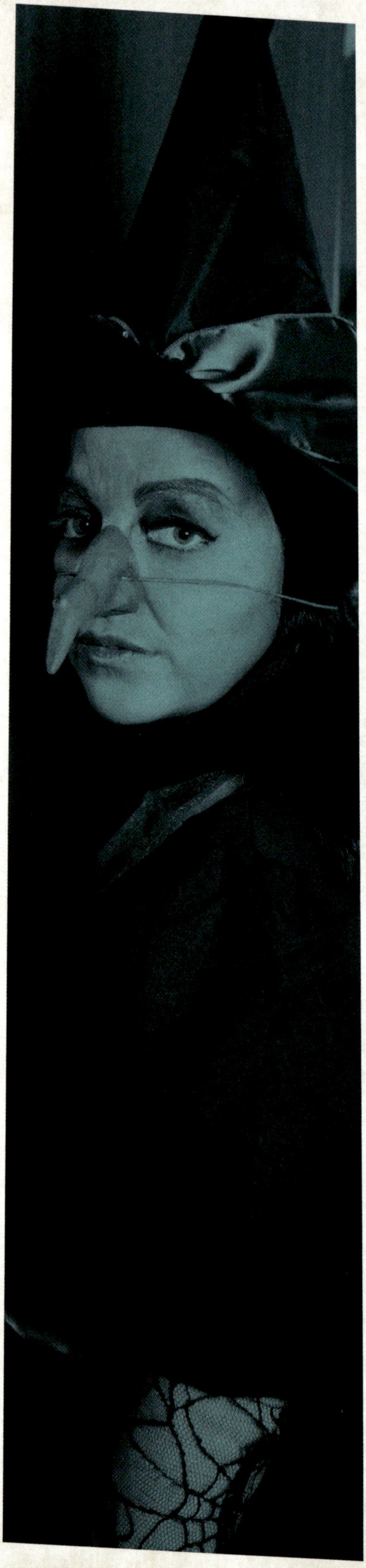
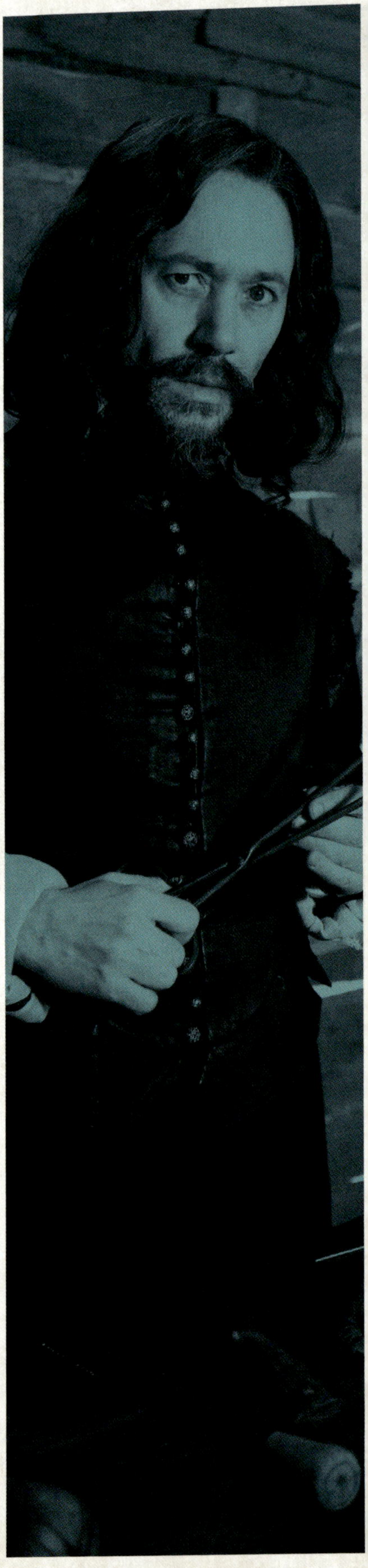

SERIES TWO

JACK WHITEHALL   JULIE HESMONDHALGH   JESSICA GUNNING   MARK BENTON
STEVE PEMBERTON   REECE SHEARSMITH

LA COUCHETTE

IN DEUXIÈME CLASSE
EVERYONE CAN HEAR YOU SCREAM...

THURSDAY 26 MARCH
10PM

BBC TWO PRESENTS A BBC COMEDY PRODUCTION AN INSIDE NO. 9 FILM "LA COUCHETTE"
REECE SHEARSMITH STEVE PEMBERTON JULIE HESMONDHALGH MARK BENTON JESSICA GUNNING
JACK WHITEHALL SCREENPLAY BY STEVE PEMBERTON & REECE SHEARSMITH
EXECUTIVE PRODUCER JON PLOWMAN PRODUCED BY ADAM TANDY DIRECTED BY GUILLEM MORALES

BBC TWO

La Couchette

- Series **2**
- Episode **1**
- Directed by **Guillem Morales**

During the summer of 2014, Pemberton and his family went to France on holiday. Rather than fly or drive, they took the train, spending a few days in Paris before boarding an SNCF sleeper to Bourg-Saint-Maurice. 'I'd never done it before, so it was quite romantic,' he remembers. 'Because there were five of us, we had our own compartment and could enjoy it. We had three beds, one on top of another, on either side, and each one had a place to put your toiletries, a little pillow and a little blanket.'

'It's like being cryogenically frozen,' laughs Reece.

'I didn't get much sleep,' admits Steve, 'but, as I was lying there, I was thinking, "I love this."' So much so that, once he was back in the UK, he suggested a sleeper cabin might make a great setting for an *Inside No. 9*. 'I didn't know what the story was, but I said, "Imagine it with different people." It's so intimate, and had shades of "Sardines" as well. We knew there were six bunks, so we had six characters. It was an exercise in an enclosed space and the nightmare of other people. So we piled it full of largely monstrous characters.'

ABOVE: The episode poster for 'La Couchette' was designed by Matthew Burlem.

They discussed Agatha Christie's train-based whodunnit *Murder on the Orient Express* but decided they didn't want the episode to be about a murder per se. However, both liked the idea of there being a dead body – for comedic reasons. 'The body rolling out [of the bunk] and landing and the others having to put it back, and that horrible notion that they decide it's better to leave it and sit out the night,' says Reece. 'That was a really strange and ghoulish dilemma we thought was interesting to explore. And then the surprise at the end when you realise there *had* been a murder.'

After having managed to get through an entire episode with only a single line of dialogue, they decided to try something similar with the opening five minutes or so. 'There's one man trying to get to sleep, another man coming in, making the noise. When you are writing comedy, you tend to be dialogue-led. You want to get the characters down. You want to get the funny things they're saying. But "A Quiet Night In" had been a good lesson. So we said, "Let's just do visual storytelling and enjoy using some of those techniques."'

As with 'Sardines', the characters in 'La Couchette' are introduced in ones and twos, 'giving them all their moment', says Steve. 'And because it was a European train, we didn't just want a load of English people.' Already inside the compartment when 'La Couchette' begins is Maxwell (Shearsmith), a prim and proper Englishman who, we later discover, is on his way to a job interview at the World Health Organization. For now, though, Maxwell is in his bunk, wearing pyjamas and an eye mask, trying to sleep. 'He's got a routine and doesn't want it interrupted,' says Reece. 'And then to put him in with Jorg, this monstrous, noisy German, was the basic comedy of it. Then we had this idea that Maxwell was going to be late for this very important appointment. And we thought, "Maybe Jorg can be up for the same job."'

ABOVE: Left to right: Kath (Julie Hesmondhalgh), Jorg (Steve Pemberton), Les (Mark Benton), Shona (Jessica Gunning), Maxwell (Reece Shearsmith) and Hugo (Jack Whitehall).

Next to arrive are Les (Mark Benton) and Kath (Julie Hesmondhalgh), a Yorkshire couple travelling to their daughter's wedding, who irritate Maxwell with their chat about who's in the top bunk. They're soon followed by Jessica Gunning's Shona, a foul-mouthed and smelly Aussie backpacker – 'I haven't had a shower since Prague' – talking loudly on her phone, before, finally, she's joined by her 'date' – fellow traveller and ex-English public schoolboy Hugo (Jack Whitehall), who's stowed away onboard. While they didn't write the character of Hugo specifically for Whitehall, they definitely had him in mind. 'This is what he does,' says Reece. 'We knew he's a massive fan. So we thought, we'll ask him. Might not be free ...'

He was. 'Jack jumped at the chance,' says Tandy. 'Remember, we had the first series out there. So it was a lot easier to get people to sign up to what we were doing. Particularly with the reviews we'd had, the likes of which I've never seen. "The best television in two decades." And they got even better with the next episode.'

'La Couchette' pushes the taste boundaries with ribald one-liners and toilet humour, which is more in keeping with Shearsmith and Pemberton's earlier work. 'There is something about an enclosed space with people in it, bodily functions or anything we secrete becomes amplified, amongst strangers,' laughs Steve. 'It just tickled us. And it is quite a childish trait. We've always done it, all through *League*, all through *Psychoville*, we've never not done that. We could have written this as a drama. In fact, all the *No. 9*s you could write that way. But it's come out of BBC Comedy. It's a comedy show. We are known for doing comedy.'

Tandy says it felt like the gloves were off with series two, with Pemberton and Shearsmith pushing

ABOVE LEFT: Although they didn't write the character of Hugo specifically for Jack Whitehall, Reece and Steve definitely had him in mind, and were delighted when he jumped at the chance.

ABOVE RIGHT: Julie Hesmondhalgh's Kath enters the compartment.

themselves and the show to even greater extremes, both in terms of subject matter and storytelling. 'They absolutely pulled it off with "A Quiet Night In". And "La Couchette" was like an extreme version of "Last Gasp", again revolving around the moral dilemmas surrounding a dead body.'

'I've seen people describe *No. 9* and say, "They're great, but they're not funny. Don't go there for laughs, because they're dark,"' ponders Reece. 'It's what people take from them. But this one we thought was out-and-out funny.'

Initially, Pemberton wanted to play the part of Les, not Jorg, who reviles the rest by taking a dump in one of Kath's shoeboxes. They offered the role to a well-known German actor, who turned it down because 'he didn't want to do the defecation scene', reveals Steve.

'It was at that point we discovered the Germans who were available to work in this country didn't have a sense of humour about their national characteristics,' says Tandy, 'so Steve ended up playing him. The shitting in the shoebox scene is the greatest thing I've ever filmed. Absolutely. Way out there. But completely within the spectrum of stuff they'd done on *League*.'

Shona was based on the girlfriend of someone Pemberton and Shearsmith had gone to Bretton Hall with, and a character they'd created in their pre-*League* days called Hippie Critical. 'I remember travelling in Thailand in my mid-twenties,' recalls Steve. 'But I was on my "holidays" and other people were on a "trip"; so I was a "tourist" and they were "travellers". People were talking about how ill they'd become and would revel in how much they stank. It's so not me, so I wrote down all these notes for a character called Hippie Critical, but we never did anything with it. So a lot of that came back, the sense that the ill-er you got was a badge of honour. Then we had a friend who had an Australian girlfriend who was absolutely lovely, but there was a bluntness to her, and a revelling in it.'

The seventh character was Yves, the corpse. He was played by George Glaves, who came from an extras agency. The only requirement was that he be 'light enough we could manhandle the body,'

ABOVE: Reece and Steve as Maxwell and Jorg.

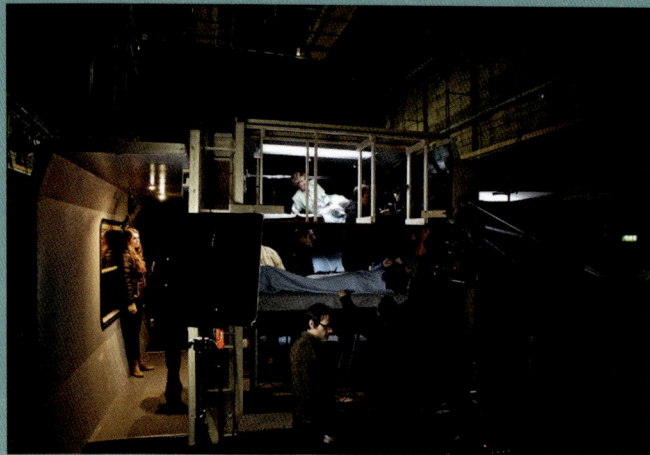

says Steve. 'But we decided to credit him because he was there with us all week.'

Having done such a superb job on the first series, David Kerr had been everyone's choice to direct the second, but he was busy. 'David doesn't quite get the credit he deserves for directing all six episodes of the first series,' says Steve. 'From slapstick comedy to dark drama to Gothic horror, he managed to keep the whole series feeling fresh and every episode unique which is an amazing achievement given our budget and schedule. He really was a fantastic collaborator and we were very sorry to lose him for series two.'

With the benefit of hindsight, Tandy, Plowman and the boys decided that six episodes was maybe too much for one person to take on, and decided to split the series up into three blocks of two episodes. 'That enabled me to keep a plurality of creative voices in the director's chair, and make sure we had little breaks, so Reece and Steve could draw their breath before doing the next couple,' recalls Tandy. 'It also allowed us to do rehearsals, getting the design team refreshed and thinking about a whole new palette and tone. Reece and Steve said, "We'd be quite interested in doing some." I was happy to let them do two, so we needed another couple of directors.'

'We asked Matt Lipsey, who'd done *Psychoville*, but he was working on something else,' says Steve. 'So we had to cast around and find some new people.'

Among them was Guillem Morales, the Barcelona-born director of psychological horror *Julia's Eyes*, a film Pemberton had, coincidentally, just watched. 'When I saw his name on the list, I went, "He's great visually. Let's meet him."'

'I was a big fan of *Inside No. 9*, a *big* fan,' Morales says. 'I met Jon Plowman, Steve and Reece, and Adam; we talked about *Julia's Eyes*, we talked about the show. I really liked them and I suppose they liked me.'

'We liked his personality, we liked how he talked about his work,' confirms Steve. 'He was clearly an auteur, someone who had ideas about shots. And we got a good feeling from him and his enthusiasm. Sometimes that's all you need, to feel someone gets it and wants to do it. We felt assured Guillem knew our past work, and knew British comedy.' Indeed, despite being raised in Spain, Morales was steeped in it. 'There was a TV channel that showed all these old classic British comedy shows,' he explains. 'So I grew up watching *'Allo, 'Allo, Fawlty Towers,* even *Doctor Who*.'

'Guillem hadn't got any television credits in this country, but he seemed to be so on point in terms of tone and thinking about the show, we had to take a gamble,' recalls Tandy. 'We put him at the beginning of the run, thinking, "If it all goes wrong, somebody can take over." But it absolutely turned out to be one of the best creative decisions we've ever made.'

Morales went to film school in Spain, where he shot almost all of his films on 35mm film stock, using short ends, partial rolls of unexposed film left over during a production and kept for later use. As such, he learned to be very precise in his filmmaking, only shooting exactly what's required, and needing minimal takes. 'His shooting ratio is incredibly low,' says Tandy. 'He's so efficient, so

ABOVE: The set was mounted on Ford Transit springs to simulate the rocking of a real train carriage.

compact. He does these amazingly detailed storyboards. He knows exactly what shot he wants for which line. It's an extraordinary skill to have.'

'I've never worked with a director so sure of how he wants it to look,' concurs Reece. 'He has it all storyboarded, every single detail. In one way, that's great for producers, because you're not doing the scene over and over. In others, it's quite scary because you're locked into what you've got. But he's nearly always right. I don't think there's been a point where I've gone, "That's not what we imagined." You feel safe in their vision and it becomes its own art, because it's through the filter of him. It was a punt on Guillem, but he's really brilliant.'

With all the action taking place inside the confines of an SNCF sleeper compartment, there was never a question of shooting on a real train. Production designer Simon Rogers (*The Thick of It*) dove into his own memories of Interrailing in the eighties to create a steel-framed set that was slightly larger-than-life size, which he built at Twickenham Studios, pulling plans from a French trainspotter's website and having real train parts – ladders, latches, door handles, net curtains and windows – sourced from a French breaker's yard and shipped to England. 'Because the cast were in bunks for the whole time, we needed to come up with a robust cantilever system to make it safe for them to lie on,' says Rogers. 'They were a bit wider than normal to make it more comfortable, and they needed to stay in place while we took the walls away.'

Each wall could be hoisted out to allow access for the camera, which was mounted on a special arm with a remote head. 'We split the action into five scenes, and each day we would spend our time working our way round the set, in a clockwise fashion,' says Tandy, 'sticking the arm in from each side, and picking up all the angles, removing one wall at a time on chain hoists. The first day was incredibly slow, but we got faster at it, until each wall change took about twenty minutes.'

To simulate the carriage's rocking and swaying, Rogers mounted the corners of the set on Ford Transit springs, so both carriage and actors moved, while the camera was locked. 'It was quite top-heavy and pretty much moved of its own volition,' says Rogers. Matthew Scrivener, the first assistant director would rock the set gently during takes with his foot.

'It was a very small amount, but gave us a very fluid feel, enough for all of the artists to brace themselves realistically. To the extent that poor Jack Whitehall got motion sickness on his first day, and had to jump off the set and be sick at one point,' reveals Tandy.

'He was mortified,' says Steve. 'He came out of the toilet and Sheridan [Smith] was in the studio having a wig fitting. He'd never met her before and was all, "Hi, pleased to meet you," while he had sick dribbling down his chin.'

ABOVE: The cast on set between takes.

RIGHT: A section of the detailed storyboard created by director Guillem Morales.

ACT 2

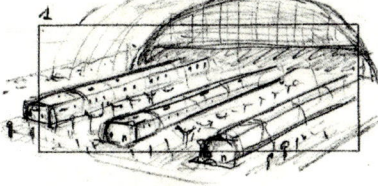
1

2 A
STATION ASSISTANT

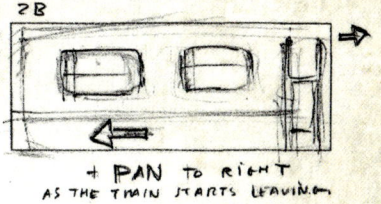
2 B
+ PAN TO RIGHT
AS THE TRAIN STARTS LEAVING.

2 C
TRAIN PULLING OUT OF THE STATION

3 A
GUARD WALKS ALONG

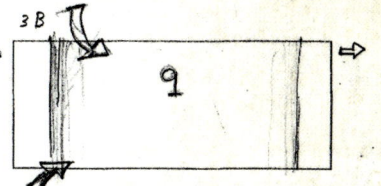
3 B
9
DOLLY IN + PAN TO LEFT
tracking him

3 C
9
"LA COUCHETTE"

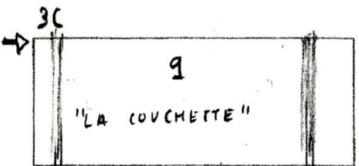

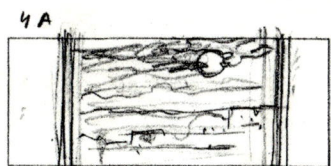
4 A
WE SEE TRAIN MOVING THROUGH
THE WINDOW...

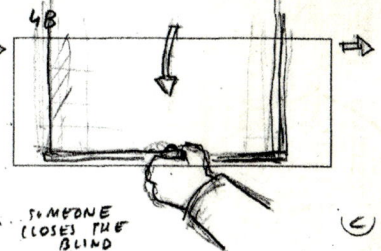
4 B
SOMEONE
CLOSES THE
BLIND

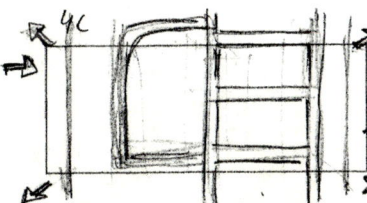
4 C
DOLLY OUT

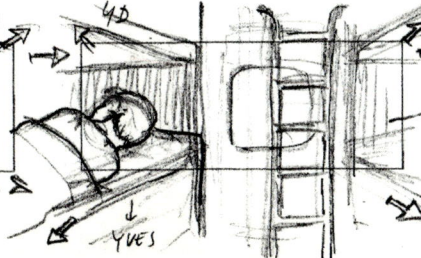
4 D
YVES

4 E
MAXWELL'S HANDS,
CHECKING HIS WRISTWATCH

4 F
MAXWELL PREPARES TO GO TO BED.

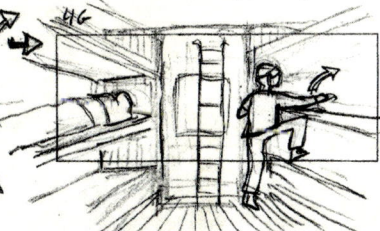
4 G

5 A
MAXWELL TAKES ONE LAST
LOOK AT YVES.

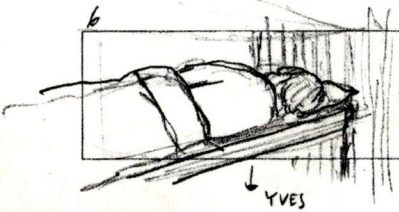
6
YVES

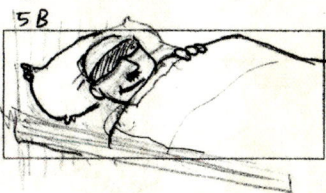
5 B

7 A

Because the bunks were stacked vertically, many of the shots involved a lot of travel in the vertical plane, rather than side to side. Having the jib arm allowed Morales to get all manner of interesting compositions and angles, with his camera moving effortlessly around the bunks in a circle, up and down, or in a U-shape, as well as deep shots looking down into the compartment. 'We had to be very precise,' says Morales. 'We had to know every single shot in advance otherwise it would have been a mess.'

'La Couchette' wasn't just Morales's first experience in TV, it was his first experience of comedy, as all his previous work had been in the horror or thriller genres. 'What amazed me is you instantly see if something works or doesn't work, because it makes you laugh. In horror or drama, you get the stuff and think, "If it's edited in a certain way, this is going to work." But with comedy, you've got an immediate reaction. That surprised me.'

As did certain aspects of British humour. He recalls Mark Benton's Les taking off trousers to reveal his pants in one scene and being shocked. 'They were absolutely tiny. It was so ridiculous, they were so tight and I called, "Cut." I went to the costume department and said, "My God, what have you done? They're tiny. It's ridiculous." And they said, "He chose them." And I started understanding. That's the attitude in British comedy. It's funny, but deep down there's a lot of pain. That was my first experience. I really enjoyed it. I enjoyed the rhythm. Horror and comedy share the same rhythm.'

BELOW: Mark Benton as Les.

Hugo: I love all that shit. Have you done
          India?
Shona: Yeah, it was awesome. I got hepatitis.

Part of what makes 'La Couchette' – which picked up the coveted Rose d'Or comedy award – so tense and unbearable (in a good way) is the sound design. 'The first ten minutes is about someone trying to sleep, nothing else,' says Morales. 'So the point was to annoy him. And what annoys you when you're trying to sleep are noises, sounds. So that door had to be very, *very* annoying. And the zip, of course.'

'Everything is magnified,' says Reece. 'The zip. The relentlessness of that. There was a lot in the soundscape of this episode that really helps the comedy. I remember we got an email from Russell T. Davies saying he loved "the savagery of that door" when it opens and closes as people are creeping in.'

'We spent a lot of time working on that door, making sure we got a real sliding effect,' says Tandy. 'And we used exactly the same recording every time, so it was this repetitive sound, always cutting into action.' As for the zip, they wanted it to sound like an electric chainsaw. 'We recorded so many different ones and had maybe four goes at mixing it. It was the thing that gave us the biggest problem on the sound front.'

In the end, it all added up to the perfect opener for series two. 'It reaches this climax where we wanted the audience to think that Kath had been so unsettled by what had gone on that she potentially had thrown herself off the train,' says Steve. 'It was definitely designed to be unbearably loud and in your face. We wanted the audience to come away from that thinking, "I need to shower" or "Thank God I'm not in that compartment."'

TOP: Filming in progress.
ABOVE: Steve and Reece in costume.

The 12 Days of Christine

■ Series **2**
■ Episode **2**
■ Directed by **Guillem Morales**

'**T**here were two premises in the notebook, completely separate,' says Steve of the genesis of 'The 12 Days of Christine'. 'One was: "Can you tell the story of a relationship over twelve years?" The idea was a structural thing; you'd have January, then go forward to the following February, then the following March. There was something interesting about that because you could hook each scene into something relevant. New Year, Valentine's Day, Mother's Day, Easter, May bank holiday. June, July, and August were a bit tricky. That's why we made it her birthday and a summer holiday. September is first day back at school. Then you're into Halloween, Bonfire Night and Christmas. That was one idea. Another was: "Could a story be the last few seconds of someone's life flashing before them?" In a hospital, with lots of visitors. It was two ideas that had been percolating for a while, and then we went: "They could be the same story."'

ABOVE: Christine (Sheridan Smith) and her father Ernie (Paul Copley).

The most critically acclaimed episode of *Inside No. 9* thus far, and the one that put the show on the map, 'The 12 Days of Christine' packs one hell of an emotional punch, thanks in no small part to a remarkable performance by Sheridan Smith as the eponymous Christine. We're introduced to her on New Year's Eve, as she arrives back at her high-rise flat with Adam (Tom Riley), who she met at a fancy dress party – she's dressed as a nun, him a fireman. Over the next twenty-nine minutes, we witness the ups and downs of her life, including marriage, motherhood, a parent with dementia, divorce and death. Although, this being *Inside No. 9*, nothing is quite what it seems, and scenes are interspersed with unexplained and unsettling interludes involving broken eggs and a mysterious man (Shearsmith). Initially, we wonder whether Christine has early onset dementia like her dad, Ernie, but, eventually, she realises she's dying – the result of a car crash – and everything we've witnessed are her memories. 'We knew it wasn't particularly funny,' says Reece. 'There would be characters in it that are funny. And they might say funny things. But we thought the ending was strong. It's a puzzle, really, that you're watching.'

While they had the end in mind from the start, the breakthrough came when they hit upon the idea of a strange man popping up throughout. 'We didn't know if she'd been knocked down or was going to be in the car herself, but knew there was a figure who was involved in the accident, who would almost be the last person she saw,' explains Steve. 'She didn't know who he was, so it was scary. We thought, "That's good, let's sprinkle it in." Not make anything of it. But she'll open a door and the man will be there. And then we'll cut.'

As with 'The Understudy', the boys found having a fixed structure – twelve calendar-based scenes – made the writing easy. 'It was the last one we wrote for series two and we were under a bit of pressure to come up with another. We wrote it in about a week and sent it in, and of all the scripts we've written, very little changed from the draft we handed in. So it had a purity to it, even though on the page it felt like it could be slight. A scene about putting a cot up. A scene about packing a suitcase. We'd been through these things. We'd had children. There was lots we could draw on. It flowed out of us.'

'We were just thinking about what happens to you over the course of your life: losing a parent, marriage, children, the struggles with all these things,' says Reece. 'We wanted it to be the stuff anyone could relate to. Like lying awake, listening to your baby cry, thinking you can't go in every five minutes. And then, in the end, you get up. It was all very relatable. And yet we're thinking, "Is it all a bit drab? Is this *EastEnders*?" But it amounted to something very affecting because that ending really tore people's hearts out.'

Once they'd written a draft, they did another pass, peppering it with moments that only make sense on a second viewing, such as the broken eggs or the blue flashing lights. 'It's all there, in plain sight, and you haven't realised you've seen all these clues,' says Reece. 'That's something we've started to

Sheridan Smith   Tom Riley   Michele Dotrice   Paul Copley
Reece Shearsmith   Steve Pemberton

INSIDE No. 9
The 12 days of Christine
Thursday 10pm

BBC TWO

ABOVE: The episode poster for 'The 12 Days of Christine' was designed by Matthew Burlem.

The 12 Days of Christine   73

"That's brilliant news!" "I know, isn't it!"

Could be RELATIONSHIP one month & one year on = life flashing before eyes.

START on alarm? Loud beep, crash — ~~coming in~~ door flies open & They're coming in from a New Year's Eve party. Fancy dress? He's a Fireman — comes her in. Start of their relationship.

By the end she's saying "You're going too fast!" Pull out to reveal it's a crash & it's been her life flashing before her eyes.

Push in on door. Then cut inside. We hear noise of them coming up. Push in on eyehole (spyhole) then it becomes a white light & we go to door banging open. She comes in & puts some loud music on & people are banging on the ceiling for her to shut up.

Later she's banging on the ceiling when someone else plays music. carefree youth giving way to miserable middle age.

A mystery man who she sees — turns out in the end to be the man who crashes into her.

DEC — ~~husband~~ has a photo album of memories + "it's like my whole life flashing before my eyes. Oh no. I know what it is now." STRAIGHT into the reveal. Pull out to reality — she's in a car crash.

> **Christine: I know, but thirty-five, divorced and working in a shoe shop with my gay best friend. It's hardly the Cinderella story, is it?**

use and think is a good conceit or device, where you are one step behind the puzzlement of the main character, and so you're intrigued and want to keep watching.'

They emailed the script to Tandy and waited. Three hours later he replied with: *My God. That is amazing. Thank you.* 'And we were like, does he mean the fact we've written it is amazing? Or is he going, "My God, *this* is amazing,"' recalls Steve. 'We talked about it for ages. Then when we met up to talk about it, Adam said, "I cried when I read it."'

'It was a genuine moment of having your breath taken away by a script,' says Tandy, welling up at the memory. 'It was an extraordinary piece of writing to land on people's desks.'

'We knew it was powerful, but I don't think we felt, "Shower us with rose petals, we've written a classic,"' laughs Steve. 'We just thought, it's a good ending. It's a good premise. It really took our breath away how people responded to it. I think people reading it were more affected than, perhaps, we were.'

The storyboard panels contain the following handwritten notations:

3F — A: Took us three days.

2J — C: Ha, look!

4B — B: Tony Tiger!

2K — C: Oh, my god, you've got everything. It's almost like my whole life...

2L — DOLLY IN.

2M

SEQ 26 / 1A — DOLLY OUT — CHRISTINE OPENS HER EYES ABRUPTLY

1B

2A — THE CAR STEREO IS PLAYING "IT'S TIME TO SAY GOODBYE" — JIB UP

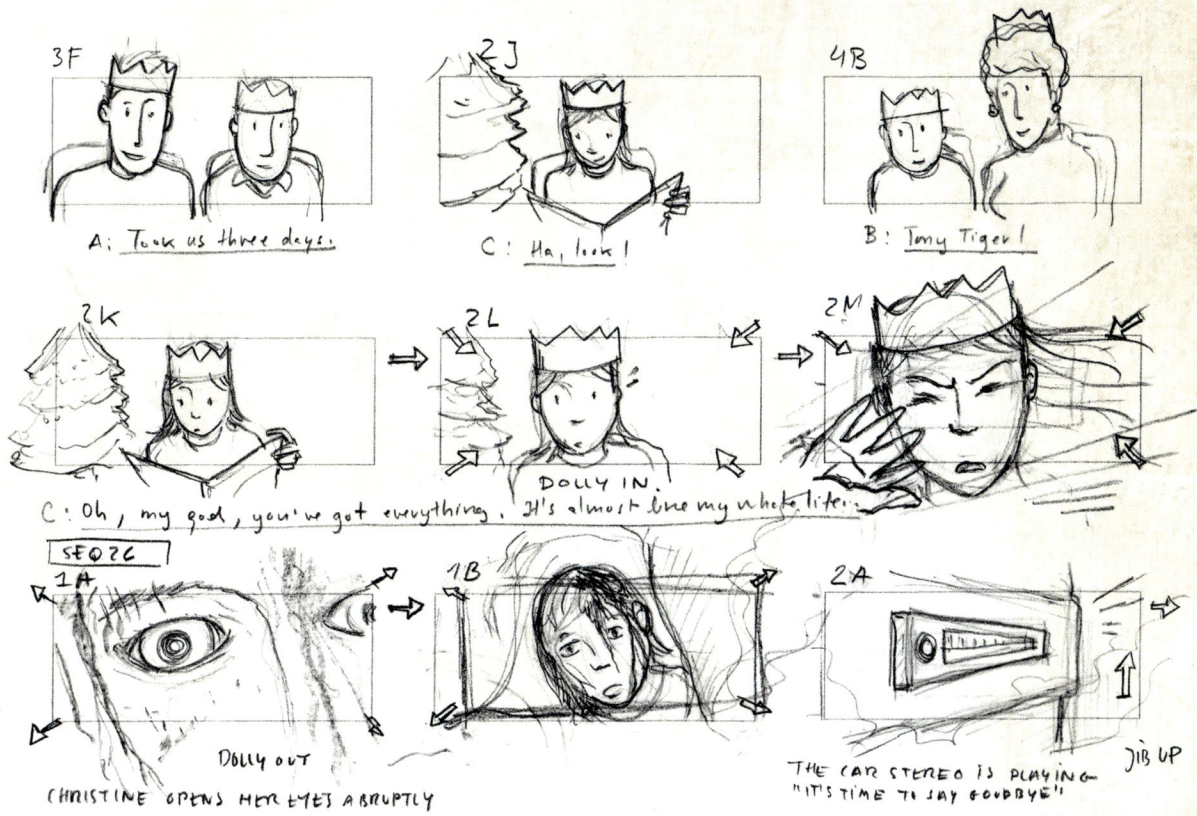

Actress and singer Sheridan Smith was the only choice for Christine. 'She has a relatability, a fragility and a warmth,' says Steve, who co-starred with her in *Benidorm*. 'All of those things were so essential to tie this story together. She's always very busy, so we had our fingers crossed, and thankfully she saw something in the script that she loved as well.'

Playing Christine's parents were Michele Dotrice, star of classic seventies sitcom *Some Mothers Do 'Ave 'Em* – 'She was so lovely and motherly and they had a really strong bond,' says Steve – and Paul Copley. Riley, who'd worked with Shearsmith on an episode of *Marple*, starred as boyfriend-cum-husband Adam, while Stacey Liu, who'd been in *Psychoville*, was cast as Christine's flatmate Fung. They wrote her as a maths student in order to shoehorn in a line about number theory and quantitative divisibility, with Fung pointing out, in the second scene, that Christine has been with Adam for thirteen months. 'We didn't want captions saying, "One month and one year later,"' says Steve. 'We wanted it to come out and for you to almost think, "What's the timeframe here?"'

Humour is provided by Bobby (Pemberton), Christine's co-worker at a shoe shop. 'Their relationship was a way of smuggling in funny lines, and was very lovely and very real,' says Reece who, initially, wasn't going to appear until Tandy convinced him to play the stranger whose connection to Christine isn't revealed

TOP: A section of director Guillem Morales's storyboard for the episode.

ABOVE: Sheridan Smith on set.

until the penultimate scene. Casting Shearsmith had an unexpected benefit. In the Valentine's Day scene, Christine mentions receiving a card from an old boyfriend who committed suicide. The photograph we see of him in her album looks like a young Shearsmith, although it's not. Nor was it a deliberate red herring. Rather it was a fortuitous choice that helped with the episode's dream-like logic. 'Similarly with the father's dementia,' says Steve. 'That was not put in there to make you second-guess whether Christine had dementia.'

As they'd spent almost the entire art department budget on 'La Couchette', production designer Simon Rogers was forced to get creative, not only repurposing another show's set as Christine's flat but reworking the interior to mark the passage of time. 'A lot of information can be carried in single items of dressing,' says Rogers. 'So a stereo being updated, a new rug or some new cushions actually give quite a lot of meaning in terms of the period having shifted.' The overall colour palette was based on the skin tones of a corpse. 'So bruised purples and greens and greys. Obviously, colours of sadness, too, which were part of the decision-making process to tell the story of a woman who was actually dead.' Even the flashing blue lights on the Christmas tree were hand-painted to match those of the police car at the end, while composer Christian Henson included the open-door chime of an Addison Lee minicab throughout the score. 'So you're there in the car with her,' he says. 'We never lie with the music. We always tell the truth.'

Most *Inside No. 9* episodes are shot in five days. 'Christine' was six, due to the large number of hair, make-up, costume and set dressing changes required each day. (They also needed to film the aftermath of the accident that claims Christine's life on location.) 'There was time for Sheridan to be in the make-up chair for an hour. No more than that,' says Tandy. 'But she's a real pro. She spends the time prepping the scene. Never didn't know her lines.'

Given Smith's busy schedule, she wasn't available for a read-through, so Morales met with her beforehand to discuss her ideas for the character and how she wanted to shoot. 'Some actors want to go fast. Others want more time. She said to me, "Go for the close-ups first."'

'Sheridan's a very sensitive performer and gives everything in every take, so for her it's better to start with close-ups,' says Tandy, 'because you get more emotional truth and intensity from the first take than the last. Usually an actor will build to that. You start wide then finish on their close-up, when they're rock solid on lines and know where they're going with the performance. With Sheridan, we did it the other

ABOVE: Sheridan Smith speaks to director Guillem Morales between takes.
RIGHT: The filming schedule for the episode, drawn up by assistant director Matthew Scrivener.

		--- END OF DAY 21 -- Tuesday, January 20, 2015 -- 3 6/8 pgs.				

DAY 22 - WED 21ST JAN - 1100-2200 (SR:0754 SS:1630)

SFX DAY

E/11	INT	FLAT NO 9 - LIVING ROOM Christine & Adam try to assemble the flat pack cot	Day 5	1 2/8 pgs	32, 33
E/13	INT	FLAT NO 9 - JACK'S BEDROOM Christine sees Jack is missing, Adam has him	Night 6	7/8 pgs	32, 33, 101

LOCATION MOVE

B/1	EXT	FOGGY STREET A row of imposing Victorian terraces on a foggy day	Day 1	1/8 pgs	
E/26 SFX	EXT	BLOCK OF FLATS Emergency services lift Christine from her wrecked car	Night 13	3/8 pgs	1e, 32, 103
E/28 SFX	EXT	BLOCK OF FLATS Christine is laid on the gurney	Night 13	1/8 pgs	1e, 32
E/30	EXT	BLOCK OF FLATS The paramedics try to save Christine	Night 13	2/8 pgs	1e, 32
E/32 SFX	EXT	BLOCK OF FLATS Jack & the stranger look on as paramedics work on Christine	Night 13	3/8 pgs	1e, 32, 103
E/1	EXT	BLOCK OF FLATS Establisher	Night 1	1/8 pgs	

--- END OF DAY 22 -- Wednesday, January 21, 2015 -- 3 4/8 pgs.

DAY 23 - THURS 22ND JAN - 1000-2100 (SR:0753 SS:1632)

E/17	INT	FLAT NO 9 - LIVING ROOM Christine is upset, Ernie comforts her, Zara enters	Day 9	3 1/8 pgs	32, 35, 36, 37, 102
E/14	INT	FLAT NO 9 - LIVING ROOM REDECORATED FLAT - It's Christine's birthday	Day 7	3 5/8 pgs	2e, 32, 33, 35, 36, 37
E/15	INT	FLAT NO 9 - BEDROOM CORRIDOR A blindfolded Christine hears squeaking bedsprings	Day 7	3/8 pgs	32

--- END OF DAY 23 -- Thursday, January 22, 2015 -- 7 1/8 pgs.

DAY 24 - FRI 23RD JAN - 0900-2000 (SR:0752 SS:1633)

VFX DAY?

Later start for Child hours?

E/23	INT	FLAT NO 9 - BATHROOM Christine runs Jack's hand under the cold tap	Night 11	2/8 pgs	32, 103
E/22 VFX?	INT	FLAT NO 9 - HALLWAY Christine burst in with a tearful Jack	Night 11	2/8 pgs	32, 103
E/24 VFX?	INT	FLAT NO 9 - LIVING ROOM Marion arrives, Jack's hand no longer has a burn mark	Night 11	2 3/8 pgs	32, 33, 35, 103
E/21	INT	FLAT NO 9 - JACK'S BEDROOM Christine finds the Stranger holding Jack	Night 10	2/8 pgs	1e, 32, 102
E/19	INT	FLAT NO 9 - BATHROOM Christine & Bobby do their make-ups, was that Adam?	Night 10	2 1/8 pgs	2e, 32, 33

way around. Most people don't want to have to deliver the most important shots right at the beginning of the day. But she got wrung out.'

As the episode goes on, the more unsettling it becomes. Given his background in horror, Morales effortlessly ramps up the spookiness via flickering lights, broken eggs, and the appearance of a dripping wet Shearsmith in steamed-up spectacles and a see-through raincoat. 'That was all Guillem,' says Reece. 'He said, "I want you in a translucent outfit so you look a bit ghostly, and we can't make out the shape of you."'

'That character should be wrong in that place,' says Morales. 'I don't know why I thought about the transparent raincoat. It was like a jellyfish. And I wanted him to be wet because it's an interior scene and he's from the outside, from the real world.'

The evening before they were due to shoot the final scene, Smith had been booked to appear on the National Television Awards and was given permission to leave early. Nevertheless, her car got stuck in traffic and she missed picking up her award. 'She stayed out late partying and the next day we were doing the Christmas scene,' recalls Steve. 'But she came in and sat down and gave that incredible performance.'

Filming the scene, in which Christine is handed the book of her life (with photos of the real Sheridan) before she bids goodbye to her family and friends, who are gathered around the dinner table, was hard on everyone. 'Sheridan is pure emotion and is able to pour it all out in such an easy way,' says Morales. 'So everyone was crying. Michele was crying. I was crying.'

In fact, there wasn't a dry eye among the gathered crew. 'People were upset,' recalls Reece. 'I remember sparks [electricians] coming up and going, "I've never seen anything like this." And I was like, "What you on about?" I mean, I got it, but it was very interesting to see. It really had an effect on people.'

'It was impossible to work and keep an objective eye on what you were doing,' says Tandy. 'If you watched a monitor, you were in bits.'

After an episode that moves at a gallop, Morales insisted on slowing things down as Christine finally understands what's happening. 'It was important for her to be, "Now I'm in control. Now I'm going

ABOVE: Ernie (Paul Copley), Adam (Tom Riley) and Bobby (Steve Pemberton).

RIGHT, TOP: Steve and Sheridan Smith in their characters' Halloween costumes.

RIGHT, BOTTOM: Steve, Sheridan Smith and Reece pose for a photo after filming.

to take my time to say goodbye to the people I love."' Moreover, he wanted Smith to look straight into the lens when Christine says, "Sweet goodbye. I love you," bidding farewell to the audience rather than those around the table. 'I thought that would be more powerful. And with a smile. And without crying. Sometimes, when an actor cries, it's not as powerful as an actor who is about to cry, but doesn't. Because then the audience does.'

The script called for each scene to bleed into the next, giving the episode a seamless quality with the transitions becoming increasingly unsettling and weirder. In the edit, Tandy decided to make them even more disconnected to further add to the tension and compress events, giving Morales even more time for the final scene. 'He'd done these invisible edits where you moved on and didn't realise. I said it would make more of an impact if we took those out and made it more jarring. It was all to do with keeping the audience jumpy. They needed to be confused. By taking out those soft transitions between the months, you enhanced that, because the tonal differences become much more pertinent.'

Pemberton and Shearsmith wanted Andrea Bocelli's 'Time to Say Goodbye' to play out over the closing credits, much to Plowman's disgust. 'He thought it was a dreadful idea,' says Reece, 'really mawkish and pushing buttons, which it is, but it does work.'

The first time Morales saw the final cut was at home, alone. 'Thank God no one was around, because I sobbed like a baby. I couldn't stop. And I thought, "My God, the nation will be in tears. What have we done?" It's beautiful and so sad.'

When 'The 12 Days of Christine' aired on BBC Two, the reaction was unparalleled. 'In the old days you had no way of knowing what people made of it,' says Steve. 'Now you can look on social media. And I had to take a breath, because people were pouring their hearts out about how it had touched them. But because it's *Inside No. 9*, because we're known for *League of Gentlemen* and big characters, you don't expect it. So you're blindsided. One week it's a German shitting in a shoebox and the next week it's this. It's what we love about working on this series. The ground is always shifting. It all added up to this big emotional punch, and we were absolutely blown away by the reaction. I thought, "My God, we'll never top that."'

'Yeah, it was sickening,' laughs Reece, only half-joking. 'It was like, *please* don't like it *this* much. But people were so moved. They were crying watching a *No. 9*! And it's a lot to do with Sheridan Smith, who was phenomenal and made you care about this character you'd only been with for half an hour.'

The Trial of Elizabeth Gadge

- Series **2**
- Episode **3**
- Directed by **Dan Zeff**

ABOVE: The episode poster was created by Matthew Burlem.

Immortalised by Vincent Price in Michael Reeves' 1968 horror classic *Witchfinder General*, Matthew Hopkins was a seventeenth-century witch-hunter who, along with his colleague John Stearne, was responsible for the deaths of more than 100 alleged witches in East Anglia and its neighbouring counties over a three-year period between 1644–47. It's a sordid and unpleasant slice of English history, and one that Shearsmith has a marked interest in. 'That whole world of witches, witch trials and woodcuts, I'm fascinated by. I am properly obsessed. Mark Gatiss is as well. We always laughed at the absurd language of "imps" and the obsession with "teats" and "suckling" and "familiars" being anywhere. An old woman is trapped in a prison cell and a spider walks across the room and they decide that's her familiar. That was ripe for the picking and for revelling in the ludicrous language.'

A/4	INT	BARN TO COMPLETE - The court descends into chaos, the villagers a	Day 2	4 2/8 pgs	1a, 2a, 3, 4, 5, 6, 7, 8	

--- END OF DAY 3 -- Tuesday, December 9, 2014 -- 10 3/8 pgs.

DAY 4 - WED 10TH DEC - 0800-1900 (SR:0755 SS:1551)

A/5	INT	BARN Under torture Elizabeth Gadge confesses	Day 2	3 1/8 pgs	1a, 2a, 3, 4, 5, 6, 7, 8
A/6	INT	BARN Richard denies any involvement with Elizabeth Gadge	Day 2	1 6/8 pgs	1a, 2a, 3, 4, 5, 6, 7, 8, 9

--- END OF DAY 4 -- Wednesday, December 10, 2014 -- 4 7/8 pgs.

DAY 5 - THURS 11TH DEC - 1000-2100 (SR:0756 SS:1551)

Rehearse Sc A/7 & A/8 in their entirety

A/7pt1/2 Mouse	INT	BARN Elizabeth is brought forth looking worse for wear	Day 3	3 pgs	1a, 2a, 3, 4, 5, 6, 7, 8, 9
A/8pt1/3	INT	BARN Clarke has conspired to save Elizabeth Gadge	Night 3	2 4/8 pgs	1a, 2a, 3, 4, 5, 8

--- END OF DAY 5 -- Thursday, December 11, 2014 -- 5 4/8 pgs.

DAY 6 - FRI 12TH DEC - 1000-2100 (SR:0757 SS:1551)

STUNTS/SFX/ANIMAL DAY

A/7pt2/2 Mouse	INT	BARN Warren uses Snowflake to identify Gadge as a witch	Day 3	2 pgs	1a, 2a, 3, 4, 5, 6, 7, 8, 9

Day Establisher of Barn

A/1pt1/2 Crow/Horses	EXT	ELIZABETHAN BARN Three men head past a milestone	Night 1	1/8 pgs	1a, 2a, 3
A/8pt2/3 SFX/Stunt/Mo	INT	BARN Clarke has conspired to save Elizabeth Gadge	Night 3	1 1/8 pgs	1a, 2a, 3, 4, 5, 8

--- END OF DAY 6 -- Friday, December 12, 2014 -- 3 2/8 pgs.

SAT 13TH & SUN 14TH DEC - DAYS OFF

DAY 7 - MON 15TH DEC - 0800-1900 (SR:0759 SS:1551)

B/2pt1/4 SFX	INT	**SFX DAY**			

--- END OF DAY 7 -- Monday, December 15, 2014 -- 4 2/8 pgs.

And so 'The Trial of Elizabeth Gadge' reimagines Hopkins and Stearne as Mr Warren (Shearsmith) and Mr Clarke (Pemberton), 'celebrity witchfinders' summoned to a town called Little Happens 'where, literally, nothing happens. And that being a big event for the people there,' laughs Reece. 'It was an exploration of that, of two people arriving, and apparently there's a witch in the village. One man is a terrible psycho who wants to torture women and get money. The other one is starting to feel that maybe this isn't right. And that was a great dynamic.'

Shearsmith mined real-life witch trial transcripts for the episode's rich, archaic language, with large chunks of Warren and Clarke's dialogue, as well as that of town magistrate Sir Andrew Pike (David Warner) presented verbatim. Here, it's elderly villager Elizabeth Anne Gadge (Ruth Sheen) who stands accused of witchcraft by her daughter Sarah (Sinéad Matthews) and son-in-law Thomas Nutter (Jim Howick), and will be burnt if found guilty, even though the actual evidence presented by Thomas, cobbler Richard Two-Shoes (Paul Kaye), and disgruntled neighbour George Waterhouse (Trevor Cooper) is circumstantial at best, and clearly motivated by greed, envy or a desire for more room at home. 'They've all got their own axe to grind,' says Reece. 'It's very *Crucible*-like in that they're just out to get revenge.'

The two witchfinders were named after character actor Warren Clarke, who'd starred in *A Clockwork Orange* and the 'Thirteenth Reunion' episode of *Hammer House of Horror*, and had worked with Shearsmith on the BBC comedy-crime drama *In the Red*. Alas, Clarke died just before

ABOVE LEFT: A page from producer Adam Tandy's notebook shows a sketch for one of the original ending ideas for this episode, in which all the characters were to be hanged – including a tiny gallows for Snowflake the mouse.

ABOVE RIGHT: A filming schedule for the episode.

'The Trial' was due to air, and he and Pemberton were concerned they wouldn't be able to use the names. 'It wasn't a joke on him, it was just a funny notion that Warren Clarke sounds like two separate names. My agent was the same as his, and he said, "We don't mind you continuing to use them."'

'It was a lovely homage to a great leading man and character actor,' says Tandy, who admits he prepared a list of other alternatives just in case. 'Stockard Channing was one of them.'

'The Trial of Elizabeth Gadge' was directed by Dan Zeff, who had previously helmed episodes of *Doctor Who* and *Marple*, as well as the acclaimed BBC drama *Hattie*, about Hattie Jacques and John Le Mesurier. 'The job slightly clashed with another, but I really wanted to make it work because I loved the show and loved the scripts,' says Zeff. '"The Trial" was one of the best scripts I'd ever read. So funny. But I also loved the darkness of it.'

To help Zeff prepare, the boys sent him plenty of research material, along with appropriate film references, including *Witchfinder General* and *The Blood on Satan's Claw*, Piers Haggard's 1971 horror about devil worshippers. 'I got lots of emails from Reece and learned a lot more about Matthew Hopkins,' he recalls. 'They also showed me some genuine transcripts. I'm a big fan of *The Crucible* as well; it's an extraordinary play and obviously has other resonances.'

'The Trial of Elizabeth Gadge' is neither a spoof nor parody. Shearsmith and Pemberton play the real-life horrors of the witch trials deadly seriously, and find humour in the absurdity of events as well as the colourful language. 'I didn't want people to think it was *Blackadder* or *Python*,' says Reece. 'Not that they're not brilliant, but this was a different take.

'We did do a joke pass, adding in the selfie and Richard Two-Shoes/Goody Two-Shoes gag,' he continues. 'We had "Gum Drops" as the name, initially, and it was Jon Plowman who suggested there might be room for a "Goody Two-Shoes", so we swapped out "Gum Drops" and made him a cobbler. I remember being squeamish about putting it in at all, but maybe without jokes, it would have been too bleak.'

> **Mr Clarke:** In truth, the imp was nothing but a carrion crow caught by the leg in a griddle.

'They could have gone bigger with the anachronisms, but I think they got the balance perfectly right,' says Zeff, 'because you don't want to push the comedy. There are so many funny lines but delivered absolutely straight. Jon said, "It's quite panto, isn't it?" And I remember thinking, I know what you mean, but it's also so much more than that. You needed to hit the comic beats, but the overall tone had to be quite unsettling. The stakes are really high; it's life and death, and Reece's character is at the heart of that. There's a darkness and a brittleness in him that creates this climate of fear. Then you need to care for this woman being accused, and root a bit for Steve's character. There's so much depth to the characters, as well as comedy.'

Playing the accused was Ruth Sheen, who starred in *Secret & Lies*, *All or Nothing*, *Vera Drake* and *High Hopes*. 'I was really pleased she said yes. I can never quite believe anyone says yes,' chuckles Reece. 'She has a long association with Mike Leigh and we liked that. She brought a real-world, natural performance to a very heightened, ludicrous situation.'

'I've always found her such an empathetic character and she brings such reality to the role,' adds Zeff. 'Maybe it's the Mike Leigh training, but there's no vanity in the acting. It is absolutely trying to get to the truth, and she gave it such heart. You *really* feel for her. Then she has the lovely twist.'

Cast as Little Happens' dim-witted, sexually frustrated magistrate was David Warner, a veteran

LITTLE
HAPPENS
1 MILE

The Trial of Elizabeth Gadge

film, theatre and TV actor whose glittering career includes such classics as *Morgan: A Suitable Case for Treatment*, *The Omen*, *Time Bandits* and *Straw Dogs*. Shearsmith and Pemberton had worked with Warner on 2005's *The League of Gentlemen's Apocalypse* movie but didn't, initially, consider him for this. 'We didn't want to go back to him at first because we wanted *Inside No. 9* to feel fresh,' says Steve. 'But we knew he had that twinkle. And for this character to have the authority, but also the comic chops to pull all that stuff off, we kept going, "David's got it!" And he absolutely has.'

'He's the idiot who thinks he's smarter than he is and somehow has got status in this village, but he is a figure of fun,' says Zeff of Warner's Pike, who is revealed to have a keen interest in 'licking anuses' as well as one of the witchfinders' instruments of torture. Known as the Pear of Anguish, this particular item has a bulbous end that is inserted anally. 'It came from the joke of, "You put this up until they feel …" "Ecstasy?" "No. Agony,"' laughs Steve. 'And we thought that this could be an ongoing gag for him.' The 'Pear' was based on a real torture device, which was replicated by the art department. 'I love that shot of the three of them around it. David Warner was so perfect,' says Zeff, who wanted to keep it as his prop to take home. 'But they auctioned it off for charity.'

'The Trial' was filmed in an authentic period barn at the Chiltern Open Air Museum in Buckinghamshire during a freezing cold week in December. 'We saw some barns with lovely wooden beams going across that were, in some ways, more cinematic. But they weren't feasible to film in for health and safety reasons. The barn we used was quite simple, although I loved the way the light came through the weave,' says Zeff. Nevertheless, he was concerned it might be a little too plain and had Simon Rogers add a wooden balustrade at the back. 'You hardly notice it, but it gives the

ABOVE: Warren and Clarke prepare to begin the trial.

feeling of a gallery rather than being one big square space.'

In the original script, the barn was filled with dozens of villagers, who remained throughout the trial. But since the production could only afford twenty extras for one day, Tandy asked the boys to rework the story to get rid of the majority of them, which is why Pike clears the space after an argument breaks out, and declares the rest of proceedings should be held in private. 'It ended up being a great comic moment when he sends them away because they misbehaved and can't stay for the "pricking",' says Zeff, 'but it was born out of necessity.'

'Pricking' was a barbaric practice employed by witchfinders to determine a woman's guilt by

TOP AND ABOVE RIGHT: Filming in progress in the barn.

ABOVE LEFT: Thomas Nutter (Jim Howick) and Sarah Nutter (Sinéad Matthews).

using a large needle to test whether a mole or birthmark was 'the devil's mark'. If the area didn't bleed or result in pain, it was considered 'proof' of their pact with the devil, although the blunt end was often used to lessen the chances of the skin breaking and, therefore, bleeding. To simulate Elizabeth's skin being 'pricked' required the make-up department to create a prosthetic back for Sheen to wear. 'It was an expense, but it was important,' says Zeff. 'Not to make the whole thing horribly gory, but to reveal the nastiness of that practice.'

'It's one of these episodes which has big laughs, but also this terrible cruelty,' notes Steve. 'The "pricking" we wanted to feel genuinely horrible. And by the end, she's a broken woman.'

Sheen's character is also accused of having an imp, also known as a familiar – a supernatural entity said to assist witches in their practice of magic. In this case, a 'demon known as Snowflake' is called before the court. In reality, Snowflake is a small, white mouse that

INSIDE NO 9. REVISED WITCH POKER

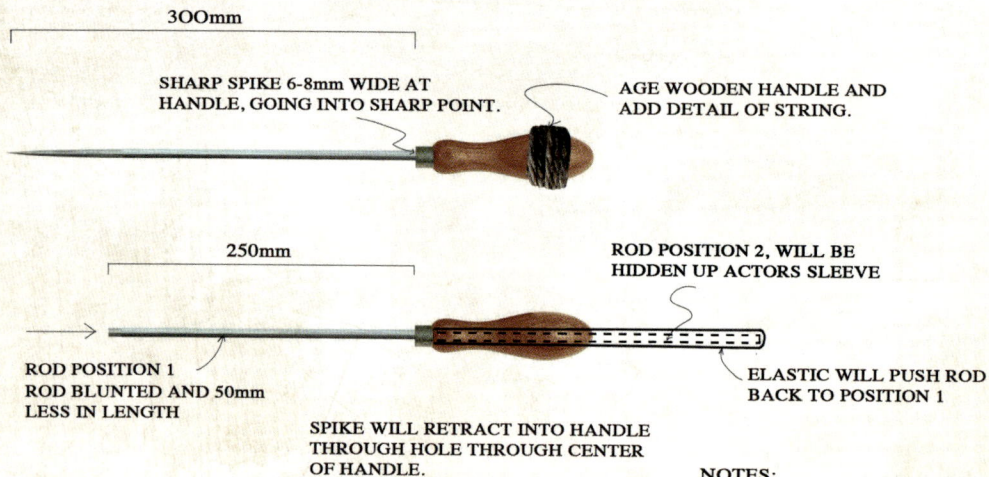

300mm

SHARP SPIKE 6-8mm WIDE AT HANDLE, GOING INTO SHARP POINT.

AGE WOODEN HANDLE AND ADD DETAIL OF STRING.

250mm

ROD POSITION 2, WILL BE HIDDEN UP ACTORS SLEEVE

ROD POSITION 1 ROD BLUNTED AND 50mm LESS IN LENGTH

ELASTIC WILL PUSH ROD BACK TO POSITION 1

SPIKE WILL RETRACT INTO HANDLE THROUGH HOLE THROUGH CENTER OF HANDLE.

NOTES:
BRIEF- TO LOOK LIKE THE NEEDLE IS ENTERING/ COMING OUT OF THE SKIN.

WE NEED 2 NEEDLES:
> ONE SHARP JUST TO BE ON A TABLE.
> ONE TO BE BLUNTED TO ENTER AND RETRACT ON SKIN.

TOP: Warren and Clarke's witchfinding equipment.

ABOVE: Prop design notes for the 'witch poker', created by production designer Simon Rogers and his team.

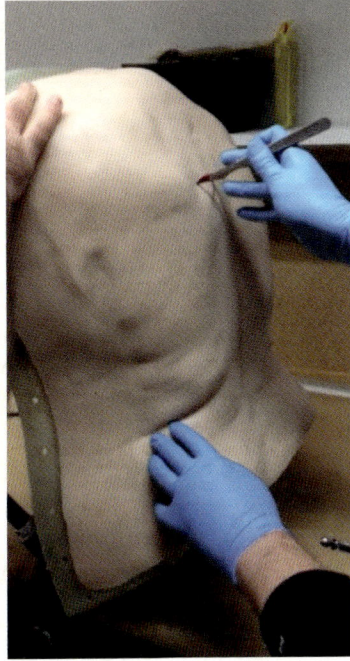

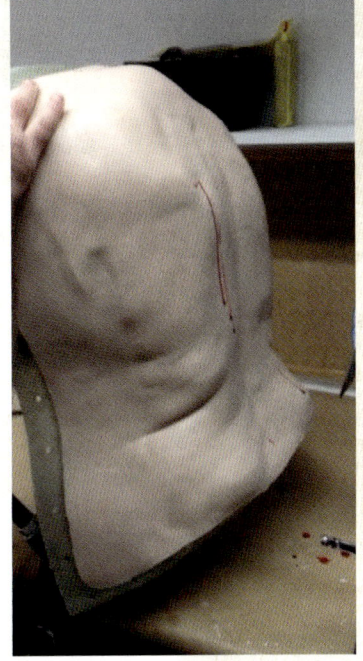

Mr Warren: The next person here to laugh will
immediately die as a witch . . .
starting from . . . now.

Clarke baits with cheese to get it to scurry towards her, thus proving her guilt. 'The mouse was hard work,' laughs Zeff. 'Although I learned how you get one to follow a path.'

When it came to the costumes, Zeff insisted on absolute authenticity. 'I wanted people to be able to "smell" them. And that is why the panto thing felt wrong to me. It was not "putting on costumes". It was authentically playing the poverty and mud and dirt. Same of the make-up. You want to almost feel you can smell the dirtiness and the bad teeth. And then Reece and Steve's characters, being the people with money, are much more coiffed and stand out in contrast.'

Despite having the standard five days to shoot the episode, which included an exterior as well as a complicated transformation effect, Zeff pushed his stars in a way they weren't used to. 'I remember Dan being very insistent on going again if he didn't think we'd got it the best it could be,' notes Reece. 'He would say, "Can I have another one?" And I was like, "What's wrong with that one?" "You could do it better." You want that from someone.'

'He was pushing all the time to have more people and wanted it to be big,' says Steve. 'The good thing about having fewer directors working on two episodes is they put everything into them. He wanted it to be really atmospheric, really authentic and for you to feel the period. And I think he pulled that off.'

'The ambition was, budget aside, to film it like a courtroom drama,' explains Zeff. 'And there's

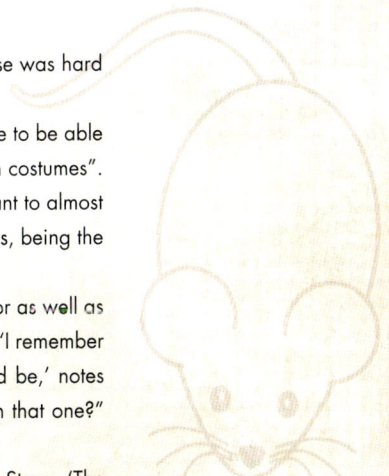

ABOVE: A prosthetic back that could actually bleed was created by prosthetic artist Kristyan Mallett for the pricking scene: here, it is tested out before filming.

A pamphlet to promote the services of
Warren and Clarke
witch finders of plenty repute

Serving the Lord in his quest to rid
England of these damnable practices.

Confessions Guaranteed!
Commended by God and the Law alike.

ABOVE: The episode inspired graphic designer Richard Wells to create this intricate pamphlet advertising the services of Warren and Clarke.

nothing more cinematic than a powerful close-up, or a shot that tracks into Reece in a moment of anger, or Paul Kaye when he's terrified. I wanted it big in terms of the emotional stakes. That's another reason why I would go again, to pull a bit more emotional power out of a scene, or get a bit more danger.' It was also a way of giving Zeff more choices once it came to the edit. 'Partly it was a way of keeping it active and moving, but I definitely got a lot of footage from my five days.'

Initially, the script ended on a more comic note and Tandy advised them to change it. In the original draft, the witchfinders find everyone guilty and hang them all. 'The mouse gets hanged, the dog gets hanged. It was gruesome, but it was a comedy payoff,' he says.

'It was too much, too extravagant,' admits Reece.

Ultimately, they opted for a double ending. The first comes when it's revealed Elizabeth has been freed by Mr Clarke, who, troubled by his conscience, has come to question Mr Warren's true motives, replacing the accused with his fellow witchfinder, who is subsequently burnt at the stake. 'There's that chilling moment where Warren says, "Tread cautiously, Mr Clarke, less you find yourself accused,"' says Reece, 'and you think, oh my God, he's going to turn on him, because he dares to question him. But then Clarke gets rid of him because he realises he's an evil man. And then we thought it would be a great moment when, after he's saved her and burnt his partner, she breaks his neck. We thought it would be a great, *literal* twist. She twists his neck, revealing herself to be a witch.'

'I don't think people see it coming and I don't think I saw it coming when I read it,' says Zeff. 'Again, on a comedy budget, you don't have time to shoot the neck twist like a proper stunt, and yet it's got to look as good as if it were a movie. A lot is in the sound. And how Ruth plays that moment.'

> Sir Andrew Pike: Tell us more of this arse-
>   kissing. How close did thou spy it?

After dispatching Mr Clarke, Elizabeth transforms into a raven and flies out of the barn, into the night. 'I wish that was a bit better,' reflects Zeff. 'It works for a quick moment, but it's not *Harry Potter*.' The transformation was achieved by shooting Sheen on a wire rig against green screen then replacing her with a trained bird. 'The trainer has the bird inside, then stands outside and gets it to fly out. It meant the height the bird could get to was slightly compromised. If we could have done the bird on green screen we might have been able to control the angle and height better. But it wasn't a disaster at all.'

'It's definitely one of my favourites,' says Reece. 'Aside from anything else, we'd not done period, and it was crying out to do a completely different era. And to really embrace the language, and enjoy that world. It is broadly funny, yet deeply upsetting. And to get Ruth Sheen. She's such a believable presence at the heart of it. She helped anchor the whole episode and made you care about Elizabeth Gadge and her plight.'

ABOVE: Reece on the monitors in the dubbing theatre during the sound dub.

Jane Horrocks   Steve Pemberton   Reece Shearsmith

COLD COMFORT

Thursday 10pm

INSIDE 9

BBC TWO PRESENTS A BBC COMEDY PRODUCTION AN INSIDE NO. 9 FILM "COLD COMFORT"
STEVE PEMBERTON JANE HORROCKS REECE SHEARSMITH
NIKKI AMUKA-BIRD TONY WAY EXECUTIVE PRODUCER JON PLOWMAN PRODUCED BY ADAM TANDY
WRITTEN AND DIRECTED BY STEVE PEMBERTON & REECE SHEARSMITH

BBC TWO

Cold Comfort

- Series **2**
- Episode **4**
- Directed by **Steve Pemberton and Reece Shearsmith**

For years, Pemberton had held on to a newspaper article about the Samaritans, a charity that provides telephone support to anyone in emotional distress or at risk of suicide, thinking that one day it might form the basis of a story. 'I don't often keep things like that,' he says, 'but within it someone talked about a call they'd had that was very harrowing, and the person seemingly took their own life on the line. Then they have to pick up the next call as if nothing has happened, and the person was a bit short with the next caller.'

ABOVE: The episode poster for 'Cold Comfort' was designed by Matthew Burlem.

Completely independently, Shearsmith had, while shooting the TV show *Stag*, come across a YouTube video of a police interview with Canadian Forces' Colonel Russell Williams. In the video, Williams sits down with Ontario detective Jim Smyth, thinking he'll be in and out in five minutes. But, ten hours later, he has confessed to the murders of several women. Visually, the video was nothing special. It was CCTV footage of the interrogation room shown in wide shot, with two other angles on the right side of frame. 'Yet you couldn't take your eyes off it,' recalls Reece, who wondered if the CCTV format was a way to film Pemberton's Samaritans idea. 'I watched it, then told everyone to, because it was so gripping.'

Another intense, claustrophobic episode, 'Cold Comfort' follows Andy (Pemberton) as he starts work at the Comfort Support Line – he is assigned booth nine – with fellow volunteers, chatterbox Liz (Jane Horrocks), emotionless Joanne (Nikki Amuka-Bird), and by-the-book supervisor George (Shearsmith). After a particularly upsetting call from Chloe, a suicidal teenager, Andy is dismissive of his next caller, Ivy, an elderly woman 'devastated' by the loss of her cat, Picasso. Later, Andy learns that Ivy has killed herself, so when Chloe calls again with the same sob story, he threatens to tell the police. But when Chloe mentions the unfortunate Ivy, Andy begins to suspect she is, in fact, another volunteer, and mistakenly believes it to be Joanne. 'At one point we thought it was Liz,' says Steve. 'Then we went, "What if it's George, who is there in plain sight, all the time, in his office?"'

Despite its serious backdrop, 'Cold Comfort' is full of humour, thanks in no small part to Horrocks' gossipy Liz. ('She's got so much ice up her fanny I call her Jayne Torvill,' she says of Joanne.) Neither Pemberton nor Shearsmith had worked with Horrocks – like Ruth Sheen, another Mike Leigh favourite – before. 'She's very versatile, very talented and naturally a very funny person,' says Tandy. 'She's a contrast to Nikki Amuka-Bird, who's got a very dry sense of humour, and is, stylistically, very different. And because there's a clash of styles in the way those two work on screen, there's tension between the characters as well.'

A surprising amount of detail was drawn from real life. 'When we enter a new world, we do a fair bit of research. And that's where we found out that an awful lot of people just ring up to masturbate, because it's a way of having another person at the end of the line. We didn't make that up,' says Steve.

ABOVE: Andy (Steve Pemberton), George (Reece Shearsmith) and Liz (Jane Horrocks).

INSIDE
Nº 9

SAMARITAN ✓   HOSPITAL ROOM

MURDER HOUSE   NAN'S PARTY

WITCH TRIAL   BACKWARDS TALE

ESCALATION MADDOX   MARRIAGE OVER 40 YRS

No 9 DOWNING ST   SPLIT SCREEN

BODY PARTS   LIFE FLASH BEFORE EYES

COME DINE WITH ME

FALSE TOOTH   FIVE NIGHT PARTY

THE GOOD SAMARITAN

THE INCIDENT - woman keeps mentioning the incident -

"without revealing what the incident was"

"do you want me to tell you the incident?"

No!

It was an abortion

Well you asked me!

No I didn't

Long story - needing a wee - held up sign to camera

"I NEED A WEE"

CALLER accuses MAN of doing something. He hangs up

ABOVE: A page from Steve's notebook with early ideas for this episode.

'Since it aired, a few people who work in that world have said it's very accurate,' adds Reece, 'which is good to hear. But also horrifying. It's one of my favourites.'

In order to mimic the police interrogation video, Pemberton and Shearsmith wanted 'Cold Comfort' to be shot with four fixed CCTV-style cameras, with the action playing out in real-time, without cuts, and all four feeds appearing onscreen simultaneously. 'Given we had such a strong view on how it should be done, we thought, let's direct it ourselves, because once you've got your frames set, it's all about the actors,' says Steve. 'Even though we hadn't done any technical directing before, we've always been partly directing everything we've done from The League onwards, because we've always staged scenes in collaboration with the directors. We've always said, "This is what we want." Either in the writing or being there on the day. So we thought, we won't compromise. Most directors wouldn't be able to bear the fact we wanted it to be static and you couldn't change the angle. And we didn't want to swap out the shots if something good was happening in one of the others.'

The episode was shot at a further education college in Hounslow. 'We found an office that we emptied out, then put all our stuff in,' says Simon Rogers. 'We made all the booths, so they were the right height, because if we bought them off the shelf they would either be too high or too low, and we needed to make sure the width corresponded to the width of the lens they were shooting on. On the surface, it doesn't seem like a huge amount of work, but it was quite involved and technical.' They used one lipstick camera and three semi-pro DSLRs fixed to stands or bolted to the ceiling. One was trained on booth nine, one high up in George's office, a third in the corridor leading to the call centre, while a fourth offered another angle on booth nine. (In addition, there are brief angles on Joanne's booth and a close-up of George in his office.)

'We decided to shoot in order to give everybody a proper arc in terms of the acting,' says Tandy. He allowed for three days' filming with a reduced crew, but the boys managed to finish in two-and-a-half.

BELOW: Michael (Tony Way).

BOTTOM: Reece, Jane Horrocks, Steve and Nikki Amuka-Bird, who played Joanne.

When 'Action' was called, all four cameras would begin recording simultaneously, with scenes playing out in uninterrupted takes often lasting up to six minutes. 'It was a bit like doing the live episode ["Dead Line"],' says Steve. 'You knew if you fucked up the take, it would be no good, because we didn't want to edit. If something went wrong, we'd stop and start again. You could move very quickly between takes.'

Pemberton and Shearsmith would review the first and last take of each scene before moving on. Given that the action played out without cuts, timing was key, with each scene having to conform to a prescribed length, 'because there was no wiggle room in the edit,' says Reece. Improvisation was kept to a minimum and dialogue cuts were made on set between takes. 'We ended up cheating very slightly. But only on the corridor outside,' says Tandy. 'We speeded that up a little bit.'

The fixed cameras produced some interesting compositional results. 'It's anti-framing,' says Tandy. 'There's a bit where George and Liz have a stand-up row in the back of shot, but we see them from their shoulders down. That was a deliberate decision. We gave Reece and Jane the note to act with their hands a bit more, because we couldn't see what they were doing with their heads.'

All the phone calls were recorded live. Off-camera callers would use a voiceover booth. 'The biggest headache was our sound recordist having to capture everything,' says Tandy. 'We had boom, radio and sleeve mikes for recording the phone calls close up. So while the pictures were incredibly simple, the sound was fearfully complex, because you need to be able to change the balance of those conversations during the show, because of the psychological input from the people calling.'

Ivy was voiced by Vilma Hollingbery, aka Mrs Wren/Mrs Ladybirdface from *Psychoville*. The other callers were played by Edward Easton, Kath Hughes and James Meehan of the comedy group Gein's Family Giftshop, who Pemberton and Shearsmith had seen at the Edinburgh Festival. The trio also appear onscreen as volunteers. Tandy, meanwhile, provides another of his voice cameos as the PPI caller.

Shearsmith voiced Chloe on set. But, worried that his voice would be too recognisable, they had Vicky Hall revoice Chloe in post-production, then had Shearsmith revoice her again, using Hall's track as a guide. Sound editor Chris MacLean and dubbing mixer Matthew Brace then mixed and matched from the separate voice tracks, extracting individual consonants, sounds and syllables from both Shearsmith and Hall to create several different versions of Chloe. 'At the beginning it's nearly all Vicky with a bit of Reece,' says Tandy. 'At the end, there's much more of Reece than her. Doing that allowed us to vary the tell, in terms of what Steve's character was perceiving.'

'It is a cheat,' admits Steve, 'but it makes the ending work.'

Throughout, your attention is mostly focused on the main image, but your eyes can't help but be drawn to what's going on in the smaller screens, be it an empty office or people walking along the corridor. 'It becomes mesmerising,' says Reece. 'Like all those clips of ghosts on YouTube, because I'm obsessed with those as well. Your eyes are scanning this very mundane-looking shot waiting on

ABOVE: Support line volunteer Andy soon finds himself overwhelmed by the calls he receives.

something terrible to happen. And that, in its own way, is dreadful.'

Towards the end of the episode, when Steve sneaks into George's office and uncovers the Chloe recordings, a hooded figure can be seen moving along the darkened corridor, into the call centre. 'The dread of the last five minutes is an extraordinary thing, helped along by the tones and drones going on,' says Tandy.

'That built in-between scenes as well,' adds Reece. 'The cacophony of the Comfort Support Line, the ringing and answering of telephones, all imbuing this very odd twilight world with pain and suffering.'

Pemberton and Shearsmith didn't want a traditional score, and instead asked Christian Henson for *musique concrète*, a form of composition made up of found sounds that are then manipulated, designed and enhanced – in this case, phone line static and the buzz of a freezer. 'It's more of a sound episode than you might imagine,' says Tandy. 'And the sound is much more complex than the vision.'

After the revelation that George is Chloe, 'Cold Comfort' still has one more sting in its tail, when Ivy's squaddie son rocks up at the call centre with a pistol and aims it at Andy. As written, there was a gunshot, and blood splattered the lens. 'The BBC was slightly nervous about the gun. They were concerned if we had the gunshot, it might be too violent,' reveals Tandy. 'Now you don't hear it, and it's more dreadful without. The trigger is tightened and you cut to black. Then you have Take That.'

As the credits roll, Take That's 'Shine' kicks in, the same song Andy sang to Chloe earlier. 'I always get very fearful about clearing music,' continues Tandy, 'but on this occasion it was very easy. Gary Barlow is big mates with Christian and was a huge fan of the show.'

ABOVE: Reece and Steve directed 'Cold Comfort' themselves.

Happy Birthday

Nana's Party

Thursday 10pm

BBC TWO

INSIDE No 9

Nana's Party

- Series **2**
- Episode **5**
- Directed by **Steve Pemberton and Reece Shearsmith**

ABOVE: The episode poster was designed by Matthew Burlem.

'Nana's Party' was one of two scripts the boys delivered to the BBC before *Inside No. 9* was officially greenlit, written to test whether the one-act, one-location idea could work as a series. 'A party is a classic way of bringing characters together, usually with the hope of everyone having a good time, which, of course, rarely happens,' says Steve. 'Then that [idea] became the eavesdropping from beneath the table, and that seemed to offer more possibilities, so we went with that instead. The idea started as an image of a head-sized box on a table and people saying, "Where's Maggie?" Maggie was the person whose birthday it was, and she wasn't there. And that being a sinister thing. We wanted family secrets to come out, and we wanted you to feel the tension of knowing somebody was under there, listening.'

ABOVE: Left to right: Katie (Eve Gordon), Jim (Steve Pemberton), Angela (Claire Skinner), Maggie (Elsie Kelly), Carol (Lorraine Ashbourne) and Pat (Reece Shearsmith).

At the time, the BBC felt the script could make a sitcom pilot, but neither Shearsmith nor Pemberton were interested in pursuing that particular route. 'I think they thought it was about a family and had a sitcom feel,' says Reece, 'not recognising that the devastating revelations that make it what it is are the very things you can't do in a sitcom, which needs to reset every episode without any earth-shattering revelations rocking the status quo.' And so they consigned 'Nana's Party' to the digital drawer and moved on.

Come series two, the boys decided to take another crack at it, giving it a flashback opening with an ambulance arriving at the house, which, says Reece, added a sense of 'danger and foreboding', even though it proves to be nothing but a cunning piece of misdirection, with the paramedic turning out to be a strippergram. Nevertheless, it was 'a fun way to pull it all together', notes Steve.

Pitched somewhere between Alan Ayckbourn and Mike Leigh's groundbreaking 1970s TV play *Abigail's Party*, 'Nana's Party' encompasses infidelity, alcoholism, sibling rivalry, abortion and pornography in a quintessential suburban setting, where a peek behind the net curtains reveals a dark underbelly. 'We try and do one of these in every series,' says Steve. 'Every house, every family, has got extraordinary secrets. It's no coincidence it's the first one we wrote, because it's all about peeling back the layers of this seemingly very ordinary family.'

After the ambulance pulls up outside the smart home of Jim (Pemberton) and Angela (Claire Skinner) and their fourteen-year-old daughter Katie (Eve Gordon), we rewind several hours to find Angela busy with last-minute preparations for her mum Maggie's seventy-ninth birthday party. Played by Elsie Kelly, who had worked with Pemberton on *Benidorm*, Maggie arrives with Angela's alcoholic sister Carol (Lorraine Ashbourne) and Carol's browbeaten husband Pat (Shearsmith), an

JIM + ANGELA   PAT + CAROL

ANNIVERSARY

ABOVE: An early sketched-out design for the fake cake from Steve's notebook.

inverterate practical joker. Hoping to get his own back on Pat for his incessant jokes, Jim has concocted a prank of his own, one that involves hiding beneath the dinner table with his head inside a hollowed-out cake, and having Angela engineer it so that when Pat moves the cake, he'll get the shock of his life. But nothing works out the way Jim hoped, as, halfway through, he and Angela switch places. 'That's when it becomes dark and nasty,' says Steve.

Suddenly, Jim's collection of *Countdown* videos is revealed to be hardcore pornography, while his longstanding affair with Carol becomes public knowledge, after a drunk Carol has a full-on meltdown, further abusing Pat – who admits to knowledge of her infidelity – before professing her love for Jim and desperation for a baby. 'It is one of the cruellest scripts we've written,' reflects Reece. 'The tragedy of Pat and Carol's relationship and how long the affair's been going on. There's that awful bit where Carol says to Katie, "You want to know what your sister would have been called?" So you assume she's had an abortion with Jim. It's horrible.'

Described in the script as 'slightly pinched and fretful', Angela is first seen vacuuming the stairs with a dustbuster, before scolding her daughter for making a mess, snapping, 'It's like a bombsite in here!' when, in reality, it's a slightly messed-up rug. 'My dad used to be like that,' chuckles Steve. 'I remember one time when he was coming home from work, me and my brothers put ten things in the room, like a bit of Kit-Kat wrapper in the corner, two tassels folded over, a picture two degrees askew, and sat back and said, "Let's see how long it takes him to come and correct everything." He came in and had this really adverse reaction. "What a shithole! Who's messed up this room?" So there was part of that in Angela we enjoyed.'

Skinner, star of the long-running sitcom *Outnumbered*, lives in the same part of London as the boys, and they would often see her in the café they'd write in, or just walking around, but neither had the courage to introduce themselves. 'She's very quiet and private,' says Steve. 'Then, when we cast her, I was with my mum outside WHSmith's and I saw her and said, "Oh, hello, you're going to be my wife." It was an excuse to actually talk to her. She's brilliant.' Not only that, she was another graduate of the Mike Leigh stable, having starred in his 1990 comedy-drama *Life is Sweet*, alongside future *No. 9*ers Jane Horrocks and Alison Steadman.

In contrast to her snobby, obsessive-compulsive sister, Carol is unhappy, embittered and self-hating. Trapped in a loveless marriage to a man she despises, and involved in a longstanding affair with her brother-in-law, Carol finally lets her true feelings be known – after one-too-many swigs of the alcohol she has secreted in her handbag inside a bottle of sun lotion. 'She's a very funny character, but also very sad and brittle, and we wanted someone great at the comedy, great at the drama and the pathos,' says Steve. The pair were friends with Ashbourne through her husband, the actor Andy Serkis, and offered her the role. 'We knew she would get the northern grittiness, but Lorraine did Carol better than we ever imagined,' notes Reece. 'We read all the parts out loud when we're writing, and she got every single nuance of the way we imagined Carol to be. That doesn't always happen. But she knew exactly how to do it. And was superb. I don't think we've ever had anyone quite like Lorraine.'

As with Angela's OCD, Pat's predilection for practical jokes was inspired by a family member. 'I've got uncles like that,' sighs Reece. 'It's wearisome and you endure it rather than enjoy it. We thought it was a funny idea that Pat is a prat at the

Carol: I want this to be my house; I want this
           spread to be my spread. I want you to
           put your sausage rolls into my oven.

beginning and you think, how insufferable, and yet, hopefully, you feel sorry for him at the end. It's quite a reversal.'

'"Nana's Party", to me, was suburbia on acid,' says costume designer Yves Barre, who worked with the boys on The League and Psychoville and reunited with them for series two onwards. 'They never hold back on colours or textures. It can be very dark. It can be very moody. It can be very cinematic. They're very open and anything goes.'

Pat's distinctive look was, according to Shearsmith, 'one I'd not done before. Strong ginger and a tight perm felt right for that character.' His pink cardigan is also the same shade as the birthday cake, which was designed to look like a face. 'We always had to remember the cake was a character, so when you look at the icing you see two eyes, a nose and a mouth,' says Steve, 'and we needed to keep the cake in frame, because Angela is underneath, listening.' Although, as it turns out, she wasn't. And hadn't overheard anything. 'Which is another surprise,' says Reece.

TOP: Steve and Reece on set.

ABOVE: This was another episode that Reece and Steve directed themselves.

'There were two directions you could shoot the cake and it look like a face,' explains Tandy. 'It was a very clever bit of design to make that work. We had it specially made. It was real sugar and did fall apart.'

Playing the paramedic strippergram was actor and model Christopher Whitlow, who choreographed his own dance routine to the *Casualty* theme. 'He came in, showed us what he worked on, and we went, "Yes. Brilliant." So we totally incorporated that,' says Steve. 'It's great when people add to what you've done. We don't tend to write a lot of stage direction or detail, so there's a lot to be filled in between the lines. That's what you're wanting your directors and actors to bring.'

'Nana's Party' was the second episode Pemberton and Shearsmith directed, although 'it was a lot more challenging than "Cold Comfort",' says Steve. 'The good thing was, the whole first half of the episode when I was under the table, I was free. There were two whole days when I wasn't needed [on camera]. So I enjoyed it when I wasn't in it.'

'There's a responsibility with directing,' muses Reece, who decided it wasn't really for him. 'Some lunchtimes where, normally, you would go to your trailer and sit down for an hour, you would have to have a meeting about this and that. It was relentless. All roads led back to us. And we don't need any more megalomania than we've already got. It's probably better to direct and not be in it. I found working with the actors more enjoyable than working with the camera. I mean, I haven't got a clue

BELOW: Steve as Jim, in position waiting for the cake to cover his head.

about changing lenses, so Stephan did all that.'

Unlike 'Cold Comfort', which was shot with fixed cameras, here the camerawork was much more traditional, designed to reflect the drama and emotional impact of the story on the characters. 'We decided the first half would be formally shot,' says Steve, 'so we put the camera on a dolly or on sticks.' But at the point when the wheels come off Jim's bus, in terms of his marriage and his various deceptions being uncovered, the camera becomes 'less controlled, more frenetic and more handheld. It's not as daring as "Cold Comfort" in terms of its shooting style, and it doesn't have the huge, emotional impact of "Christine", but I think it's a really underrated episode. We find it really funny. I mean, we love all of them, we don't play favourites, but you tend to root for the ones that have been overlooked. And "Nana's Party" has got everything in half an hour you might see in a two-hour play.'

Angela: Can you straighten those tassels,
           please, they're literally driving
           me mad.

ABOVE: Elsie Kelly as Maggie.

LEFT: Reece as Pat. Reece notes: 'Strong ginger and a tight perm felt right for that character.'

STEVE PEMBERTON   ALISON STEADMAN   REECE SHEARSMITH

SÉANCE TIME

WEDNESDAY 29TH APRIL 10PM

BBC TWO PRESENTS A BBC COMEDY PRODUCTION AN INSIDE NO. 9 FILM "SÉANCE TIME"
REECE SHEARSMITH SOPHIE McSHERA ALISON STEADMAN DAN STARKEY CARIAD LLOYD
ALICE LOWE STEVE PEMBERTON CADEN-ELLIS WALL
WRITTEN BY STEVE PEMBERTON & REECE SHEARSMITH
EXECUTIVE PRODUCER JON PLOWMAN PRODUCED BY ADAM TANDY DIRECTED BY DAN ZEFF

BBC TWO

INSIDE No 9

Séance Time

- Series **2**
- Episode **6**
- Directed by **Dan Zeff**

In October 2010, Shearsmith hosted a Radio 4 documentary called *The League of Gentlemen's Ghost Chase,* in which he and the other members of the *League* – Pemberton, Mark Gatiss and Jeremy Dyson – spent a night at the Ancient Ram Inn in Wotton-under-Edge near Bristol, supposedly one of the most haunted places in the UK. At one point, they attempt to contact the dead using a Ouija board and hear knocking sounds, noises that Gatiss later reveals were him.

Nevertheless, Shearsmith was drawn to the idea of a *No. 9* involving a séance – 'it's the spookiness side of me coming out again' – but hadn't been able to find a suitable take until he hit upon the idea of fusing the world of spirit mediums and paranormal reality series *Most Haunted* with the behind-the-scenes drama of a hidden-camera show such as *Candid Camera.* 'Needy actors, costume people; there were a lot of things we thought could be mined for comedy. The *Most Haunted* scenario was great, too, because you can do ghosts, but undercut it with the nuts-and-bolts of how you would achieve it.'

ABOVE: The episode poster was designed by Matthew Burlem.

'Séance Time', which takes its name from a line spoken by David Warner in the 1974 Amicus anthology *From Beyond the Grave*, begins with Tina (Sophie McShera) arriving at a large Victorian villa where she is greeted by 'Hives' (Shearsmith), who welcomes her in before dimming the lights and introducing Alison Steadman's blind medium Madam Talbot. As the three sit, Madam Talbot attempts to contact the astral plane, sparking all manner of spooky happenings – ectoplasm, a fire-belching candle, drawers opening and closing on their own – before a blue-skinned demon dwarf (Dan Starkey) appears, scaring the bejesus out of Tina.

Suddenly, the lights come up and Hives reveals to Tina that she's been pranked as part of a hidden-camera show called *Scaredy Cam*. Hives is really Terry, the show's presenter; Madam Talbot turns out to be a demanding diva named Anne, who's slumming it playing fake mediums during the day while appearing on stage in *Hedda Gabler* at night; while the 'blue demon' is a diminutive performer – but definitely not a dwarf – who's desperate for a drink of water and to be taken seriously as an actor. But no sooner has Tina signed her release form and been ushered out the door, than the room is reset and another unwitting 'contestant' appears.

ABOVE: Tina (Sophie McShera), Madam Talbot/Anne (Alison Steadman) and Hives/Terry (Reece Shearsmith).

LEFT: The location used for the exterior opening shots, which show Tina nervously walking up to the medium's front door.

Séance combined dub notes
2nd pass 6th February
~ 2'45 door creak
~ 3'30 music box earlier

4'20 teddy motif.
~ 4'39 handle ↓
~ 5'10 Alison moans ↑
~ foley on drawers
~ 10'20 Lose Ann sigh.
~ 6'17 Tina dialogues.
~ 7'42 T/B clicks ~ 7'38 Gemma level.
~ 7'57 T/B Gemma.
~ 8'17 × sigh♯ ♭♭.
~ 9'40 passim crew noise
~ ? sophie record scratch earlier.

~ table knock earlier.
AS: "mummy" half breath
~ 11'18 subtle music Q. ↑
~ 13'19 subtle music Q - ↑
~ 16'10 subtle music Q ↑
~ 10'28 Clive improv in monitor ↑ check.
~ 13'44 × ADR Ann.
~ 13'59 Clive ↑
~ 16'08 Door close ↑ (creak?)
~ 17'08 2× laughs.
~ 19'24 Baby
· 19'55 Gemma↑ sync.
~ 20'08 × ADR "hnh"
~ 22'20 Angry Birds
~ reverb on Amanda

table knock ↑
AS "mummy" half breath

Only this time, Pete (Pemberton), the person being pranked, isn't playing along, and everything that could go wrong does, from Pete bringing in dog shit on his shoe, to stepping on a discarded talon and yanking the prop tambourine off its wire. 'When you see Steve go through the whole process the second time, the grade has changed, the music has changed, the atmosphere has changed,' says Tandy. 'So you are under no illusions this is a piece of hocus-pocus rather than a genuinely scary thing.'

The second 'séance' is brought to a tragic end when Pete freaks out at the sight of Starkey's demon and knocks him out, an idea lifted from another YouTube video Shearsmith was obsessed with, a Halloween prank gone wrong. In it, an American high school student jumps out of a wheelie bin in a corridor with a mask on and the person he's trying to scare punches him in the face. 'He falls back in and the lid closes,' recalls Reece. 'It's so savage and kills any comedy dead.'

Terry, we quickly ascertain, is a 'monstrously egotistical' man, desperate to claw his way back on to prime time after a career setback which saw Scaredy Cam cancelled and him reduced to bingo ads, after a young boy peed himself on live TV while Terry was dressed as a gorilla. 'Three million hits that pissing boy got, and I didn't see a penny of it,' Terry moans.

'Again, that places it in a certain time,' says Steve. 'Hits on YouTube might not be what people talk about now, but then it was. It was almost like, forget making your half-hour television programmes. If you can get a clip that hits on social media, that's worth far more than labouring over these fucking Inside No. 9 episodes.'

'He is a shit to everybody,' says Dan Zeff of Terry. 'But Reece brings real depth to him. He's not remotely happy. He's driven by obsessions about other people achieving more than him or things that have gone wrong in the past, and that makes him misanthropic and unable to connect to anyone else's pain.'

'It has shades of "Couchette", in that when something awful happens, there's this sense of "How does this affect me?"' concurs Steve. 'The actress is worried about getting to the theatre and her evening performance. The make-up woman's only worried about how it looks on camera. Terry's only worried about how he's coming across. It's another group of awful people. It's us being quite

ABOVE AND LEFT: Detailed set dressing plans for the séance room, drawn by production designer Simon Rogers.

DIMMABLE GAS LAMPS ATTACHED TO WALL

ENTRANCE TO HIDDEN CAMERA AREA

HIDDEN CAMERA AREA

HIDDEN CAMERA AREA

MAIN ENTRANCE IN

GAS LAMPS ATTACHED EITHER SIDE OF FAKE MIRROR

'TWO WAY MIRROR MOUNTED TO FAKE WALL'

```
Gemma:      Can we get away with that, do you think
            . . . ? A 'shit' for two 'bloodies'?
            Seems fair enough . . . .
```

ABOVE: The detailed set plans, drawn by production designer Simon Rogers, show the séance room and the hidden camera area where the *Scaredy Cam* crew are waiting.

damning of our own industry and the egos you get. Not that we've witnessed much of it. But you do hear stories.'

'I love this episode simply for what it says about the television industry,' states Tandy, 'which is that its aim is to lie to members of the public. Even if it's some talent show which notionally has a prize at the end of it, it's mostly about how you can humiliate people for money. It's a shocking indictment of a lot of what's passed off as entertainment and television in this country.'

Alison Steadman was yet another Mike Leigh veteran. But not only had she starred in *Abigail's Party*, which had directly inspired 'Nana's Party' and was a huge influence on both Shearsmith and Pemberton's writing, she was also, at one time, married to Leigh.

'Alison has strong comic bones and clearly understood what she was lampooning,' notes Tandy.

'She's so versatile; she can play any level on the social spectrum,' adds Zeff, 'so it was all about finding the right degree of luvvieness without it feeling like caricature. She nailed that character perfectly.' (Shearsmith had previously co-starred with Steadman in an episode of *Marple*, which is namechecked here.)

Among the *Scaredy Cam* crew are hassled junior producer Gemma and disinterested make-up and hair person Amanda, played by Cariad Lloyd and Alice Lowe respectively. 'Wasted, really,' says Tandy of Lloyd and Lowe. 'We were already at the point where we could ask anybody to do even a tiny part that's only got two decent scenes, and people would say, "Yes" and we regret it four years later when we'd say, "This would be a great part for Cariad or for Alice," but they've already been in, and we have to stick to our rules and not have anybody back.'

Playing 'Blue Demon Dwarf' was Dan Starkey, best known as Strax on *Doctor Who*. 'He's used to sending himself up and was able to have a lot of fun with it, building up his part and suggesting things,' says Tandy. 'He's also had his fair share of days in prosthetics, so understands that world. We didn't want to get a dwarf. We wanted somebody who was clearly not a dwarf, and we gave him a name in the credits: Clive.'

Once again, the production returned to Langleybury for interiors. But, this being *Inside No. 9*, the budget didn't extend to having a sizeable TV crew appear onscreen, just a handful of crew dotted around and a viewing station in the kitchen. 'It's not quite as we first wrote it,' says Reece. 'It was hampered by money constraints, so the actual nuts-and-bolts of the filming is quite spare. We thought there'd be a much bigger production behind the scenes, and it's only a few light boxes and stuff to give you the idea they're filming. But we squared it with the idea that they've moved into a real house and have to do it quite mobile, because if you were tricking someone, you wouldn't say, "Come to a studio."'

When it came to staging the opening séance, Shearsmith provided Zeff with several films as reference. 'We talked about the medium in *The Others* and the way her eyes looked. And he sent me clips from *The Changeling* and *The Awakening*,' recalls Zeff. 'Not that he was saying, "You've

ABOVE: Reece as Hives/Terry, holding 'Mary', the creepy doll that forms part of the séance set.

got to shoot it like this."' In terms of camera movement, Zeff took his inspiration from the horror films of Sam Raimi. 'There's an air he gets in his camera work that I love. It's balletic. There's something about the way it moves that makes you feel there's a presence in the room. It's almost like the camera is the spirit.'

ABOVE: Alison Steadman as Madam Talbot/Anne.

Having started out as 'fake' horror, 'Séance Time' turns, first, into a behind-the-scenes comedy with pratfalls and zingy one-liners, before, effortlessly, slipping back into real horror for its final few minutes. 'So the music changes, the style of acting changes, the camerawork changes,' says Tandy.

'It's not something you get in any other show,' insists Zeff, 'that movement from horror to comedy to stupid comedy to a lovely bit of character comedy with Dan saying, "Why don't I have a name? What's my character?" There's something very human in that and painful, and then back to horror. It feels absolutely unique and difficult to pull off. With their stuff, you're carrying a very full bowl, and my job is to make sure I don't spill it. The challenge is *not* fucking it up.'

And yet the ending of 'Séance Time' proved almost impossible to crack, with neither Shearsmith, Pemberton nor Zeff feeling they quite got it right.

'It was probably slightly unsatisfying,' admits Reece.

'We spent ages trying to figure out how to end it,' adds Steve.

Various scenarios were tried and discounted. 'At one point we were going to

Anne: Did you know I was very nearly Marple?
             They said I wasn't sweet enough.
             Fuckers.

cut to the prank that goes wrong with the gorilla suit, making the boy wet himself,' remembers Zeff.

Now, after the body of Starkey's blue demon is possessed by the spirit of the little boy who, humiliated by the gorilla prank, actually killed himself, Terry sees something in the cot that causes his bladder to let go. 'I remember talking to Dan about the boy being more horrible if we stayed right back from it, and couldn't make it out,' says Reece. 'So when Terry goes in and is trying to talk to him, you don't see it.'

'Dan, Reece and Steve spent a lot of time trying to make the ending work,' reflects Tandy, 'but it was always a difficult call as to what we were trying to say. It's all about this monster who is prepared to do anything to get back on television, and the forces arrayed against him; in other words, the spirit of the dead boy. It has to play out very quickly and be clear to the audience what's happened. In a way, we had too much fun in the first half, and the story of the boy really only comes to the fore in the last five pages. So it's hard to make that land.'

In the end, Zeff suggested they finish with jump scare, as the dead boy leaps up into the lens, before cutting to the closing credits. 'That was a bit of Dan's directorial improvisational brilliance,' says Tandy. 'M. R. James would have finished with three dots or a dash and you'd be left with the horror of that moment. Unfortunately, I don't know how you do that in TV these days.'

ABOVE LEFT: Dan Starkey as Clive, the 'Blue Demon Dwarf'.

ABOVE RIGHT: Dan Starkey and Reece.

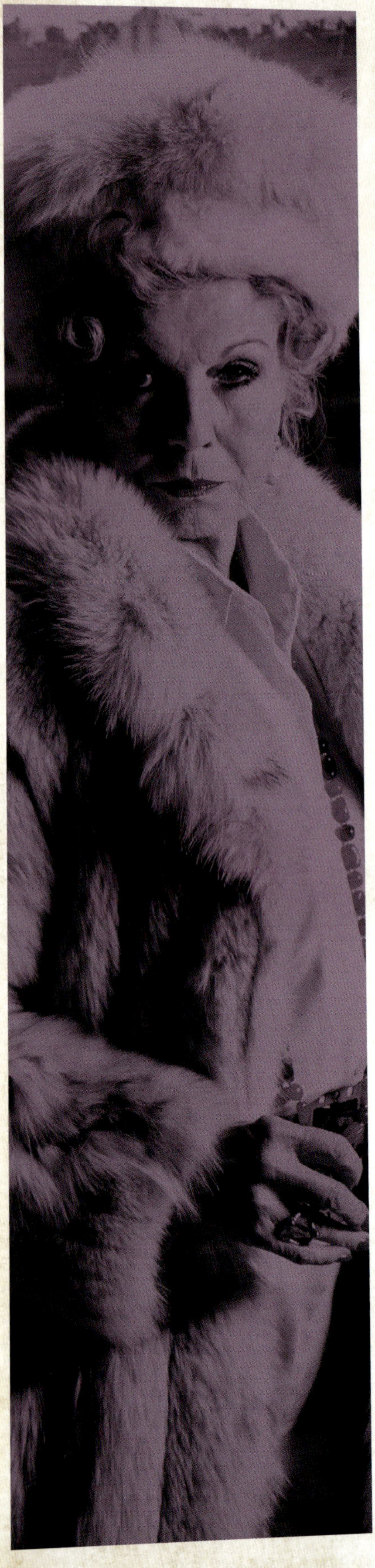
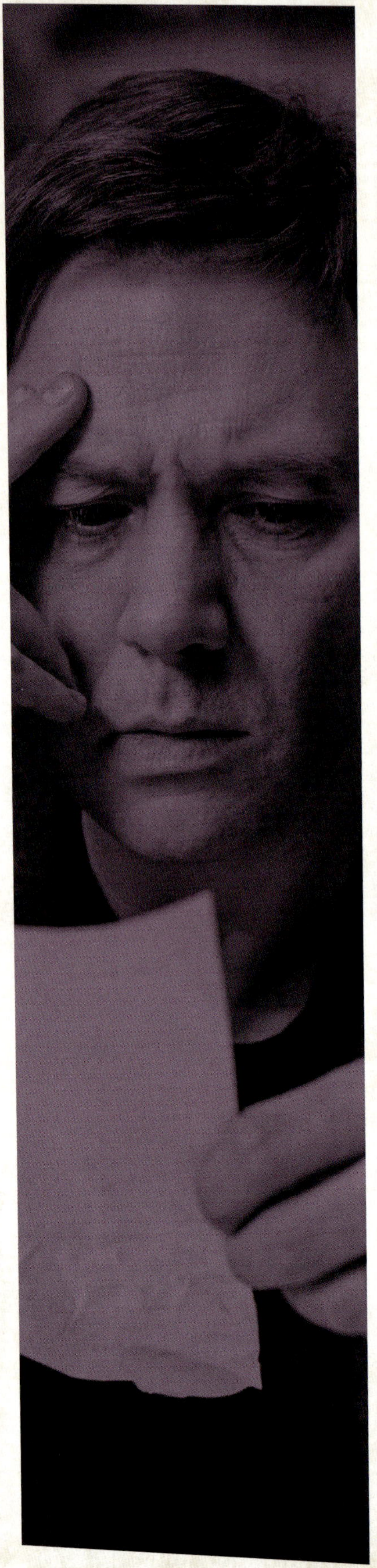
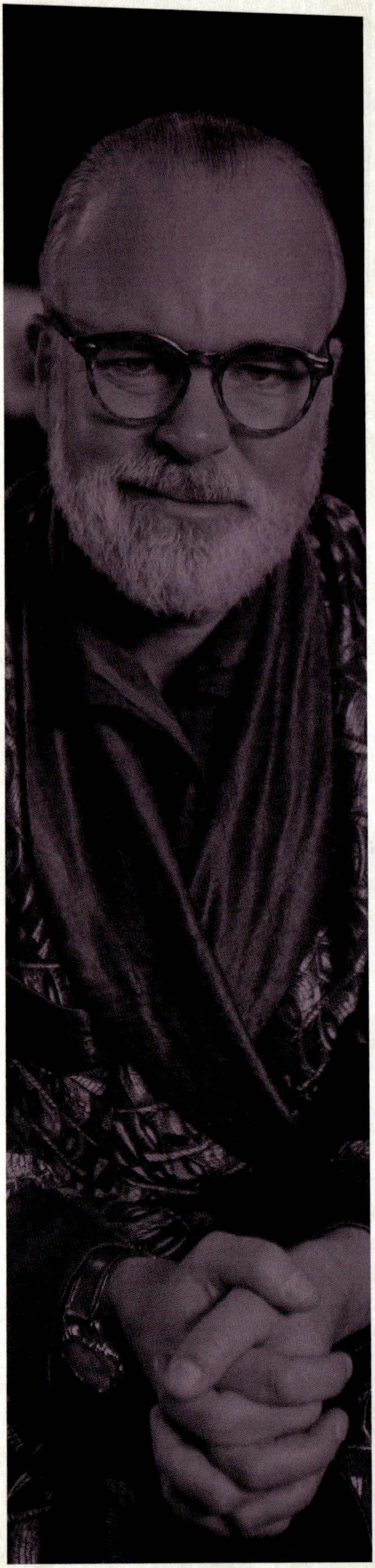

SERIES THREE

REECE SHEARSMITH   RULA LENSKA   JESSICA RAINE   STEVE PEMBERTON

Have you been GOOD? or have you been BAD?

The Devil of Christmas

...is watching you.

The Devil of Christmas

■ Series **3**
■ Episode **1**
■ Directed by **Graeme Harper**

The idea for 'The Devil of Christmas' sprang from a desire to do a 'full-on' horror episode. 'Having read about this Krampus figure, we thought it was a great basis for a story, the dark side of Santa Claus,' explains Steve. The boys quickly set to work, writing 'seven or eight pages of a family arriving at a chalet in Austria and all these spooky things happen'. But, in trying to inject humour into this festive frightener, they realised they were diluting the horror, with the tone closer to *Scooby Doo*. 'That's when we had this brainwave: let's embrace that and set it in the seventies. Immediately we made a list of all the things you see in ropey seventies television: light-as-a-feather suitcases; people eating but never eating anything; booms in shot.'

ABOVE: The episode poster was created by Graham Humphreys.

As well as injecting humour, the period setting gave them the chance to pay homage to those anthologies that had influenced *Inside No. 9*, shows such as *Tales of the Unexpected*, *Thriller* and *Beasts*. 'That's when it became exciting,' continues Steve. 'We thought, it's a spoof, a pastiche, it'll be a great exercise in recreating old television, but it didn't feel satisfying enough. Then we thought, what if a director's commentary started playing over the top and he can highlight some of the errors? Because we didn't want to overplay the mistakes, but we didn't want people to miss them either.'

Presented as an episode of a seventies anthology, 'The Devil of Christmas' begins with an English family – husband Julian (Pemberton), pregnant second wife Kathy (Jessica Raine), son Toby (George Bedford), and domineering mother Celia (Rula Lenska) – arriving at an Alpine ski lodge for the holidays, where their creepy Austrian caretaker, Klaus (Shearsmith), recounts the legend of the Krampus who punishes badly behaved children. It soon becomes apparent, however, that what we're watching isn't an old episode, as, three minutes in, the soothing tones of its director Dennis Fulcher (Derek Jacobi) and an unidentified interviewer (Cavan Clerkin) start talking over the picture in the manner of a DVD commentary. Then Fulcher asks if they can stop the tape, the images rewind, then begin again. As the programme progresses, we see unedited scenes as well as behind the scenes of the production, before, finally, it becomes clear that what we're watching is an elaborate snuff film, as Kathy – 'in reality' an actress called Penny – is killed on camera.

'It was born of our minds running to the seventies and early eighties where there seemed to be a snuff movie every week,' explains Reece of the episode's very dark twist. 'You think you're listening to a director's commentary and it ends up being a police interview. At the time we thought, "This is the most horrible one we've ever written." Because it is so savage.'

ABOVE: Klaus (Reece Shearsmith), Julian (Steve Pemberton), Toby (George Bedford), Kathy (Jessica Raine) and Celia (Rula Lenska).

SUITCASES TOO LIGHT
REVERSES WITH NO JAW MOVING
DRINK CONTINUITY UP & DOWN
FILM EXT. → VIDEO INT.
VIDEO BLUR
STUNTMAN / WOMAN OBVIOUS —
BAD WIG ETC.
ATTACKED BY DOG — ARM SUDDENLY
THICK.
5 O'CLOCK SHADOW ON ONE OF THE ACTORS
RAIN OUTSIDE & DRY INSIDE

SCARS, SCRATCHES MOVING L OR
R OF FACE
BLANK PAPER IN BOOK / NEWSPAPER

THUNDER & LIGHTNING — SAME
THUNDERCLAP
BLOOD TOO PINK / BRIGHT RED
BAD CHILD ACTING — BABY &
CHILD ALWAYS LOOKING OFF
TO ITS MOTHER
SAME WITH ANIMALS — LOOKING TO
OWNER
DAY FOR NIGHT FILMING
BACKDROP UNCONVINCING OUTSIDE
STUDIO WINDOW
BOOM SHADOW ACROSS FACES
OFFERING UP FOR CAMERA
EG. THROW IN FIRE, THEN IN CLOSER
SHOT ITS TOO PERFECT.

But even with that horrific denouement in mind, the boys were determined both the Krampus story and in-episode thriller narrative held up, and watched numerous episodes of Brian Clemens' seventies series *Thriller* for inspiration. 'They all seemed to be about a husband or a wife having an affair and trying to get rid of their partner, usually by giving them a heart attack or a scare,' notes Steve. 'So we were writing on three levels constantly.'

Once the script was finished, they sent it to Tandy for his input. 'Adam loves the technical side of television,' says Steve. 'He loves the history of television. He was a floor manager on a number of mid-eighties BBC plays, so knew all about this rehearse-record. Where you rehearse for a week, and record in a day, maybe two. He was like a pig in shit.'

But Tandy felt the script needed work. 'There are about five or six different production styles involved – and a stylistic rug pull every five minutes – and we had to make sure we were true to all of them,' he explains. 'Reece and Steve had written a lot of technical details which didn't really fit. Originally it was set over three days in the studio with a single camera, and they needed to understand the exact process.' So Tandy had a researcher search the BBC archives for studio sessions from the seventies and found the last part of an episode of *Z-Cars* and gave it to the boys. 'And like magpies, they picked all the really good bits.'

'There was some brilliant stuff in there,' says Steve. 'They would finish a scene, leave the cameras running, then wheel them across to the next bit. And you saw what happened between set-ups. The actors, as soon as the scene finished, just dropped and sat there. Not really talking very much.'

Pemberton and Shearsmith were determined 'The Devil of Christmas' should feel as authentic as possible. 'The first line in the script was, "As the camera trails along, the candles smear", which you used to get all the time,' says Steve.

ABOVE: A page from one of Steve's notebooks shows lists of their ideas for making 'The Devil of Christmas' feel like authentic 'ropey seventies television'.

'We presumed there was an app that could make it look like that,' adds Reece. 'Adam said, "There isn't such a thing. You will have to source vintage cameras."'

Smearing, or persistence trails, are a result of a bright light source burning the phosphor on a camera's cathode tube. 'There was no way of achieving it in post-production,' says Tandy. 'It had to be shot on antique cameras because modern ones use chips rather than tubes. So I thought, "Why don't we *really* go for this? They want it to look authentic, let's make it absolutely authentic."' And so to shoot the episode Tandy rented four vintage studio cameras from a company that specialises in hiring equipment as props for TV shows, and had them fitted with state-of-the-art zoom lenses.

When it came to the music, composer Henson joined in the period spirit, writing a mono score using only seventies instruments. 'A mixture of Roland synths, Solina Strings and a Wurlitzer electric piano,' he reveals, 'put through a distortion box once owned by Jimi Hendrix.'

Given that 'The Devil of Christmas' was to be shot like a multi-camera studio drama, Tandy looked for a director familiar with that way of working. 'I spoke to a few but most were quite sniffy about it,' he sighs. 'They said, "I'd really like to be doing a proper *Inside No. 9*." So I phoned the BFI, asked if they knew of anybody who was around from that period and they threw Graeme Harper's name at me. Graeme's not even retired. He's still working. So I got in touch via his agents, said, "Please come and help" and he leapt into action.'

'I was delighted,' says Harper, who started as a child actor before joining the BBC as a runner in the mid-sixties. He is the only director to have worked on *Doctor Who* during its original run as well as the revamped show. 'They knew I was knowledgeable about multi-camera studio productions where they said "Action" the moment the play started and "Cut" at the end and didn't do much editing or reshooting, even if you got camera shadows or booms came into shot, which, invariably, did happen.'

Shooting multi-camera required a different production process to the one they boys were used

ABOVE: For maximum authenticity, producer Adam Tandy hired four vintage studio cameras, which were used to film the episode.

INSET: The number 9 from the front of the cabin, drawn by art director Elizabeth Bromby.

to. 'In the old days, we would rehearse for a week, maybe two. With this we had five days in a grotty old rehearsal room in north London,' says Harper. 'All the actors came and learned their lines while they were blocking through each scene, with the sets marked out with tape and mock furniture, so they all knew how far they could go before falling outside the set or into walls. That gave me the chance to plan my camera script. Then, in the evening, I would go home and plot all the cameras' positions, so the vision mixer in the studio could cut up the shots as I'd planned. After four days, we had a technical run-through for the crew. Everything was absolutely traditional, the way it would have been done.'

'It was a bit of a learning curve for Reece and Steve because they normally expect rehearsals to be for their benefit, but here it was for the director,' says Tandy. 'It's all about trying to

```
Dennis:     Actors hate doing eating scenes . . .
            They've got to remember the continuity.
            So you'll see here. Nobody eats a
            thing!
```

create tension and mood and emotion through moving the camera, so you've got to develop your shots. If you look at Graeme's shooting scripts, you'll see a lot of detail. That's why you needed those four days in rehearsals.'

Call the Midwife's Jessica Raine – whose character died almost as shockingly in series two of *Line of Duty* – was cast as Kathy, aka Penny the unfortunate actress. 'We knew Jessica could do period and she's a proper star,' says Tandy. 'For the first twenty minutes you're not asking for a great deal of subtlety, but she's doing it with such conviction and care you completely believe she's that person, even when she's talking about thunderstorms and brushing her hair.'

Playing Kathy's mother-in-law Celia was seventies icon Rula Lenska, who had starred in two episodes of the BBC anthology *Leap in the Dark* 'so knew that world,' says Reece.

'She was a bit unsure to begin with,' continues Steve. '"Are they taking the piss?" She wanted to meet us and know it was coming from our love of all of this. And we got on like a house on fire. She was fantastic and had done exactly this kind of television before. So she got all the gags and didn't overplay it.'

That only left two roles for Pemberton and Shearsmith to divvy up: Austrian Klaus and Kathy's husband Julian. Both fancied playing the latter – 'the Simon MacCorkindale part' – but Pemberton won. 'I used the fact that in "La Couchette", I played the German and I didn't want to do it again,' says Steve.

ABOVE: Jessica Raine as Kathy.

Klaus turns out to be Kathy's lover, who, dressed up as the Krampus, literally scares Julian to death. 'I had the costume made for Reece to wear but you really don't see it,' says Yves Barre. 'It's a shame because it was like a minotaur; the horns, tongue and the legs were of a goat. When Reece got into the costume for the first time, he did a little dance, an animalistic, feral thing, which was just wonderful. But no one ever saw it.'

When it came to acting, Pemberton and Shearsmith insisted the performances feel of the period without falling into pastiche or parody, and gave Raine a DVD of 'Baby', the fourth episode of the Nigel Kneale-scripted *Beasts,* to illustrate the slightly theatrical style they were after. 'Everyone did their homework and watched old *Tales of the Unexpected* to know how to replicate the heightened performance without making it silly,' says Harper. 'Programmes from that period were made at such speed that that kind of performance was accepted. It was overacted, by usually very, very good actors. And we tried to replicate that very, very earnestly.'

'In rehearsals, Adam kept saying, "You can't enjoy this too much,"' recalls Steve. '"You can't be in *Acorn Antiques.* You've got to be in *Z-Cars."'

'I was concerned they were having too much fun, and losing sight of the dark heart of what was going on,' notes Tandy. 'When those rug pulls happen, you had to stop having your fun and start signalling to the audience that this is going to turn nasty. Because every time you do a behind-the-scenes gag you undercut the tension. It's a balancing act.'

'Obviously, we wanted it to be funny, but we could have pushed it further,' insists Steve. 'It was just finding the right level and the right intonation. Watching a lot of stuff from the seventies, it seemed like they were all at the National Theatre, proclaiming Shakespeare, so that gave you a real good clue to the rhythms. There's no naturalism going on whatsoever.'

ABOVE: Rula Lenska, George Bedford, Steve and Jessica Raine on set.

(231 ON 1)

Cue 20: Insert Director V/O

WE SEE JULIAN DIE .

[232] 3   A-B
**CRANE UP WITH THEM
AS THEY RISE AND GO
INTO A KISS. ZOOM
INTO MC 2S.**

KATHY TURNS AND KISSES KLAUS.

FLOOR MANAGER [V.O]:
Right we've got ten minutes to get the final
scene, cameras round to the bedroom
please. Dennis is coming down to the floor.

SUDDENLY WE'RE OFF!

**SEE KATHY WIPE HER
MOUTH AS THEY
BREAK AWAY + PULL
FACE
CAMERA SWINGS L-R
SEE STUDIO. FOLLOW
KATHY, MAKE-UP IN
WITH TISSUE FOR
KATHY, 2 CAMS X IN
F/G. 1+2 FLOOR
MANAGER LOWER 1/2
WALKS AHEAD, SEE
MAX STANDING IN
DRESSING GOWN AS
KATHY GETS INTO BED.
1 STAGE HAND GIVES
CHAMPAGNE BOTTLE
TO HER, 2 GLASSES**

THE CAMERAS WHEEL ROUND TO
THE BEDROOM SET. KATHY
CROSSES TO THE BEDROOM AND
GETS INTO THE BED.

SHE IS HANDED A BOTTLE OF FAKE
CHAMPAGNE BY THE STAGE HAND.

FLOOR MANAGER [V.O]:
Thanks Penny, in 5, 4, 3...

Cue 21: Insert Director/
Interviewer V/O

[233] 1   D
**MS KATHY
CAM STILL SETTLING
AS SHE SITS UP
GETTING READY**

(3 NEXT)

WALL 4

WALL 3

STUDIO SERVICING ROAD

WALL 1

WALL 2

FIRST AID

FIRST AID

CHRISTMAS TREES

TRUCKABLE CHIMNEY BREAST

BACKCLOTH OR STUDIO BLACKS T.B.A

STUDIO E
Height to underside of grid
5 meters

After four days of rehearsals, the production moved into Studio D at Elstree for a half-day camera test to make sure the vintage equipment was working properly. 'Studio D is close to Studio C, where they recorded *Beasts* and *Thriller*, so it felt like it had the right heritage,' says Tandy. Studio D had long since been converted to high definition, so the analogue equipment was patched into the gallery where Harper and the rest of the production team would sit during filming, selecting the shots.

The set was designed by Simon Rogers as if it had been made out of stock scenery. 'If you look carefully at the back walls, you can see there are seams between the flats which have tape over the top. That's how stock scenery was made and erected in the seventies and eighties,' says Tandy, 'but, bless him, Simon had the sets constructed with those seams in, so the scenery looks like it's come from a warehouse in Acton.'

'I remember putting sets together like that when I started out as a stagehand, using metal spikes and ropes, although we didn't do that for this because we never saw the back,' says Rogers. 'But we approached the set with that same spirit. Making things out of stock sizes was really important, so it felt like they'd come from the scenery store, not joining them up properly, and taping things together.'

Where things differed from the seventies were in the length of the shoot and the amount of cameras involved. 'Normally, we'd have shot it in one day with five cameras. But because we wanted to have

ABOVE: Detailed studio plans for the set, designed and drawn by production designer Simon Rogers.

LEFT: The period multi-camera shooting style required director Graeme Harper to create a highly detailed shooting script.

time to redo things, we needed two days to make sure we got everything exactly as it should be,' says Harper. 'And we had three cameras that were very old and likely to go wrong.' On the second day, one did. 'But I think it helped the process, because it made it look even crappier.' Not that they were purposely trying to make the episode look bad. 'Steve and Reece insisted everything should be natural as much as possible. Don't try to create booms dropping in. They did quite naturally. And the set wobbled. You didn't have to force things. You just let them happen.'

'It was such an act of restraint on our part,' says Reece. 'You could have easily gone for bigger laughs, with more obvious mistakes and gags. But we always had it in our minds that, somewhere, it was broadcast and it was good enough.'

'The Devil of Christmas' was edited live, with Harper and vision mixer Ian Trill calling the cuts in the gallery. 'We could finesse it but we didn't want to tamper too much, because what a drama vision mixer adds to a show is a particular look and it ends up being slightly different to what a picture editor would do in post-production,' says Tandy. 'But there were a number of tweaks we did, mainly because it was overlong.'

In the seventies, television was shot in a different aspect ratio (4:3) and resolution (576 picture lines) in comparison to today's high-definition pictures (16:9 and 1080 lines). Programmes were recorded on to two-inch video tape in an analogue format known as Quad, meaning playback wasn't as sharp or clean as modern, uncompressed digital images. 'Even if I could have found working two-inch

ABOVE: Jessica Raine on set.

RIGHT: Steve as Julian. Both he and Reece wanted to play this role, calling it 'the Simon MacCorkindale part'.

machines, the BBC (and our insurers) were uneasy about our shooting on something as fragile as old video tape,' says Tandy, who opted for the DigiBeta format instead. The problem was, the digital images came out looking too sharp and crisp. 'Normally when you record on to tape, it loses some of its definition and quality, so when you play it back, you can tell it's been recorded. Then, when it's edited, it's even softer and grainier. Ours looked like live studio pictures. They didn't look authentic.' To help degrade the images, Tandy recorded the edited programme on to one-inch tape then back on to HD to soften them even further.

The episode's final rug pull comes after Penny is chained to a bed by 'Klaus', who ravishes her. He then steps out, and a couple of crew members lay a plastic sheet beneath the confused actress, and gag her roughly. 'Jessica asked for the gag to be tied really tight. She didn't want us to take any care over her. She wanted it to be real enough in terms of the brutality of that moment,' says Tandy. Before Penny has time to process what's happening, someone else wearing the Krampus mask enters with a machete. The look of terror on Raine's face is almost too realistic. The first time they did it, 'you didn't feel the savagery,' says Steve, so they tried again, this time with Glenn Marks, the stunt co-ordinator, behind the mask. 'I remember it being very tense around the monitor, but Jessica was so good. She knew we wanted it to be horrific.'

Just before Penny's killed, Fulcher comments that it's 'always a strange moment, when you see them realise what's going on'. The implication, somewhat chillingly, is that he's done this before. To voice Fulcher, they cast stage legend Derek Jacobi who, famously, also narrates a well-loved children's TV show. 'We thought, how funny that the voice of In the Night Garden is the director of a snuff movie,' chuckles Reece.

'We were going for somebody who could do a plummy voice, but also had a lot of intensity and emotion,' says Tandy of Jacobi. 'We were so lucky to get him. It wasn't a huge amount of work. We'd already edited it with a guide voiceover, because we needed to make sure all the backwards and forwards worked and had the right length for him to fill.'

'I remember showing him that last scene,' says Steve, 'and he said, "Oh dear." He looked really upset at how savage it was.'

'The end was vile,' agrees Harper. 'It was a shock. And I hope it did shock people.'

'I read a few things at the time, saying, "It looks like it's coming from people who hate television," and I thought, that's a really interesting way of looking at it, because it's quite the opposite,' says Reece. 'It was absolutely our adoration and love that inspired it. It was a love letter to that way of working and that style.'

'The Devil of Christmas' was broadcast on Boxing Day 2016, as a Christmas special, separate to the rest of the series, which came out the following spring. 'We could have said no,' says Steve. 'But we saw it was a good opportunity to get two lots of publicity, and we did, because it's such a different thing to have on at Christmas. It's an anti-Christmas special.'

21st February 2017 – 22:00

THE BILL

REECE SHEARSMITH
STEVE PEMBERTON
JASON WATKINS
PHILIP GLENISTER

BBC TWO PRESENTS A BBC STUDIOS PRODUCTION AN INSIDE NO. 9 FILM "THE BILL"
REECE SHEARSMITH ELLIE WHITE STEVE PEMBERTON JASON WATKINS PHILIP GLENISTER CALLUM COATES
WRITTEN BY STEVE PEMBERTON & REECE SHEARSMITH DIRECTOR OF PHOTOGRAPHY STEPHAN PEHRSSON EXECUTIVE PRODUCER JON PLOWMAN PRODUCED BY ADAM TANDY DIRECTED BY GUILLEM MORALES

BBC TWO

INSIDE NO 9

The Bill

- Series **3**
- Episode **2**
- Directed by **Guillem Morales**

There used to be a café near where Shearsmith and Pemberton live and work called Feast that they would visit 'literally every day for lunch' while writing. 'We would sit and spot all the people who were always there and say, "Look at him. He's always there." Little realising *we* were the ones who were always there,' laughs Steve. 'This was the first script we wrote for series three, so we were just meeting up to have our initial discussions, looking through the notebooks, talking over ideas. And on this particular lunch, we overheard a conversation between three older people, two women and a man, about whose turn it was to pay the bill. And there was something about the inversion of it, because jokes about paying the bill are about *not* paying, and this was: "No. It's *my* turn."'

ABOVE: The episode poster for 'The Bill' was designed by Rob Treen.

'"Put it away, Margaret. You got it last time. Now, Margaret. I *insist*,"' recalls Reece. 'We thought, that's really funny. The argument is about wanting to pay, the magnanimity of it. And we said, "Could that be a *No. 9*? Is there a way of keeping that going for half an hour and building a massive argument out of it?" And we came back to the office and started to think about it. How do you go around in circles with that? How do you keep it interesting? And how does it escalate?'

'In a way, it was even more restrictive than the wardrobe [in "Sardines"],' continues Steve. 'Because with the wardrobe, you could have people coming in and out, whereas this was round a table. Very often with *No. 9*, it's: "This is the challenge if you choose to accept it." Can you keep going for thirty minutes with four people arguing about this bill? What are the elements? What's beneath it? Of course, it's not about the bill, it's about other things. So what's the rivalry between them? And you flesh out the characters. A bit like with "A Quiet Night In", we said, "Let's start writing and see how we get on." We didn't know the ending. We had no idea they were all going to turn out to be conning Craig.'

'The Bill', which won Shearsmith and Pemberton the Television Craft BAFTA for comedy writing, takes place, late at night, in a tapas restaurant in an unspecified northern town. Loaded Londoner Craig (Philip Glenister), in town on business, has been taken out by Archie (Shearsmith), Malcolm (Pemberton) and Kevin (Jason Watkins) following a badminton match, but a major row breaks out between Archie and Malcolm over who should pay – tight-fisted Kevin suggests splitting it – to the consternation of the East European waitress Anya (Ellie White). As Archie, Malcolm and Craig attempt to cajole, bully and fight for the right to pay, the script explores themes of toxic masculinity, ego and metaphorical dick-swinging, eventually descending into violence and bloodshed when the men engage in a game of stabscotch, which ends with the waitress's throat being cut by Craig.

'We like writing arguments, we like writing this kind of banter, which is on the edge of an argument, and then exploding,' says Steve.

But, this being *Inside No. 9*, Anya isn't really dead, and the whole evening has been an elaborate

ABOVE: Reece and Steve as Archie and Malcolm.

con designed to swindle Craig out of £200,000, with penny-pinching Kevin the ringleader. The boys took inspiration for the con from David Mamet's *House of Games*, although admit to being unsure it was the right way to go. 'There are a lot of What Ifs?' says Reece, 'but it did give you an ending. And a great surprise as well, with the reversal of Jason's weedy character being the Prof.'

'The thing about cons is that real ones are done in such detail and the characters are really elaborate,' says Steve. 'So it's a very detailed backstory they've worked up about the rivalry between them and how this argument escalates, because they've got to get Craig to fever pitch. We reverse engineered from that and said, "Everything you've seen before is a lie." And the little tilt of Jason's glasses at the end, where suddenly he's in charge and we melt into the background, was perfect.'

Not everyone agreed. 'I remember when we showed it to Guillem, he was disappointed,' continues Steve. 'He said, "I love this story and I don't like the fact none of it's been real."'

'It felt a bit contrived, to be honest,' says Morales. 'I'm not saying it feels contrived now, but reading it, all that palaver about who pays the bill was becoming more and more outrageous and silly. And threatening. And when they kill the waitress, I thought, "Well, now they don't have to pay the bill." Clever but awful. But I didn't see the end coming. So I said to them, "We should give some tiny clues, because otherwise it's the most elaborate trick ever." So we added some moments, telling the audience, "There's something else going on here." Otherwise *Inside No. 9* just becomes about the twist. And it's not. It's the change of the tone. That's the beauty of the show.'

'We always made sure we had enough reactions and looks, so we could dial up or dial down for people who are watching for a second time to see we aren't pulling the wool over their eyes and everything is in plain sight,' explains Tandy. 'So you get the occasional lift of an eyebrow or somebody saying, "No, don't say that, say this." All of that is to do with the underlying con, rather

ABOVE: Left to right: Craig (Philip Glenister), Archie (Reece Shearsmith), Anya (Ellie White), Malcolm (Steve Pemberton) and Kevin (Jason Watkins).

RIGHT, TOP: Tension builds as the diners argue over who is going to pay the bill.

RIGHT, BOTTOM: The restaurant's menu.

CRAIG: What do you mean 'different types of piss'? There aren't 'different types of piss'.

than the overt, on-the-surface version of the dialogue, which is mostly jokes. And if you watch again, you can see that undercurrent developing as it goes on.'

In addition to being set in an unnamed northern town – 'You want everyone to think that it could be where I live, that's my local restaurant,' says Steve – the script makes much of the north-south divide, with Craig from London – 'He needed to be the mark who's come in [from elsewhere]' – and Archie and Malcolm proud northerners who won't back down. (Archie even feigns a terminal illness to engender sympathy and therefore pay.)

'We're from Yorkshire and Lancashire, so love all of that northern banter,' laughs Steve. 'We knew there was going to be some rivalry between Malcolm and Archie over who wanted to have the largesse of paying, because we had Jason's character as the mean one, and we had a lot of fun with that.'

As for Craig, the boys couldn't quite land on how to play him. 'We wrote a version where he was a posh twit amongst all these northern blokes. As a counterpoint, we wrote a version where he was a bit more laddish,' explains Steve. 'And then we thought of Phil and – boom! – it was clear. I'd known him for years, since he was a student at Central [School of Speech and Drama]. When Phil said yes, we went back over it. While we never write for people, once you've cast them you can make sure it's going to fit.'

Best known for his portrayal of DCI Gene Hunt in *Life on Mars* and its spin-off, *Ashes to Ashes*, Glenister is pitch perfect as the flashy, loud-mouthed Londoner who falls into the trap set by Kevin, Archie and Malcolm. 'Whoever played that role had to be large enough and powerful

number n!ne

TAPAS·RESTAURANT·BAR

enough otherwise he'd be swamped,' says Tandy. 'Jason, Reece and Steve are all great actors, but they're all playing slightly beta males. And Phil is being made to look like the alpha. He tells the sexist jokes and is flashing his cash around. And that's what they're trying to encourage him to do, because the flashier he becomes, the more he becomes intent on showing them he's got money.'

Jason Watkins had worked with Shearsmith and Pemberton on *Psychoville*. 'A brilliant actor,' says Steve. 'Brilliant with comedy and very, very detailed.' So much so that he insisted on a tiny wallet for his character to keep his carefully folded discount vouchers and cash in. 'He was incredibly good with the props,' says Tandy. 'We were seeing a master at work. He was really careful about character detail, costume detail, prop detail. Always got the jokes. He was amazing.'

'It comes from working in theatre,' insists Steve. 'He wanted ownership of that stuff and knew what was funny about it. Phil is a different beast. He's got his sides [that day's script pages]. And just before "Action" is called, he's still looking at them. Then he puts them down and gives a very natural, brilliant performance. Whereas you know Jason has worked out all the details and has been practising how he's going to unfold this five-pound note that's never been unfolded in years. He and Phil were a great contrast.'

Playing the small, but crucial, role of Anya the waitress was Ellie White, whom Pemberton had seen in a BBC Three pilot called *People Time*. 'Stupidly they never commissioned it as a full series, but she played different characters and was fantastic. Very, very funny. It's really exciting to spot new people. And I knew she could do the accent.'

When the cast assembled to do a read-through, it came up short. 'We wrote it thinking it was a normal half hour and when you do it at pace, it's fifteen minutes long,' recalls Reece. Worried it would underrun, Tandy asked the pair to write a couple of extra pages of dialogue, just in case, although they weren't needed. 'During the first rehearsal they were so quick, so fast, they were enjoying it so much,' says Morales. 'But I was thinking it's not going to be short, because that's not the pace. There are going to be moments of pause. When you're filming, you film what they say, and what they *don't* say.'

Despite its northern setting, they shot in a members' restaurant next to a nightclub in Hendon, north London. 'We scouted various locations and I liked that best because it was so crazy and over the top,' says Morales. 'There were paintings and lamps everywhere.'

Since 'The Bill' takes place entirely at night, the crew had to cover the windows with acoustic blankets during daylight to keep the light and traffic noise out, while Morales would have his camera

TOP: Reece as the prickly Archie.

ABOVE: Ellie White as waitress Anya.

RIGHT, TOP: Craig, Archie, Kevin and Malcolm battle for the bill.

RIGHT, BOTTOM: Philip Glenister as Craig.

aimed into the restaurant. When it got dark, the blankets could be removed and Morales could shoot towards the window, with Glenister's character on camera. Unfortunately, the restaurant was also on a bus route, so every time a London bus or black cab passed behind Glenister or stopped outside, they would have to cut. A few made it into the episode, but Tandy used spot colour correction to change the indicator signs from white to the bright orange LED signs you get on buses/taxis up north, and even changed the colour of the bus lighting in order to make it look like it wasn't from London. 'Tiny little details; I'm not sure anybody would ever notice, but you'd be surprised at the care we take.'

Filming around a table is a chore for cast and crew alike. It requires multiple set-ups to capture all the various angles, and necessitates actors sitting down for long periods of time. 'It's exhausting and quite relentless,' says Reece.

For Morales, the challenge was: how do I make the episode visually interesting? 'I said we have to be with them and be part of that conversation,' he remembers. That meant putting the camera on the table, very close to the cast. 'Sometimes that's a bit uncomfortable for the actor, but they are in front of the camera delivering the performance or the emotions to the camera, not the other actor. And the camera is the audience.'

Morales asked for a table with a hole in the centre and a special camera mount, but was told it was too expensive. What they could afford was two different-sized tables. 'We had a big one and a little one. One was five feet in diameter, the other seven,' says Tandy. 'So when the camera is outside the circle and you're seeing the group, it's

Seq	Scene	Panel
2	100	1

Seq	Scene	Panel
2	90F	1

Action Notes
CRAIG tries to grab the knife from ARCHIE and pulls his arm backwards from the table

Seq	Scene	Panel
2	100A	1

Seq	Scene	Panel
2	90G	1

Dialog
Get off!!

Seq	Scene	Panel
2	100B	1

Action Notes
ARCHIE's arm swings backwards over CRAIG'S shoulder...

Seq	Scene	Panel
2	99A	1

Action Notes
...passing right in front of ANYA.

Seq	Scene	Panel
2	90H	1

Seq	Scene	Panel
2	99A_1	1

KEVIN: Archie, one question. It's just that, I didn't actually touch the knife, so technically I think I probably owe less.

the small table. And when you're inside the circle, turning round, looking at the actors in close-up, it's the large one. But because of the lenses you are never aware of that.' Occasionally, there wasn't even a table.

'It feels completely dynamic. It feels action-packed. And that's down to Guillem,' says Steve. 'The genius of it is when it's finished, you don't realise you've just been watching four people sat around a table.'

To further ramp up the tension and threat, Morales and Stephan Pehrsson used a subtle trick that 'you're not aware, but you *feel*,' says Morales. 'Every five minutes we turn off one of the lamps, and if you compare a shot from the first five minutes to another twenty minutes in, you will notice the difference. It's becoming gloomier and gloomier, and darker and darker, and you don't know why. But the audience feels something is coming, which is the *Inside No. 9* thing.'

As the con reaches its climax, the diners engage in a game of stabscotch – otherwise known as 'nerve', 'pin finger' or 'five finger fillet' – 'because we needed a knife to come into play. Or they do,' says Reece. Filming the game, which involves a sharp knife and actors' hands, was another challenge. 'You can use a blunt knife, but people will notice,' explains Morales. 'The other way is to do it very slowly then speed it up, but you won't believe it. It was clear we needed both the hand to be real, and the knife to be real, and the only thing to do was to shoot the elements separately, then put them together. And so that's where digital effects are great.'

The production ran out of time on the day, however, and so, several weeks later, during the filming of 'Private View', they set up a table for Tandy to finish shooting the scene.

Anya's throat-cutting required a prosthetic neck rig and fake blood and was no less testing. 'We only had one go at it and Ellie was like, "Oh my God, what a responsibility,"' recalls Morales.

'We did a rehearsal off-set, just to show her what was going to happen, and she found it genuinely scary to have all that blood coming out,' adds Tandy.

The episode ends with another meal and another con, only this time Craig is now part of the gang. Some viewers didn't like the coda. 'They were like: "WHAT?! Don't believe it,"' recalls Reece, although the script does seed the fact that Craig's more than a little bit bored with his lot in life.

'He just loved this experience, and so thought, why not?' insists Steve.

LEFT, TOP: A page from director Guillem Morales's storyboards.

LEFT, BOTTOM: Jason Watkins as Kevin.

BELOW: To achieve the tension-building shots around the table, a camera was placed in the middle.

BOTTOM: The eponymous bill.

ALEXANDRA ROACH　STEVE PEMBERTON　REECE SHEARSMITH

THE RIDDLE OF THE SPHINX

28th February – 22:00

BBC TWO PRESENTS A BBC STUDIOS PRODUCTION AN INSIDE NO. 9 FILM "THE RIDDLE OF THE SPHINX" ALEXANDRA ROACH STEVE PEMBERTON REECE SHEARSMITH MUSIC BY CHRISTIAN HENSON WRITTEN BY STEVE PEMBERTON & REECE SHEARSMITH EXECUTIVE PRODUCER JON PLOWMAN PRODUCED BY ADAM TANDY DIRECTED BY GUILLEM MORALES

BBC TWO

INSIDE 9

The Riddle of the Sphinx

■ Series **3**
■ Episode **3**
■ Directed by **Guillem Morales**

Since his early twenties Pemberton has been fascinated by cryptic crosswords. 'Over the years I'd always have a go and would maybe get one or two answers,' he explains. 'You'd look at the clues as a layman and think, "What the hell?" And it makes you angry, because how on earth can you get this answer from this clue? But I always loved the challenge of it. And when I was in *Benidorm*, the late Kenny Ireland and I used to sit around and do the *Guardian* one. It's a very good group activity for a load of actors with time to kill.'

On 9 March 2015, Pemberton appeared as a guest on a *Comic Relief* episode of the BBC Two quiz show *Only Connect*, presented by Victoria Coren Mitchell. 'The question setter is called Alan Connor and when Victoria and I got the train back together we started talking about cryptic crosswords. She said, "Alan's written this book called *Two Girls, One on Each Knee: The Puzzling, Playful World of the*

ABOVE: The episode poster was designed by Graham Humphreys.

Crossword," and later she sent it to me. It was about the history of crosswords, but it was also a guide to solve cryptic crosswords. Suddenly, everything came together. And in the same way as I thought, "Can you develop an episode around four people wanting to pay a bill?", I started to wonder, "Can you dramatise completing a crossword?" That was the challenge. Can you create a story out of it? Within it, obviously, you wanted a mini tutorial. You wanted one of the characters to be telling another what the clues are, what to look out for. So while it could have turned into a Ted Talk, it was a case of one of them is a crossword setter, the other is someone who doesn't know how to do crosswords …'

'The Riddle of the Sphinx' begins with Nina (Alexandra Roach) breaking into the office of Cambridge University Professor Nigel Squires (Pemberton), who publishes cryptic crosswords in the student newspaper *Varsity* under the name The Sphinx. Nina is soon discovered and, for the next fifteen to twenty minutes, the episode becomes a battle of wills reminiscent of Anthony Shaffer's *Sleuth* and Ira Levin's *Deathtrap,* with a dash of George Bernard Shaw's *Pygmalion* and a splash of Willy Russell's *Educating Rita* thrown in for good measure, as Squires schools Nina in how to solve a cryptic crossword. 'I imagined it as a two-hander that went this way, then that way, so you were never sure who had the upper hand, and it kept switching,' says Steve who, once again, started writing without a clue where the story was heading. 'I knew Nina was acting dumb in order to get him to open up. But then he was aware of her plan and has double-crossed her. It flowed out. It felt labyrinthine. Although I was unsure what anyone was going to make of it.'

'I thought it was a great idea,' says Reece, who, unlike Steve, isn't a fan of cryptic crosswords. 'It was intriguing. I think everyone can't help but get drawn into solving a puzzle. However much they might not want to. It's a bit like magic in that respect.'

Once Pemberton settled on a name for his crossword setter – 'Everyone has a pseudonym and

ABOVE: Steve as crossword expert Professor Nigel Squires, aka 'The Sphinx'.

I was surprised there were no Sphinxes' – the rest of the plot slotted neatly into place. In Greek mythology, the Sphinx is said to kill and eat anyone who can't answer her riddles, but is bested by Oedipus who, famously, killed his father and married his mother. 'I was thinking, "This two-hander is great, but it's only going to take you so far." So to have a new character who is holding all the cards, and a third act where things get turned on their heads again, was brilliant.'

That third character was fellow Cambridge don and Nina's professor, Dr Jacob Tyler (Shearsmith) who has alerted Squires to her plan to murder him – she blames him for the death of her brother who killed himself after losing to Squires in a crossword competition – but is secretly plotting revenge of his own. For Nina, real name Charlotte, is revealed to be Squires' daughter, and the product of his affair with Tyler's wife that led to their divorce. And Tyler's revenge involves cannibalism, murder and suicide. 'It's got a very, very dark heart and a relentless ticking plot, and Reece's character coming in two thirds of the way through dials it up to a whole new level, as the layers of the conspiracy get peeled away like an onion,' says Tandy. 'I talk about rug pulls a lot, but usually in terms of style. This is all about content. You don't really get to know what's going on without going through a lot of rug pulls and revelations. It becomes worse and worse, leading, ultimately, to cannibalism. And so the legend of the Sphinx is actually quite important.'

'There was that brilliant line where Reece's character says, "I want you to eat her." And it didn't feel gratuitous, because it's coming out of Greek tragedy,' asserts Steve. 'We're not doing anything that hasn't been done thousands of years before us. Of course, many people did find it gratuitous. Having started out as a thing about a crossword and being very *Pygmalion*-like, it ends with him carving her bum. It's one of my absolute favourites. Really quite theatrical. A single set. Real time.'

'The themes were huge,' says Reece. 'And it felt really exciting. You never knew where you were.

ABOVE: Reece (playing Dr Jacob Tyler), Alexandra Roach (playing Nina) and Steve (playing Professor Squires) on set with director Guillem Morales.

The shifting sands of it being all about wordplay and puzzles and things not being as they seem was very allegorical. Revenge is always the greatest of plot drivers.'

Directing 'Sphinx' was Guillem Morales who describes the script as '*Educating Rita* written by two psychopaths. My first impression was: what the fuck? *Really*?' he laughs.

Concurrent with writing the script, Pemberton had to compile the crossword, his first, since the clues (and answers) were integral to the plot. 'There were certain words that were key,' he recalls. 'Asphyxiation was one, then pufferfish. So the idea about this particular poison which seizes you from the inside was there from the beginning. I remember there were lots of notes

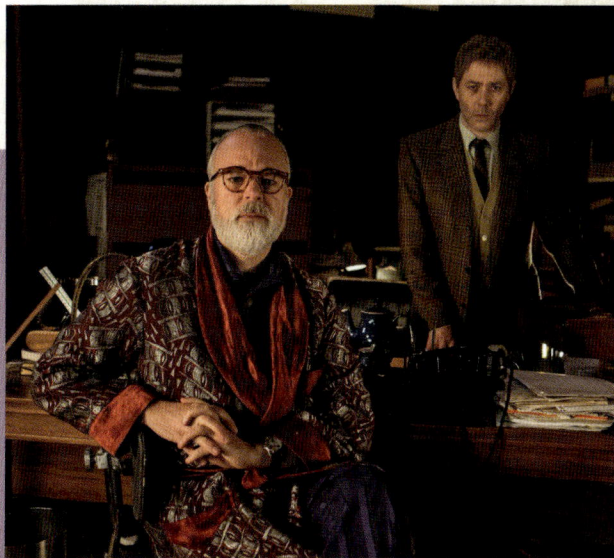

```
Jacob Tyler:        I think I'll take a bit off
                    the rump.
```

and jottings out of the plot, which I don't normally like to do. I like to feel it. But you had to have this crossword in order to build the episode around it, which meant you couldn't wing it. There was a lot more sitting and figuring out what the plot was, then doing the crossword, then doing the script.'

While reading Connor's book, Pemberton discovered the concepts of Ninas, hidden words within crosswords, 'where you find something going diagonally, just coincidentally, from the other clues'. The term was coined for *New York Times* cartoonist Al Hirschfeld, who smuggled the word 'Nina' into his cartoons in honour of his daughter. 'A bit like us and our hare, people enjoyed spotting the hidden Nina,' says Steve, who named Roach's character after her in tribute, and incorporated one into his crossword. 'I wanted there to be a reveal where, hidden within it, you had the words: "I swapped cups"' [referring to the cup of poison ultimately consumed by Nina].

Pemberton sent the crossword to Connor who they later engaged as a consultant 'to be sure we weren't cheating', says Steve. 'There were some he said, "I wouldn't do that" or "That wouldn't be allowed." We changed most of them, but sometimes it suited the plot, so the clue for asphyxiation wouldn't have been allowed in a newspaper, but it worked so well the fact it was a mixture of the Sphinx and the letter.'

Gonville and Caius College, Cambridge stood in for the exterior of Squires' building, while his cluttered office was yet another room at Langleybury House. 'It was a big, wood-panelled space on the ground floor that must've been the headmaster's office when it was a school and didn't look like it's part of a Gothic revival mansion,' recalls Tandy. 'It looks academic. So it made sense to build what we wanted into that room.'

'It was empty, so we had to dress and paint everything,' notes Morales. 'It was like having a set.'

'Simon Rogers and the art department did a brilliant job,' says Steve. 'It really felt like my character had been there for years. All we wrote was that there was a board with the crossword on, and a small

ABOVE: Steve and Reece as Squires and Tyler.

tea-making area with a stove. The rest they came up with.'

'We completely dressed it and changed the whole thing,' says Rogers. 'John Sorapure, the director of photography, really liked the idea of dark blue walls which, at that time, wasn't a colour I'd used on sets, but I've used a lot since. With props, you want to be able to tell a little bit about the character, so the old Apple II computer suggests a level of liberal academia. Obviously, the accumulation of his academic life needs to be on show, to give some visual hints about who he is and what he's done. It's a set I was really happy with. It's always about providing lots of detail to fill the frame, add mood and, hopefully, meaning.'

The room had three large windows that were cloaked off during the day to simulate night. To add atmosphere, Morales asked for dramatic *Frankenstein*-style lightning and lashing rain. 'That was great, that element of the Gothic,' says Reece. 'Like lightning effects by God.' Morales also asked for a Sphinx statue that sits atop a cabinet, and a giant crossword and large blackboard on which Squires and Nina write down the answers. 'In the script it was a notebook. They were sitting at the table doing the crossword and I thought, "It needs to be bigger and more dynamic." Because apart from the cannibalism, apart from the Greek tragedy, apart from the awful revenge, it's an episode in which you can learn how to solve crosswords. And you've got the perfect teacher in Professor Squires.'

Roach (*Sanditon*), however, is dyslexic, which made memorising her character's long speeches as well as writing the answers on the large crossword difficult. 'She said it was a nightmare,' reveals Reece. 'It was really scary for her because she had to, at speed, fill in all these words. She spent ages looking at the clues and did a brilliant job.'

While the 'I swapped cups' Nina had been intentional, during filming Pemberton noticed another: 'RIP NHS.' 'And because my character was called Nigel Squires, we thought that's so close to RIP Nigel Squires. So we added the line, "Isn't your middle name Hector, by the way?"'

ABOVE: Director Guillem Morales with the blood-spattered crossword.

Guardian cryptic crossword

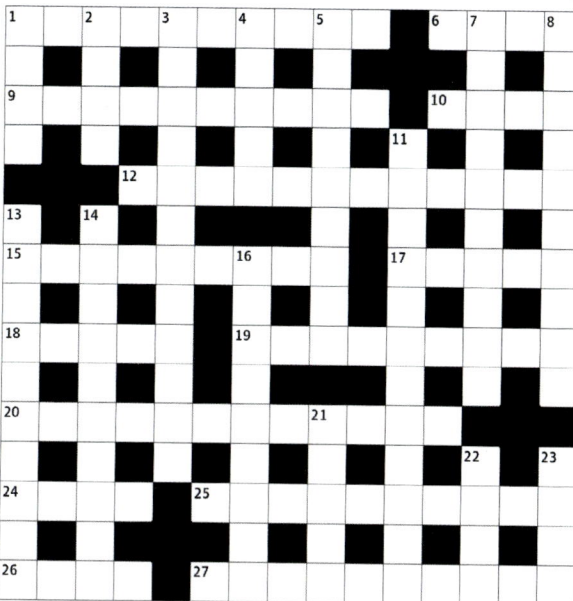

No 27,132 set by Sphinx

Across

1 To wound and wander, destitute (4,3,3)
6 Springs soldiers quietly within (4)
9 Degas evacuated and bathed before putting big picture in bog (10)
10 Untangle for a natural hairdo (4)
12 I hear an American poet solved the riddle of the pseudo hotel patron … (7,5)
15 … some smart aleck, no wit allegedly (4-2-3)
17 Hitherto, two notes are joined (2,3)
18 Tory leader on board for English flower (5)
19 Gets and holds down (9)
20 You might at Halloween see Robert on top of slapper, drunk (3,3,6)
24 Land is endlessly sacred (4)
25 Strength of support arranged inside unopened truss (10)
26 Periods where Fry's sons choose SATS, some say (4)
27 Associates fool with first workers (10)

Down

1 Indian product of French-Italian agreement (4)
2 Cover sound like a 50 cent song (4)
3 Why, say, a setter here is disturbed about a Spanish uncle — it's enough to take one's breath away (12)
4 Preliminary drawing of drink from the barrel, say (5)
5 Knocked back beer and wine, then put on a French undergarment (9)
7 Catch a train before poisonous bite (10)
8 Little pot, good for putting on (5,5)
11 Could George first digest bananas, before eating good Italian breakfast dish (4,8)
13 Hawk's equipment has a double catch (10)
14 Dickens character who undertakes to be a coffin maker (10)
16 Upset, as pedants often follow cuts (3,6)
21 Malaysian township, whence traveller returns to capital (5)
22 Frankfurter's number one bun? Don't start! (4)
23 The Origins of a Species popularised savage serpents (4)

There was, however, another Nina that neither spotted, until an eagle-eyed viewer pointed it out. 'You can read "one lepus", which is Latin for hare. People think we were prophetic. "You hid the hare." No we didn't,' laughs Reece. The actual hare can be glimpsed inside a cabinet, next to a Squires family photo that the camera lingered on at one point, although the shot was cut because it was deemed too much of a clue. 'As a result,' says Tandy, 'the hare isn't that obvious.'

Through Kenny Ireland, Pemberton had met Hugh Stephenson, crossword editor at the *Guardian*, and arranged for the Sphinx's crossword to be published in the newspaper on the day the episode aired. 'We were hoping for the scenario of someone doing it in the morning, going to work, then stumbling upon watching it that evening, and thinking, "I did this crossword this morning,"' laughs Steve. 'But then you got people in the forums who were rating the Sphinx and his clues. It's amazing how intensely they get into it. "Well, I would never have allowed that. This is clearly the work of an amateur." It was insane.'

Not that it's put Pemberton off: he has since written a couple more cryptic crosswords for the *Guardian* as well as one for the third episode of the Steven Moffat/Mark Gatiss BBC serial *Dracula*. 'The thematic thing of a crossword is cloaking your intentions. You want people to read the clue and not spot what's right in front of them. That's what's so delicious about it. And it's exactly the same thing that we do, day in, day out, writing *Inside No. 9*.'

ABOVE: The crossword Steve created for the episode was printed in the *Guardian* on the day the episode aired — under the pseudonym 'Sphinx'.

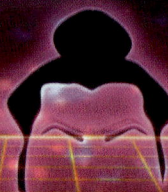

Empty Orchestra

■ Series **3**
■ Episode **4**
■ Directed by **Guillem Morales**

The idea for 'Empty Orchestra' first took root in Pemberton's mind when he was working on *Benidorm*. 'I got into karaoke being there,' he remembers. 'They all do it, in every single bar. Never, never thought I would do it. Or enjoy it. And I found I absolutely loved it. We would do it almost every weekend.' And having just finished his run on the show, karaoke was 'very fresh in my mind' when he and Shearsmith began discussing doing an episode where pop song lyrics would drive the story – 'essentially, a sung-through version, but not quite a full-on musical' – although they decided to put a pin in it. For now. 'You needed dialogue,' says Steve.

Nevertheless, a Japanese-style karaoke booth rather than a crowded bar felt like the perfect locale for a *No. 9*. 'A dedicated room, tiny. When you walk in you think, "How the hell am I going to spend five

ABOVE: The episode poster was created by Rob Treen.

minutes in here, with up to eight people?" Then, once you start, you're begging for an extra hour when it's finished,' continues Steve. 'The question then was, "Could we tell a story with these songs?" And a bit like with the crossword, we had to know the songs in advance because they inform everything, so we knew we had to get them cleared. We weren't allowed any American ones. I knew I wanted "Titanium"; that was such a great one to go out on. We wanted a variety of music. We wanted a rap song, or one with rapping in. Asked for Pitbull. Couldn't have it. Went with "Wham Rap" which fit really well, because it's the crap white guy's version. So we went back and forth before we wrote it to find out what songs we could have.'

'From the word go, it was a hard ask,' admits Tandy. 'The guys gave us a list of pop songs they wanted. Half the stuff wasn't clearable. So we had to come up with others they could lift lyrics from, in order to do the meaningful doubletalk, where the lyrics are said to people. I can't remember which ones are substituted from their original picks because they did such a great job of weaving it all together. My excellent production co-ordinator Kate Scarborough liaised with business affairs and the music copyright team and sorted it all out. We didn't need recordings, but permission to use the copyright. And we couldn't change any of the lyrics. Because then it becomes a burlesque. And we couldn't afford to re-record the tracks. So we had to find a karaoke company that had them all on its repertoire. They actually re-recorded a couple they didn't have, so we had tracks and lyrics for all of the songs.'

'Empty Orchestra' – the title is the literal translation of the Japanese word 'karaoke' – is set in a bar in London's West End, as work colleagues Greg (Shearsmith), Fran (Sarah Hadland), Connie (Tamzin Outhwaite), Janet (Emily Howlett) and Duane (Javone Prince) celebrate the promotion of their boss Roger (Pemberton). 'Office workers was a dynamic we hadn't done before,' says Steve. 'We decided

ABOVE: Left to right: Fran (Sarah Hadland), Janet (Emily Howlett), Greg (Reece Shearsmith), Duane (Javone Prince), Roger (Steve Pemberton) and Connie (Tamzin Outhwaite).

there was going to be an affair, office politics and some bullying. Fancy dress was almost secondary, although you do associate office parties with dressing up.'

Four are dressed as famous singers: Amy Winehouse, Michael Jackson, Boy George and Britney Spears. 'They're all iconic looks,' says Steve, 'but we thought it would be funny if the boss is in a shirt and tie and has made no effort whatsoever, other than a flashing red nose.' Shearsmith's Greg is dressed, incongruously, as a sumo wrestler. 'It's a small room so I thought, "Let's have a massive fat suit in there, that's funny,"' says Reece, who'd never done karaoke before. 'It was slightly uncomfortable because sitting down was a bit ungainly.'

'It was a lot of visual storytelling, and, wherever possible, using the song to tell the story,' explains Steve.

After having co-directed two episodes of the previous series, Pemberton considered directing this and 'Diddle Diddle Dumpling'. 'I had a very strong idea about "Empty Orchestra" and I would have done it very differently. But I realised I'd be in seventy per cent of the shots and I didn't want to be in it all the way through and direct. It's too much.'

In the end, they 'foisted' 'Empty Orchestra' on Morales, who was already directing four episodes

ABOVE: Reece as Greg singing with Tamzin Outhwaite's Connie.

SINGLE PIXEL RGB LED
SURFACE MOUNTED TO
BOTTOM EDGE OF
CEILING PIECE RECESS

LED FITTING AS
DOWNLIGHT TO
ILLUMINATE DRAPES

SINGLE PIXEL LED
SURFACE MOUNTED TO
TOP EDGE OF LOW WALL

LED FITTING ATTACHED
TO REAR OF TOP WALL AS
UPLIGHT FOR DRAPES ALL
ROUND

of the series. 'Because the scheduling was going to be so hard, it couldn't be anybody who wasn't ultra-prepared, and I knew Guillem would do a good job. But I did have to beg him,' says Tandy.

'Steve said, "Do you have anything else to do?" "No. Okay, I'll do it,"' recalls Morales, who then spent the Christmas break 'creating all the blocking and storyboards. As always, it's more work than you imagine, because there are so many details you have to consider. And when I watch the episode, you can't tell how difficult it was to make. Maybe it's because I am not really a fan of karaoke, it felt like a nightmare; I felt trapped there. Reece felt that way as well. For me, karaoke is hell.'

'It's a *lot* of people's idea of hell,' laughs Steve. 'And when I watched it back, I thought, "I bet people think it *is* hell." This room is somewhere you can never get out of.'

For a brief moment, they did toy with that particular get-out. 'But then we said, "Let's keep it real." Because it's a very upbeat, joyful ending. The baddies are vanquished. They get their comeuppance,' says Reece.

'What was great was saying, "Let's do the opposite of what you expect." The right people prevail. Which is a twist in itself,' notes Steve.

Since filming in a real karaoke booth was impossible because they're too small, the production team ended up building it as a set at Shepperton Studios. 'Simon [Rogers] made the set out of pretty much nothing,' says Tandy. 'It was a minor miracle he was able to bring it together for the budget we had, which was not a lot. We'd run out of money.'

Much like the train compartment in 'La Couchette', the booth had floating walls to allow access. 'They were barely walls,' laughs Rogers. 'We managed to cobble together some flattage and cover it in glittery fabric. It was a combination of karaoke booths I'd been in over the years, drunk at three o'clock in the morning, and adding a little bit of LED to suggest they're all quite pissed, so it feels quite disorientating. It's a musical as well, essentially, so it needed to have an elevated and heightened aesthetic. But that was an example of working with a lot of shiny, reflective surfaces and

ABOVE: Set design plan for the karaoke room, designed and drawn by production designer Simon Rogers.

some practical lighting to give some colour and detail to the set.'

When it came to the cast, Pemberton and Shearsmith were looking 'for people who could sing. If you had six people like me who are caterwaulers, it would be almost unbearable,' says Steve. 'So we asked for a list of good musical theatre people and Sarah and Tamzin were both on it.' Pemberton had appeared with Outhwaite in an episode of *Hotel Babylon.* 'We'd wanted to work with Sarah and Tamzin for a while,' says Tandy. 'What we didn't know was they were already best buddies, were a bit of a double act and ultimately unstoppable on set. Whenever they started singing, they turned into two party girls. And it was their energy that got us through the week. They were amazing. They gave everything. We were all shattered by the end of it, but those two got us through.'

Duane was played by stand-up comedian and performer Javone Prince. 'He gave a really sensitive and ultimately emotionally knowing performance,' notes Tandy. 'He starts out as this big, larger-than-life character. But, by the end of it, he has become this gentle giant who has an emotional connection with somebody he had no clue held a torch for him, and the honesty of that moment really comes across.'

Emily Howlett's Janet was written as deaf. 'We thought it would be really interesting to have a deaf character in this situation,' says Steve. 'And then, of course, we wanted a deaf actress to play the part. Not only would that help make it authentic, but it would fill in gaps we didn't know.' But finding a deaf actress who was able to sing proved tricky. 'It's beyond quite a lot of profoundly deaf actors and actresses who've got some speech, to be able to produce enough range in their voice to sing,' says Tandy. 'Emily did a lot of work to make sure she could do it and gave such a great performance.'

'She had no way of knowing how songs work, in that you go up at this bit, down in this bit,' explains Steve. 'So she had to visualise how a tune worked, how a melody worked. She worked with a friend who taught her, almost visually, that song.' During rehearsals, Pemberton asked Howlett what it would be like for her to step into a karaoke booth. 'She said it would be hellish. And the only way she would know what was going on or what people were singing, would be to feel the vibrations. That's why you see her turn her hearing aid down, because there's no point. We thought that was lovely.' So lovely, in fact, that they reworked the ending to take it into account, ultimately making the episode more of a love story and less of an office night out. 'In the script it said, "They see each other across the room. He approaches. They kiss,"' Steve continues. 'Now, when Duane approaches, she thinks he is going to make her feel the vibrations, but he says, "Feel this. My heart is beating because I'm with you." That came from us talking to Emily and to Guillem.'

TOP: Steve on the monitor.

ABOVE: Tamzin Outhwaite's wig is adjusted between takes.

On the first day of filming the lighting board broke and shut the production down for more than half a day. 'And we only had a five-day shoot,' says Tandy. 'I think we started at about 3 p.m. on the Monday.' To make up time, cast and crew needed to do an hour of overtime, every day. 'We did twelve- to thirteen-hour days that week. It was a big cast, lots of angles. Thankfully we had Guillem to carry all of that in his head. His storyboards were a lifesaver.'

This was especially the case as there was so much visual storytelling to register, with furtive looks across the room speaking volumes. 'There were a lot of details, and a lot of things happening at the same time that had to be co-ordinated,' says Morales. 'The storyboards kept us focused on what we needed, what was missing, because it was a puzzle that was shifting and becoming more and more complicated over the five days.'

Despite the confined space, Morales mounted his camera on a dolly and shot with wide-angle lenses to be close to his actors, while Pehrsson employed a different lighting set-up for each song. 'You're not really aware of it, but there are these subtle changes,' says Reece. 'People bring so much to what we've done to lift it off the page.'

To record a clean audio track for the dialogue, the cast were recorded separately from the music. Most of the time there was no music on set. The cast wore earpieces to hear the songs they were singing or miming to. 'When you saw them dancing with no music it was very weird, like the silent disco in the Shard,' says Morales.

'Singing was nightmarish,' recalls Steve. 'In karaoke, the music's blasting out and even if you can't sing, it's fun. But here no one could hear the music other than you. We kept having to remind everyone, "Speak up, pitch up, you're talking over the music." Everything has to be at that level, even though there's no sound. The other tricky thing was we had a monitor in most of the shots with the lyrics on, and they had to match exactly what we were singing. Technically very difficult, but we were blessed with a cast who were so up for it.'

Unfortunately for Howlett, she proved too good a singer. 'It wasn't as terrible as it should have been,' insists Tandy. 'We were pretty naughty, because you want to feel an awkwardness that they've played this horrible trick on her. So we ended up having to shift her vocal time very slightly.'

'To make it more cringeworthy,' adds Reece.

In fact, Tandy had to tweak most of the singing. 'Authenticity was an issue. When the sound guys did the first mix, they made the vocals too good, and I had to quietly go to them and say, "You have to rough it up a bit. It's got to sound like they're singing karaoke rather than dropping into a musical number." It had to feel like the singing was real, not lip-synced. But I love the emotional depth of the episode. The love story at the heart of it is really lovely. And it says something about the ability of *Inside No. 9* to go *anywhere*.'

BELOW: Although the other characters are all dressed as pop icons, Reece and Steve liked the idea of Greg wearing an unexplained and ungainly sumo suit, while the gloomy Roger's only concession to the fancy dress theme is a flashing red nose.

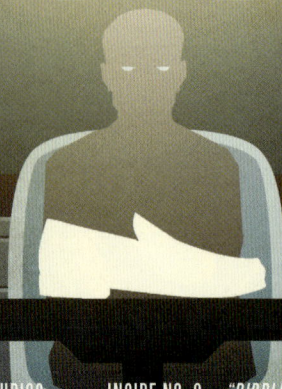

REECE SHEARSMITH   KEELEY HAWES   STEVE PEMBERTON

DIDDLE DIDDLE DUMPLING

14th MARCH – 22:00

BBC TWO PRESENTS A BBC STUDIOS PRODUCTION AN INSIDE NO. 9 FILM "DIDDLE DIDDLE DUMPLING"
REECE SHEARSMITH KEELEY HAWES ROSA STRUDWICK STEVE PEMBERTON DANNY BAKER MATHEW BAYNTON
DIRECTOR OF PHOTOGRAPHY JOHN SORAPURE WRITTEN BY STEVE PEMBERTON & REECE SHEARSMITH EXECUTIVE PRODUCER JON PLOWMAN PRODUCED BY ADAM TANDY DIRECTED BY GUILLEM MORALES

BBC TWO   INSIDE No 9

Diddle Diddle Dumpling

- Series **3**
- Episode **5**
- Directed by **Guillem Morales**

'**W**e'd written "The Bill", "The Devil of Christmas" and "Private View" and were on a roll,' recalls Steve. 'One day, as I was walking to the office, I passed this black shoe, next to a tree. I didn't stop. I carried on walking. But my mind was thinking about obsession. What if a person got so obsessed with the shoe, like it was a lost pet? We've always found obsession very, very funny. So I came in and said to Reece, "I've just had an idea."' The pair trooped around the corner, snapped a photo of the shoe with their phones, then returned to their office and started writing. 'We knew it was not about the shoe. We didn't know what it was about. But we knew this guy had issues and this obsession was covering for something else.'

'Diddle Diddle Dumpling' – which takes its name from the nursery rhyme 'Diddle, Diddle, Dumpling,

ABOVE: The episode poster was created by Rob Treen.

RIGHT, TOP: Left to right: Sally (Rosa Strudwick), David (Reece Shearsmith) and Louise (Keeley Hawes).

RIGHT, BOTTOM: Keeley Hawes as Louise.

My Son John' – is the tragic tale of stay-at-home dad David (Shearsmith) who finds a single, discarded dress shoe on the street outside his home. Bringing it inside, he embarks on a quest to return the shoe to its rightful owner – a quest that includes the creation of a website as well as an appearance on Danny Baker's radio show – to the concern and distress of his wife Louise (Keeley Hawes), their daughter Sally (Rosa Strudwick) and friend Chris (Pemberton). But David's obsession with finding its owner masks a deep-seated grief. Sally was a twin, and her brother died. And while Louise has moved on, David can't. Or won't. As the seasons pass – accompanied by Vivaldi's music – David and Louise's relationship deteriorates completely and he is sectioned for violent behaviour, after beating up Mathew Baynton's Ted who, at Louise's instigation, claims to own the shoe. Although, ultimately, we discover that David was the person who left the shoe there in the first place. 'It's very Bergman-esque,' says Tandy. 'It's about unhappy people having existential crises.'

Playing David's long-suffering wife was Keeley Hawes, star of *Ashes to Ashes*, who had just arrived back to the UK after filming *The Durrells* in Corfu. 'She'd been away for months,' explains Steve, 'and her agent said, "This script has come in." And Keeley said, "Oh God, I hope I don't like it. I hope I don't want to do it. I just want to come back and have Christmas." But she read it, really liked it, and said, "Damn, I've got to do it now." And to get someone of her calibre was fantastic.'

ABOVE: Reece as David with Steve, who played Chris.

RIGHT: Rosa Strudwick as Sally.

David: I'll get it. No, you get it. Ask them exactly whereabouts they lost it. And don't mention the size.

'Keeley gives an extraordinary performance,' says Tandy. 'Although, ostensibly, the episode is about Reece's character's descent into madness and, ultimately, violence, you have to admire the skill with which she portrays the hidden grief of a woman dealing with the death of her son with just a look, a pause or a glint in the eye which speaks volumes.'

As the shoe-obsessed, mentally fragile David, Shearsmith is equally extraordinary, delivering, arguably, his most heartbreaking and affecting performance. 'He's going to pieces while she's keeping it together,' says Tandy. 'It's an amazing exploration of bereavement and grief, and the two of them do sterling work.'

Originally, David and Louise's house was number nine, with the shoe a size ten. But Tandy said, '"You're missing a trick here. Make the shoe the number nine." You expect the house to be number nine but, when he shuts the door, it's actually twenty-two. It's two twos, because of the symmetry. That's the first clue.'

As for the shoe itself, there were numerous conversations about the style, colour and whether it had laces or not. 'In the end we thought, slip-on, because it would be easier to have been lost, somehow,' says Reece.

'I didn't particularly like that shoe and tried to change it,' says Morales, who was, however, delighted with the amazing mid-century modern house in Hampstead, north London, that the production team found to film in. 'We wanted something with a lot of personality, a lot of character, and when we saw that one, it was obvious, it was so special. We loved the colours. We loved the shapes. It was retro. It was very Kubrick. It was absolutely cinematic.'

Besides a few furnishings and the erection of the garden wall on which David finds the shoe, Morales shot the house as is, with its wooden floor, deco stylings and cool colour scheme reminiscent of Stanley Kubrick's adaptation of Stephen King's *The Shining*. 'It did feel like the Overlook [Hotel],' says Reece. 'That's why Guillem chose it. He knew the aesthetic he was after.'

Stephan Pehrsson had shot every episode of series one and two, but wasn't available for either 'The Riddle of the Sphinx' or this, so Tandy approached John Sorapure, who he had worked with on the BBC Two comedy *W1A*. 'I wanted to bring on different camera

people to give us different looks,' he recalls. 'And when John, Guillem and I sat down in a café in Waterloo one evening to talk about "Diddle Diddle Dumpling", the two of them had, on reading the script, come up with exactly the same idea about the way to shoot it, which was very formally, with symmetry in every frame.'

'We have to see the world through David's point of view, so the frame became really important,' explains Morales. 'He's grieving and missing the other twin. So everything has to be symmetrical. Visually, it shows you the psychology of the character and how he lives in that house and how he is dealing with grief. And then I decided to force the style more, and go a bit Kubrick, a bit Wes Anderson. Really trapping the actors in the frame.'

'He designed it so beautifully,' says Steve. 'Everything was very formally but symmetrically shot. It's one of the best-directed episodes.'

That sense of the symmetrical extended beyond shot composition and into set dressing, with 'Diddle Diddle Dumpling' the only *No. 9* to feature a pair of hares, one on either end of a long sideboard.

With the episode taking place across an entire year, Pemberton and Shearsmith used Sally's paintings to mark the passing of the seasons. For one transition, a painting blows against the windows and when it's taken down, we've moved on a season. Morales shot it in reverse. 'It took forever,' says Steve, 'but really worked.' The biggest problem was how to create four distinct seasons when the episode was filmed during one week in February. 'We didn't have access to spring or summer, so it all had to be created using tricks,' reveals Tandy. 'We were literally sticking plastic blossom on trees in order to make springtime happen and changing the grade and putting sweat marks on costumes to make it look summery.'

The dark heart of 'Diddle Diddle Dumpling' is set in a backdrop of domestic normality, one inspired by Pemberton and Shearsmith's adopted neighbourhood in north London. 'The yummy mummies, the yoga mat, and Planet Organic gags are very specifically Muswell Hill,' admits Steve.

'It felt like real conversations you might have. Or sneaking a look in another child's book bag to see whether yours is reading at the same level,' laughs Reece. 'It was a shame; originally we had a young character called Gertrude who said, "Do you have any passata?" "No, we've got ketchup." "Oh no." She went unfortunately.'

The script for 'Diddle Diddle Dumpling' was six pages too long when the boys handed it in. 'I

TOP: Mathew Baynton as Ted.

ABOVE: David's behaviour becomes increasingly erratic as his obsession with the shoe grows.

knew we were going to have problems with it,' recalls Tandy. 'Although it had those great arguments, with huge energy, it's also had a lot of creeping horror and psychological moments where you're on Reece as he descends into madness.'

As originally scripted and, in fact, shot, the episode concluded with David sectioned and Chris having moved in with Louise and Sally. Chris hands Louise a DVD he got from the police, containing CCTV footage that shows David was responsible for putting the shoe in the street in the first place. She sits there, watches it and breaks down. 'Keeley was amazing,' says Morales.

But the scene was cut. 'In the edit we couldn't find a way of telling that story in twenty-nine minutes,' reflects Tandy. 'So there was no option but to take out that final section. It was slightly unsatisfying to end it the way we did. If I'd stuck to my guns, we would have had a proper ending.'

Now, the episode climaxes with David, his hands covered in blood, having attacked Ted. Although some viewers jumped to the conclusion that David had killed his daughter, so she could be with her sibling. 'Much darker than we ever thought,' adds Reece. 'I wish we *had* thought of that. It's horrible.'

> **Louise:** I just wanted it to be over. Who cares? Who cares who took the fucking stupid shoe!

In an effort to incorporate some of the original ending, editor Joe Randall Cutler laid the CCTV footage of David, along with a still of him wearing the shoes, over the closing credits. 'It was an extra little flourish,' says Reece. 'We'd never had anything like that before.'

'It is a remarkable episode, and is remarkable for lots of reasons,' says Tandy. 'Number one, it demonstrates how a really good script can be made into something even more amazing, through the collaboration of people behind the scenes. That episode looks like no other we've made.'

'Diddle Diddle Dumpling' is also much funnier than people credit. 'I remember being slightly annoyed that people missed the absurdly funny nature of what the episode is about,' says Reece. 'Maybe it's because it's so strange. That awkward dinner party is one of the best scenes in it. It's excruciating, but hysterically funny.' And when Hawes' Louise puts the shoe on the dinner table and says to her husband David, 'I bet you can't not talk about it for two minutes', and he can't, you don't know whether to laugh or cry. (Hawes' line was lifted from Richard Attenborough's movie *Magic*, a favourite of the boys.)

'It's another one about mental illness,' says Steve. 'I guess that's what stopped some people finding it so funny. Because it is desperately sad.'

ABOVE: The shoe supplies this episode's 'number nine'.

MORGANA **ROBINSON** MONTSERRAT **LOMBARD** REECE **SHEARSMITH**

STEVE **PEMBERTON** FELICITY **KENDAL** FIONA **SHAW**

private view

21st MARCH – 22:00

BBC TWO PRESENTS A BBC STUDIOS PRODUCTION AN INSIDE NO. 9 FILM
"PRIVATE VIEW" MORGANA ROBINSON MONTSERRAT LOMBARD REECE SHEARSMITH FIONA SHAW STEVE PEMBERTON FELICITY KENDAL JOHNNY FLYNN MURIEL GRAY
WRITTEN BY STEVE PEMBERTON & REECE SHEARSMITH EXECUTIVE PRODUCER JON PLOWMAN PRODUCED BY ADAM TANDY DIRECTED BY GUILLEM MORALES

BBC TWO

INSIDE NO 9

Private View

- Series **3**
- Episode **6**
- Directed by **Guillem Morales**

As with 'Last Gasp', 'Private View' fused together two separate ideas into one. First, there was the notion of doing an Agatha Christie-style murder mystery 'with a set of people who don't know why they've been gathered', says Reece. Secondly, there was an idea they had about body parts, and the parent of a child who donated his organs keeping tabs on the people who got them and seeking revenge.

Paying homage to the 1973 horror *Theatre of Blood* – a favourite of Shearsmith and Pemberton who, alongside Mark Gatiss and Jeremy Dyson, provided a commentary for the Arrow Blu-ray release – as well as the literary oeuvre of Agatha Christie, 'Private View' is a macabre morality tale. In it, an eclectic group of hand-picked guests – celebrity-obsessed former *Big Brother* contestant Carrie (Morgana Robinson), pompous critic Maurice (Shearsmith), humourless health-and-safety officer

Kenneth Williams (Pemberton), Irish dinner lady Jean (Fiona Shaw) and visually impaired author of erotic fiction Patricia (Felicity Kendal) – are invited to an east London basement gallery for the opening night of *Fragments*, a retrospective exhibition by the late sculptor Elliot Quinn (Johnny Flynn). There to greet them are nurse Neil (Peter Kay), hired to help Patricia, and tattooed waitress Bea (Montserrat Lombard).

Before you can say Miss Marple, they find themselves trapped inside and being picked off one by one by an unknown assailant. 'It's a real jigsaw, this kind of writing, because you want everyone to be a suspect,' says Steve. 'But in the way we didn't want to pastiche the Krampus story with "The Devil of Christmas", we did allow ourselves to have fun with this. It is very much "comedy horror". We wanted a real mixture of characters. We knew we wanted someone who's quite pretentious. Someone who'd never been to a gallery before. Someone who was very officious. And having an ex-*Big Brother* contestant, we knew we could mine loads of comedy from that.

'They all are being punished for their specific vices, which are linked to the organ they were given,' he continues. 'You don't genuinely fear for any of the characters because they're all ridiculous. It's a really fun episode. Cartoonish and *Scooby-Doo*-ish in a way.'

'Sometimes you think, "Great story, but what gives you the comedy?"' says Reece. 'Here, the comedy came easy.'

As did the choice of director. 'We knew Guillem would love this because he's a horror aficionado,' says Steve. 'And, visually, he brought a *giallo* element – the leather gloves and red lights of early seventies Dario Argento films.'

'I'm not that big a fan of Argento and *giallo*,' admits Morales, 'but I liked the nightmarish feeling [Argento's] *Suspiria* had, and thought it would be good for this. It was a difficult script in the sense that the tone was weird. And I thought a more dreamy, nightmarish feel would help glue all the

ABOVE: Steve and Reece as gallery visitors Kenneth and Maurice.

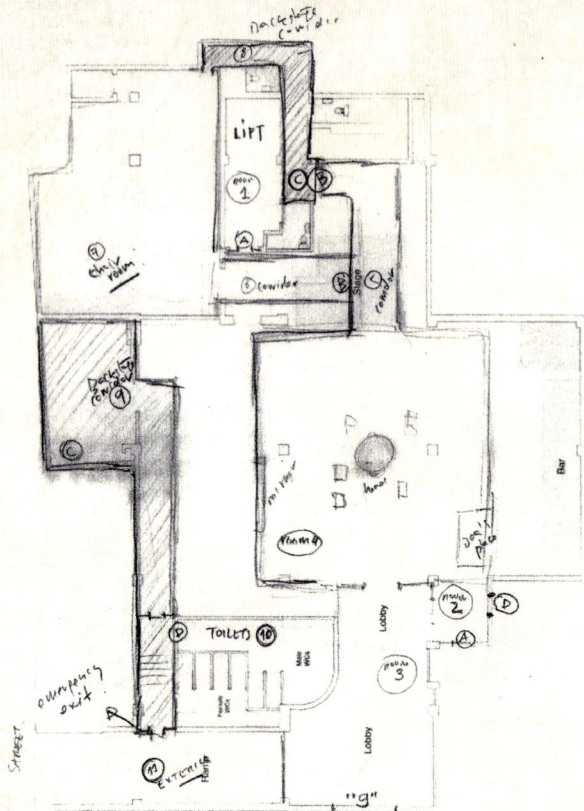

different elements together. Of all the episodes I've done, it's the weirdest.'

The cast is headed up by comic superstar Peter Kay, whose BBC show *Car Share* Shearsmith recently appeared in. But, in the manner of Janet Leigh in Alfred Hitchcock's *Psycho*, Kay is the first character to be killed off. 'It was great to get him to come in and do that cameo,' says Reece. 'You thought he was going to be the main thing. And he was our Janet Leigh for the day. Although I don't think we made much of him being in it.'

That was because they couldn't. 'Peter was adamant he didn't want his name to be publicised, so we didn't get to mention his involvement at all,' says Tandy. 'It was a big secret. I had to take him out of the *Radio Times* listing and off all the paperwork.' Still, the sight of Kay, bleeding out in a sticky pool of blood while Shearsmith kicks him was worth the press blackout. 'He did such a favour for us, because he had barely anything to do,' says Steve. 'But even the little he had, he improvised. The line "Spilt me Ritz" was completely him on the day. That wasn't in the script.'

Playing duplicitous Jean, who appears, initially, to be a dotty old lady but turns out to be Elliot's mum and the killer, was Fiona Shaw. 'We'd written it as a funny northern lady so Fiona didn't immediately come to mind,' says Steve, who had worked with Shaw on a BBC adaptation of *Gormenghast*. 'But we knew we wanted someone who, in that final speech, is almost Medea-like, and Fiona Shaw popped into ours heads.'

'We needed someone you thought could commit the murders,' adds Reece. 'We didn't want someone old and frail. Fiona's tall and a strong presence. And we enjoyed revealing she was the murderer before the end.'

Felicity Kendal, star of classic seventies sitcom *The Good Life*, was cast as haughty novelist Patricia, who, in meta-fashion, comments on the tropes of murder mysteries while appearing in a murder mystery, while Montserrat Lombard became the third *Ashes to Ashes* star to appear in the series after Philip Glenister and Keeley Hawes.

The boys' favourite character to write, however, was Morgana Robinson's attention-seeking *Big Brother* contestant who utters the immortal line, 'I'm a celebrity, get me outta here!' 'It was at a point where reality television was on the wane and you realised these people had a one-year cycle before they were replaced,' notes Steve.

Pemberton and Shearsmith take more of a back seat in 'Private View', with the former playing council officer Kenneth Williams – who, despite his name, has never seen a *Carry On* film. 'He brought lots of comedy being a health and safety officer in a murder mystery because suddenly everything is a hazard,' notes Reece. The character's appearance – leather jacket, shirt and tie, ponytail – was based on someone they knew who worked at a television production company. 'It was,' says Steve, 'a weird combination of things.'

Shearsmith's Maurice was inspired, physically at least, by theatre director Trevor Nunn. Maurice is the only one to escape Jean's murder spree, although some viewers were confused as to how. 'You leave things to people's imaginations and assume they'll join the dots, but sometimes they won't buy it unless they've seen it,' considers Reece.

'We thought it was fine,' says Steve. 'You see him struggling, and the next thing he's got out and killed her. We thought it was obvious what happened. But lots of people went, "I don't get it. Can someone explain?"'

Rounding out the cast as the late artist who appears as a disembodied projection was Johnny Flynn, who had co-starred with Shearsmith onstage in *Hangmen*. 'We almost asked Mark [Gatiss] to do it, but he was too old,' says Steve. 'It needed to be a younger person.' And finally, novelist and TV presenter Muriel Gray cameos as herself, reporting on the exhibition. 'She's a big fan of the show, so was delighted to come along,' says Reece.

'Private View' was filmed in an old industrial laundry in Hackney, east London. 'It was a big black box with block pillars and that allowed us to put up dividing walls to create a space which looked like a gallery,' says Tandy. As for Elliot's artwork, it was designed, much like the painting in 'A Quiet Night In', to satirise and lampoon the pretentiousness of contemporary art. 'It's the absurdity of "What is art?" and so a lot of arms and legs stuck together becomes a thing you ponder seriously,' says Reece. The blood on the floor was a nod to Richard Wilson's oleaginous installation *20:50* –

ABOVE: Left to right: Patricia (Felicity Kendal), Kenneth (Steve Pemberton), Jean (Fiona Shaw), Carrie (Morgana Robinson) and Maurice (Reece Shearsmith).

'obscure reference but someone will have got it,' notes Steve – while Kay's corpse was a homage to the hyper-real sculptures of Ron Mueck, both of which Pemberton had seen at the Saatchi Gallery and at the Royal Academy. 'They were very specific things rooted in modern art.'

Mostly, the artwork was what Simon Rogers and the design department could create in the time and budget available, both of which were lacking. 'We filled it with a load of old shit, glued together, wrongly, and painted,' Rogers laughs. 'I mean, we've all been to enough gallery shows where you think, "I could have done that." And that's what we did. But we made sure none of it was that good. Although I was really pleased with the mannequins.'

'Simon's team worked very, very hard to produce something which, I think, stands up quite well on camera,' says Tandy. 'But we struggled. There's no doubt about it. It was a hard shoot. And we missed the trick with the blood. The floor was black so the red didn't show up. In retrospect, we should have put down white flooring. There were a few things we didn't get quite right, but we got enough of the scale, colour and tone.'

'It was the last one we filmed so the budget had been spent,' remembers Steve. 'It's one of the hardest things for a designer to do, create a massive space with original art, each piece of which would have taken an artist months to do. So of course you have to do shorthand, which is where the mannequins come from. One wall is a big broken mirror and another is a sort of *Guernica* with body parts.'

'Sometimes things aren't quite as you imagined them. But it sort of works,' reflects Reece.

What they didn't skimp on were the onscreen deaths. While the script detailed each murder, the boys relied on Morales to make them *memorable*. 'That's the game we have. Reece and Steve expect me to make their ideas more horrible. I don't know if it's a healthy relationship. But it's the

ABOVE: Felicity Kendal as Patricia, the visually impaired author of erotic fiction.

relationship we have. Every time they send something to me I'm thinking, "How can I make it more interesting, more horrific, or weirder?"'

When Kendal's partially sighted author is discovered in a toilet stall with her eyes gouged, Morales wanted it to be just like the scene in Hitchcock's *The Birds* when Jessica Tandy finds her husband with his peepers pecked away. (He suggested the idea not knowing that Adam Tandy is Jessica's nephew. 'That's how I found out.') First we see a tear of blood slowly fall from behind her sunglasses, as if she's crying, before they're removed and the full extent of her mutilation is revealed. 'Felicity was slightly freaked out by the prosthetic eye make-up we had to put her in, but she played along marvellously,' says Tandy. The tear was produced digitally by visual effects house Double Negative. In the script, Lombard's waitress was strangled by a telephone cord in the lift. Morales suggested the phone being shoved down her throat as well. 'The smoke and sparks were all him,' says Steve. 'He was very clear, visually, about what he wanted.'

'You haven't got ninety minutes or a two-act play to kill everybody off,' says Tandy. 'You've literally got twenty-nine minutes to set the scene, kill everybody and get to a resolution. So it's got to happen like clockwork. There's barely any room for jokes. It's death after death after death. In a way, the relentlessness of that is the thing that keeps it going.'

While the amount of music required varies from episode to episode, 'Private View' needed forty-four minutes in total. 'I was not only writing the score; I was also writing the diegetic music,' explains Christian Henson. 'The different art installations have different bits of music and they had to overlap, so there were several scores stacked on top of each other.'

'Private View' was yet another horror finale, albeit comedy-horror. But apart from 'Empty Orchestra', series three had all been rather dark in subject matter or tone. 'I got an email from Jon [Plowman] saying, "Whatever you write next, please have it be a bit lighter and have some jokes in it,"' recalls Steve. 'And I think that was in our minds when we started series four.'

'I am very much of the opinion that *Inside No. 9* is a proper anthology that doesn't have to be funny every week,' says Tandy. 'Jon and I slightly disagree on that point, but it's a fine line.' Nevertheless, series three proved to be watershed for the show, after all eighteen episodes were made available on BBC iPlayer. 'A lot of people found it before season four, binged the whole lot, and couldn't wait for the new series.'

ABOVE LEFT: Steve with Montserrat Lombard, who played waitress Bea.

ABOVE RIGHT: Reece and Steve with Peter Kay, who played Neil. Kay's cameo appearance in the episode was a closely guarded secret.

SERIES FOUR

JAYCANN AYEH   REECE SHEARSMITH   RORY KINNEAR   BILL PATERSON
MARCIA WARREN   STEVE PEMBERTON   HATTIE MORAHAN
HELEN MONKS   TANYA FRANKS   KEVIN ELDON

ZANZIBAR

ROOM 911

£50

TUESDAY 2ND JANUARY, 10PM

Zanzibar

- Series **4**
- Episode **1**
- Directed by **David Kerr**

L
ike so many great ideas, 'Zanzibar' began down the pub. 'We had
a meeting with Jon Plowman and Adam and said we were keen to try
something different,' remembers Steve. 'Jon said, "Have you thought about doing
a farce?" Of course, we had touched on it with "A Quiet Night In" and "Nana's
Party", but the thought of doing a classic farce was appealing. In fact, one of
the very first ideas we'd had – and started writing – was about a celebrity and
his double. The celebrity had fallen on hard times and the double was trying
to get his career back on track to help his own. That seemed quite farcical. But
when you think of a farce, you tend to think of the classic door-open/door-close
scenario. So we came up with a hotel corridor. We didn't want to do a hotel
room; we wanted a corridor, because you have endless doors.'

ABOVE: The episode poster
was designed by Christopher
Clegg.

They started by listing all the characters who might be in a hotel. There was the businessman who's come to attempt suicide. A man planning to propose to his girlfriend. A bellboy. A maid. A prostitute. 'And we knew we'd have one actor playing two parts,' says Reece. But this being *Inside No. 9* they decided to switch it up a little, by showing the 'off-bits' of a farce rather than the farce itself. 'We imagined there was one happening *inside* the rooms and we were seeing the bits when they went *outside*. That felt like a twist. We did a lot of preparatory work. But something about it felt almost too easy, like how we felt writing "The Devil of Christmas" without the framework of the interrogation. Then Steve said, "What if it's Shakespeare?" Suddenly that unlocked it. It became literary, and allowed you to do all those great tropes like speaking in soliloquies. It elevated it, rather than dragged it down.'

'That's not to decry farce, because farce is one of the very hardest things to do,' continues Steve. 'Every episode of *Fawlty Towers* is a mini-farce and they spent months working out the precision of all that. But it felt like it wasn't *Inside No. 9* enough. The twins idea allowed the theatricality. And the second we had that, it came alive and we realised we could switch between verse and prose. Because one of the things we were aware of was that half an hour of verse, of iambic pentameter, could become gimmicky and annoying, especially if we used a lot of rhyming couplets, which we wanted to enjoy.'

'We looked at Shakespeare and how clever he was, and were trying to be as authentic as possible,' says Reece. 'But it was hard. I remember once thinking, "Fucking hell, why have we done this to ourselves?"'

'It was a labour of love,' reflects Steve. 'Every time you thought of a joke or a funny line, you had to make it fit within this rhyme scheme. There are ten syllables in iambic pentameter, so we spent a lot of time precision-tooling everything. It was double the work we would normally do. But I think it's one of the most joyful episodes of *Inside No. 9*. That's not hard,' he laughs. 'It's not a crowded field. But you do have a big smile on your face when you watch it.'

The story takes place on the ninth floor of the Hotel Zanzibar, as identical twins Prince Rico (Rory Kinnear) and Gus (also Kinnear) – separated at birth and unaware of the other – check in, the former with

ABOVE: Amber (Hattie Morahan), Gus (Rory Kinnear), Robert (Steve Pemberton) and Alice (Marcia Warren).

SHEIK
SECURITY

SHEIK DOUBLE   DRINKS &c.

MARRIAGE PROPOSAL (CAKE) VAMP 1
VAMPIRES   VAMP 2

(PROSTITUTE)   (HITMAN)   KEY CARD TO
                                      ALL ROOMS

OLD ALZHEIMER MAN   YES DYING TO
SON   BUT HER MEMORY — SHE
REP SUICIDAL?   HAD HER HONEYMOON
.ALABASTER?   FAKE GUN   IN ONE OF THE ROOM
MARRIAGE / DOCTOR WITH   BUT HE COULDN'T DRINK IT
RUSSIAN + KIDNEY
WRITER / NEEDING QUIET   SUICIDAL

BUSINESSMAN / WIFE TURNS UP TO SURPRISED

EMPTY ROOM   WAITER / CHAMBER
                           MAID

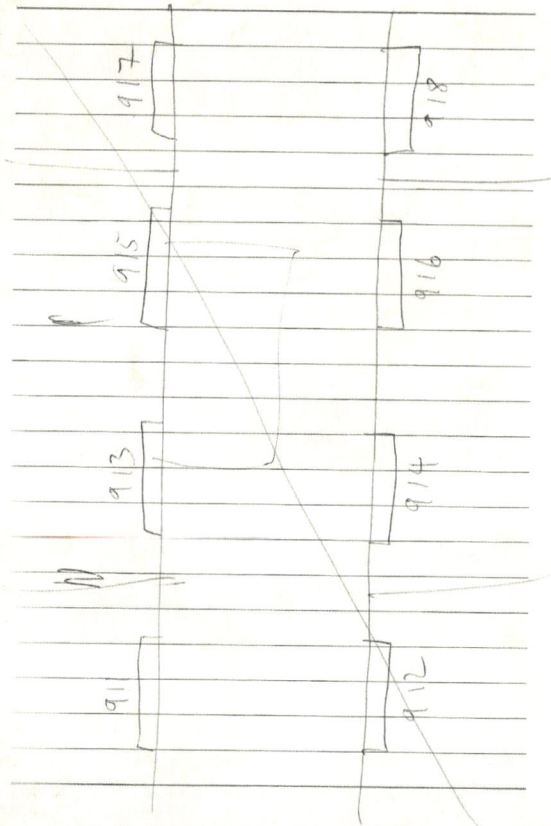

Alice: Well, I know my door begins with number nine. Oh, this one's open, guess it must be mine.

---

his duplicitous bodyguard Henry (Shearsmith), the latter with his uptight and unhappy girlfriend Amber (Hattie Morahan). The action is farcical and furious, encompassing both comedy and tragedy, with star-crossed lovers and mistaken identity, a murder plot and love potions, and a coterie of ridiculously entertaining characters including Jaygann Ayeh as jaunty bellboy and narrator Fred, attending to his guests' every desire, from apple tarts to, well, tarts; Bill Paterson as the suicidal Mr Green, who turns out to be the twins' father; Helen Monks as the perky chambermaid Colette; Marcia Warren as doddery old Alice; and Tanya Franks as Tracey the prostitute, aka Red, who specialises in watersports.

'We knew who the characters were and that there were loads of possibilities for confusion,' says Steve, 'so the actual writing wasn't so much about plot as getting the lines right. And you could have a scene in prose where the chambermaid, bellboy or even the prostitute speak in non-verse, because they were "low characters", so that was a relief. "Can we talk plainly?" "Oh yeah." "Thank God for that." In fact, we put that in.'

Nodding its muffin cap to a plethora of Shakespeare's works – *As You Like It*, *A Midsummer Night's Dream*, *The Comedy of Errors*, *Hamlet* and *Othello*, among others – 'Zanzibar' is, indeed, one of

ABOVE: A page from one of Steve's notebooks shows early ideas for the episode, including a sketch of the hotel corridor.

the most heartwarming, effervescent episodes of *No. 9* despite its assassination subplot and talk of golden showers. The name 'Zanzibar' just 'popped into our heads,' says Steve. 'It sounded exotic. It just felt right,' adds Reece.

When Tandy received the script, he was delighted. 'It was a surprise when this arrived on the desk, but they were pushing an open door. I love this sort of thing,' he enthuses. 'It's rhyming couplets, rather than strictly Shakespearean iambic pentameter, but I thought it was very clever and had great possibilities for casting. And, in my mind, I was thinking that we should probably shoot this like an old BBC Play of the Month.'

David Kerr was back to direct two episodes, having been busy during the filming of series two and three. 'There's a part of me that would love to do nothing other than *Inside No. 9* because, creatively, it's a dream gig and Reece and Steve are the perfect collaborators,' he says. 'I couldn't believe my luck when I read "Zanzibar". It's a truly original, formally inventive film and yet, selfishly, seemed to be speaking to so many sides of me I couldn't resist. I studied classics, Latin and Greek, and iambic pentameter. I'd done a bit of acting in Shakespeare. And I'd directed [the BBC's 2016] *A Midsummer Night's Dream*. So the language side of it was massively appealing. But so many of the themes felt Shakespearean. You've got the threat of violence, revenge, twins, mistaken identity, families being reunited, and the sense of an ensemble as well. So often, *Inside No. 9*s tend to be two or three people in a room. Here we were trying to bring a bigger cast to bear on a story, and it felt more like a play than many of the others, because you could almost do this on stage.'

This time around, Pemberton and Shearsmith wanted actors with experience of Shakespeare and comedy. And for the dual role of the Prince and Gus, they decided to let someone else shine. 'Because Reece and I play all the main male characters in late middle-age, there's not a lot of room for our contemporaries,' says Steve. 'In this there were plenty of good characters you could play, so we decided we wouldn't take the big, juicy role, we would try to get somebody else in. And Rory was perfect.' A former member of the Royal Shakespeare Company, Kinnear won an Olivier Award for his portrayal of Iago in a National Theatre production of *Othello*. 'He did a famous *Hamlet*, he's done *Macbeth*, *Othello*,' continues Steve, 'and he was great because he was very throwaway with his delivery. He wasn't giving it a big National Theatre performance. We wanted to find the subtleties within that. And he really came into his own.'

Despite a long and distinguished career in film, TV and on the stage, Bill Paterson had never done Shakespeare before. 'He was enjoying the fact he got a soliloquy,' says Reece. 'He said, "No

ABOVE: Steve as Robert with Marcia Warren as his mother, Alice.

one's ever asked me before." I said, "Now you're going to be getting *Lear*,"' laughs Steve.

Kerr, who'd directed Kinnear in an episode of *Beautiful People*, had also worked with Paterson on a short-lived TV series called *Ed Stone Is Dead*. 'Bill is one of those actors we take for granted because he's been brilliant in so many different things. What I loved was how he tapped into the pathos of his character. There is a mournful quality to him that plucks at the heart strings in the middle of this daft mayhem.'

Marcia Warren had starred in the London stage adaptation of *The Ladykillers* and was a suggestion of Jon Plowman. 'She played the slightly borderline dementia of the character so brilliantly and in a way that made it adorable and empathetic. And was game for the silliness of it,' says Kerr. Hattie Morahan was another ex-RSC actress and is married to Blake Ritson, aka Justin in *The League of Gentlemen*, while Jaygann Ayeh had only recently graduated from RADA. 'He was about to go into *Hamilton* and was on the verge of stardom and greatness,' says Tandy.

'He seemed so natural and cheeky we couldn't resist,' says Kerr. 'A bit like "Sardines", you wanted as many different energies and character types as you possibly can fit in one space.'

Shearsmith took the small but memorable role of Rico's bearded bodyguard. 'It was my stubble,' he insists, 'but then it was darkened and had that weird look. And I dyed my hair fully black, which I'd not done before. I'm forever trying to think of a new look. And that Cockney accent felt right for the part.' Pemberton plays Robert, Alice's son, and 'a real mummy's boy who was there to try to jog his mother's failing memory by recreating a piece of her past. The fact he was so fey was a nice contrast to Amber's sexually charged temptress. It was nice to play someone so well-meaning and sweet.'

And finally there was Kevin Eldon, whose stage hypnotist Vince inadvertently entrances the wrong person. 'It is the rule, and it should be the law, that Kevin Eldon should be in anything funny, because he'll make it funnier,' says Kerr.

ABOVE: Hotel door hangers for the Zanzibar, created by trainee art director Beth Hiley.

Z

DO
NO
DIST

Z

PLEASE
SERVICE
MY
ROOM

Given the complexity of the action, Tandy felt 'Zanzibar' required a proper rehearsal rather than just a read-through. 'I'd done a bit of farce in theatre and know the only way you can make it work is to be absolutely rock-solid on moves and lines, so you don't have that argument on the day about who's coming out of what door when. So I made everybody rehearse like it was a theatre piece. I say "made", but I think everyone realised we needed to do that. We marked out the corridor on the floor of a community hall in Shepherd's Bush and plotted the moves for the entire piece so that when we got to the studio, David knew where to put his cameras, and the nuances of the performance had more or less been cracked.'

'I'm so glad we were able to do that,' says Kerr. 'You want to feel all your actors are in the same film. And there is a risk with something where the language is heightened and the antics quite theatrical that you end up with a mismatch of tones. It gave us a chance to make sure we were all playing at the same level.'

Both Kerr and Tandy had hoped to shoot in a real hotel corridor, but, after visiting several, realised any location would be too much of a compromise. 'All modern hotels when you get out of public areas and into the room floors are very narrow, and we needed to find something with scale,' explains Tandy. 'It was clearly impossible to find a hotel that was going to let us film for a week. We would also have needed to buy out an entire floor and even then wouldn't be able to redecorate. For all of those reasons, it became clear the only way to do it was to build a set. It wasn't something I wanted to do. But, in the end, it gave us the opportunity to do something very special in terms of look.'

'We didn't want there to be any seediness or scariness,' says Steve. 'We wanted it to be a high-end hotel, edging towards the magic realism of *The Grand Budapest Hotel*, with strong, bold colours. We didn't want it to be a realistic hotel corridor. They're very dark, often.'

'It wasn't *Barton Fink*,' adds Reece. 'We wanted a cheery place.' So while the Hotel Zanzibar

ABOVE: Filming in progress.

Conceptually brilliant ... the cast of Zanzibar. Photograph: Sophie Mutevelian/BBC

Inside No 9.3 Zanzibar

3/6 D1

3/6 D1

rey/ brown 2/pc
bone self pattern &
y cream self strip
/B , 2× buttons'd
pel , flap pockets .
straight leg, centre

cotton, flat collar
button front. L/s w/ Blu

Tanya Franks

CHANGE 1

3/4 D1

3/4 D1

CHANGE 1

Helen Monks

CHANGE 1

Marcia Warren

CHANGE 1

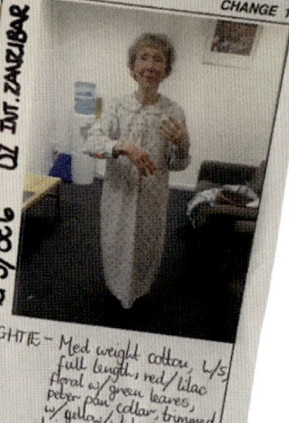

EP3/Sc.2   INT. ZANZIBAR

EP3/Sc.7   D1   INT. ZANZIBAR

EP3/Sc.6   D1   INT. ZANZIBAR

- Bright coral bodycon mini
dress, w/ coral floral
lacing detail @ chest &
ribbon lace. Spaghetti straps
- Beige fur short jkt, w/
flat collar~ 3 × drk brown
lrg circular buttons @ CF,
sage green/cream flower
smooth under collar~ L/S
- Gold metallic stiletto, pointed
toe.
- Large pink/grey/greige/red
floral tote w/ greige lining.
Pepper corsnetig, leopard-print
scarf tied to strap
- Rose gold metal ribbed strap
with gold face & leopard print
backing.
JKT - Rows of small circular
silver studs w/ diamanté centres.
Dangling pendant detail w/ pearl
ERG - Eg Ruby studs

- White circular frame, diamanté
studs & cream/grey opaque bead

ZANZIBAR

JKT - Cadbury's purple, heavy
polyester brill...

PRON - Small white cotton
pinny. Rectangular w/
frill edge. Long white

NIGHTIE - Med weight cotton, L/S
full length, red/lilac
floral w/ green leaves.
Peter pan collar, trimmed
w/ yellow/white lace. trimmed
hem. Button fastening @
chest

SLIPPERS - Navy terry towelling
slip-ons w/ L/s &

exterior was, in reality, that of The Langham in London's Portland Place, the corridor was built at Pinewood Studios under the auspices of production designer Dennis De Groot (*That Mitchell and Webb Look*). 'David is very good at look and Dennis is a very experienced designer. So we got this great-looking set, full of deep teals and creams,' says Tandy. De Groot's budget only stretched to one corridor and a solitary bedroom, so he put the latter on wheels to allow it to be rolled up and down the corridor as and when needed, even during takes. 'It was a very clever, theatrical approach to solving a problem,' says Kerr. The theatricality also extended to the costumes. 'The problem there was the corridor,' says Yves Barre. 'It was a very limited location. So it's all about creating a moment, and it's all about the silhouette. Everything was soft and a bit heightened, like a very commercial West End comedy.'

Given the constraints of shooting in a long, rectangular space, Kerr approached the episode in much the same way as 'A Quiet Night In', opting to shoot with long masters, and 'have the camera take us on to the next bit of action, minimising the number of visual cuts.' But while longer takes mean fewer set-ups, it's also something of a high-stakes game 'because, if you're doing a two-minute take and someone fluffs a minute-and-a-half in, you have to reset and start again. It's an all-or-nothing approach to filming. But I got to the end of that week and didn't want it to stop. I was having such fun with this bunch of actors and the heightened language. It felt like if this were a play, we'd be looking forward to a long run.'

'The last quarter of it is quite relentless. It's all in iambic pentameter, and we wanted it to have the manic energy you need with a farce,' says Steve. 'The other really good addition to this was Christian's music. Some episodes have very little music, but here it's almost throughout, giving you a rhythm and a pulse. You don't really notice it, but it's there. There are a lot of doors opening and

Prince Rico: But all this talk of murder makes me wince! Like this iambic foot, you're stressed, I'm not.

closing and a lot of separate scenes, so having that beautiful music helped tie it all together.'

'My parents are actors and my grandad founded the actors' union, Equity, so there is quite a bit of "jazz hands" wanting to get out,' laughs Henson, 'which is why I enjoyed "Zanzibar" more than any other episode. Most music these days, in drama, tends to be really subdued. What's really different about *Inside No. 9* is they allow me to go for it. And more often than not, that seems to work.'

'Half an hour goes by like that,' concludes Steve. 'Yet you've had so many plots, and so many resolutions. It's quite exhausting when you think about how much plot there is in it.'

Bernie Clifton's Dressing Room

- Series **4**
- Episode **2**
- Directed by **Graeme Harper**

'I remember saying we should do a two-hander, because we hadn't done one,' recalls Reece. 'And even then, it ended up not being. But we thought a faded double act as a conceit might be funny, because you'd have comedy in it, with the pair talking about what they used to do.'

Given that neither wanted to wear heavy old-age make-up, they decided their fictional double act would have been famous in the eighties, an era that brought us the likes of Little and Large and Cannon and Ball. 'It was the arse end of variety, when those kinds of shows were dying out and that style was being overtaken by alternative comedy,' says Steve. 'So we thought, what if they just got their big

ABOVE: The episode poster was designed by Andy Bottomley.

television break, having done years and years of live shows, then it all fizzled out for them?'

'Bernie Clifton's Dressing Room' sees Tommy (Shearsmith) reunite with his old comedy partner Len (Pemberton) after three decades, for a special one-off performance in front of an invited audience. But the incident that caused them to fall out in the first place, and resulted in Tommy leaving the business completely, soon comes back to haunt them. Back then, the pair were known as Cheese and Crackers, a name inspired by a real-life double act called Cheese and Onion. 'I remember seeing them when Mark and I were starting drama school in the mid-eighties,' says Steve. 'Now I'm older, I would probably enjoy watching them, but, at the time, we wanted to rebel against these awful Seaside Special variety acts who used to have one good hour that they would tour around the country. Television eats material quickly, so you need to work hard on new stuff, and you felt some of these double acts were living off that good hour.'

Another source of inspiration was *The Story of Light Entertainment*, a BBC documentary series that devoted a whole episode to double acts. 'That's where that line about Mike and Bernie Winters came from,' says Steve. 'You hear stories about how so many double acts couldn't stand each other and would only speak on stage. So watching that was really instructive and gave a lot of good insight into the stuff we could bring into it.'

The incident that caused Tommy and Len to fall out was, itself, inspired by an infamous *Celebrity Big Brother* episode from 2014 in which Jim Davidson goaded fellow contestant Coleen Nolan. 'He very slyly says to one of the other people, "Go and ask her about Frank Carson's dressing room." So this person gets up and asks, "What happened in Frank Carson's dressing room?"' recalls Steve. 'She exploded: "How dare you! How fucking dare you?" And it was like, "Wow, what *happened* in Frank Carson's dressing room?"' laughs Reece. 'So we thought we'd call it "Bernie Clifton's Dressing Room".

ABOVE: Reece and Steve as Tommy and Len, aka Cheese and Crackers, old comedy partners.

We would allude to what happened and eventually you'd find out what it was. It was completely based on wanting that feeling in our thing.'

But neither man felt that, on its own, the dressing room incident was enough of an ending for a *No. 9*. 'We knew they had a falling out, and the reconciliation of these two people standing in a church hall, with years and years between them, was a really powerful image,' reflects Steve.

And then it hit them. Len is dead. Tommy is there for the funeral. And the whole back and forth between the two former partners is Tommy working through his regrets and issues, having the arguments and, ultimately, the reconciliation he never got to have in real life. Also, the incident is actually a classic piece of misdirection, with misery guts Tommy seemingly to blame for dissolving the partnership, but, in actual fact, he did it to protect Len, who was becoming an alcoholic and a monster. 'He wanted to keep it going, but knew he had to do the honourable thing and stop, so Len wouldn't kill himself in the process of becoming increasingly famous and off the rails,' says Reece.

While they loved the notion of Len being a figment of Tommy's imagination, both were slightly hesitant, wondering if it was too similar an idea to 'The 12 Days of Christine'. 'Are we doing the same wrapped up in a different way, which is what we think about with every single script,' says Reece. Ultimately, they decided it wasn't. 'You're with the living person, as opposed to "Christine" where you are with the dying person,' says Steve. 'And we went, "It's too good. It's too right."'

To direct 'Bernie Clifton', Tandy asked Graeme Harper back. And having worked on a succession of variety shows over the years, Harper 'recognised' Tommy and Len. 'I'd seen them, I'd met them, I knew these people. I understood that world,' he says. 'It was a lovely piece of drama, trying to get inside these two people who really are in love with each other, but had a bitter divorce. What I really wanted was to show the genuine side of their feelings to each other. Steve played a very gentle, kind, lovely soft

ABOVE: Lyrics for the song that closes the episode, 'Tears of Laughter', which Reece and Steve co-wrote with Christian Henson.

comic who, underneath it all, was quite manipulative and me, me, me. Whereas Reece's character was sharp, to the point and knew exactly what was going on and how he was being played.'

'Sentiment, that's the thing that makes this work,' agrees Tandy. 'And the fact there's nothing more important than showbiz. They had a falling out, and Reece's character gave up the business – he couldn't bear the pain of doing it any more – and is very resistant to the idea of doing the old routines. But Len makes him, for old time's sake.'

When it came to Cheese and Crackers' routines, the boys were keen to show that what's acceptable in comedy has changed over the decades. 'We thought it would be funny if they had a list of impressions you can't do any more,' says Steve. 'Clearly Len's not racist, but he doesn't see the problem with doing funny voices to get a laugh, and Tommy is way ahead of that.'

Not that every routine was meant to be awful. 'We wanted it to feel like it's in their bones,' says Reece. 'Ten Brown Bottles is a classic variety act, so we had to be able to do it with our eyes closed.'

'Ten Brown Bottles, the silent comedy stuff, and the bit with the hat and coat: we wanted those to be good,' says Steve. 'We didn't want you to be groaning all the way through. Of course, some of it's terrible. The ventriloquist act, we wanted to be *really* bad.'

ABOVE: Reece on set.

'We wanted to get into the truth of these people, and their routines didn't need to be over-rehearsed,' says Harper. 'It was much more interesting the more spontaneous their reactions. Steve and Reece know each other very well. They can almost read each other. And I don't think they over-rehearse any of their stuff in order for it to be fresh when it comes in front of the camera.'

Cheese and Crackers' 'interview sketch' was actually based on one the boys performed together in the early days of *The League of Gentlemen*. 'We used to do shows at the Canal Café Theatre,' recalls Steve. 'As well as character stuff, we used to do funny, daft sketches, one-offs we would call them. We had this job interview sketch where they get caught up in all these accents, so we adapted the one in this from that. I think it was Graeme who said, "Can we do hats?" Because hats seem to be a very classic thing. We resisted for a while, but it elevated it.'

'It made it more like a routine,' agrees Reece. 'And even though we'd done it in the early nineties, it felt ancient.' So, too, were the flyers of Cheese and Crackers, which used twenty-year-old photos of Shearsmith and Pemberton. 'They were *League of Gentlemen* flyers,' says Reece. 'It was very poignant and bled into our past.'

After the reveal that Len is, in fact, dead, Tommy talks with Len's daughter Leanne (Sian Gibson) before returning to the church hall. There, the pair perform their signature song and dance number. 'In the original script, they did a slow dance to a Neil Sedaka song because they both love Neil Sedaka; I've no idea why,' says Tandy. 'But I know from previous dealings his music is pretty much unclearable, so I had to get the boys off that idea.'

Instead, he suggested something akin to Morecambe and Wise's classic 'Bring Me Sunshine', tapping choreographer Nicola Kean to work out a dance routine to accompany a song co-written with Christian Henson. 'Morecambe and Wise were trained dancers,' notes Harper. 'These guys were meant to be the same, maybe second- or third-rate versions, but this was their song. And it had to look

ABOVE: Steve in Len's costume for the Cheese and Crackers ventriloquist act.

good. For them to be able to do it like a *Strictly Come Dancing* performance, they would have had to rehearse, just that routine, for a whole week. We didn't have that. They spent about an hour and a half to two hours a day for a week. And on the third day, they got it.' They broke the dance down into eight sections, which Harper would shoot until they were perfect. 'It was tricky to learn,' says Reece. 'But it was good to give you that authenticity. And it did.'

As they start dancing, the lights dim and the hall transforms into a stage with coloured lights and a follow-on spot. 'It's a really lovely moment and a remarkable transition,' says Tandy, who convinced Harper to film the final moment in which Len disappears using a moving motion control camera, 'which I regretted, because it took half a day to get that one shot. And we had to get this enormous motion control camera into the church hall.'

'It's very sad when it cuts back to the reality and Tommy goes off to Len's funeral,' says Reece. 'But it's lovely to see them back together, doing what they did, on happy terms, rather than this war that you've watched play out, when they're shouting at each other about the reality of what happened and him being an alcoholic. I remember the vicar came in and was watching the monitor during that bit, and he was like, "I thought it was a comedy."'

As with 'The 12 Days of Christine', the reaction to 'Bernie Clifton' when it aired was extraordinary. 'A lot of people didn't see the twist coming,' recalls Tandy. 'There was that collective gasp on Twitter of, "Oh my God, he's not there. He's a ghost." We knew it was a great episode, but I don't think anybody expected it to have the emotional impact it had.'

'It really touched people. In unexpected ways,' says Steve, who won a television BAFTA for Best Male Performance in a Comedy Role. 'Again, we are never really ready for that kind of reaction. But I got a lot of emails about it. I had one from the daughter of Chas Hodges, of Chas and Dave – I think her dad was pretty ill at that point – saying how much she liked it.'

'A lot of the old comedians really liked it,' adds Reece. 'It was a proper nod and they got that. And Bernie Clifton, eventually, saw it. He said he was apprehensive about what it was, because he knew this thing was coming on with his name in the title. And he thought, "I know what happened in my dressing room, but what have they decided happened?" But he loved it.'

'He came to our dressing room when we did *The League of Gentlemen* tour,' remembers Steve. 'It was our love letter to comedy and those kinds of variety acts. We celebrated that era, as well as saying, "These are the shortcomings of it," and we told a story about loss and reconciliation. People found it very moving. We got a lot of comments from people who'd lost loved ones who said it really helped them.'

TOP: Filming in progress.

ABOVE: Reece and Steve in costume.

ONCE REMOVED

ANYTHING COULD HAPPEN IN THE LAST 10 MINUTES

MONICA **DOLAN**   DAVID **CALDER**
NICK **MORAN**   STEVE **PEMBERTON**
REECE **SHEARSMITH**   EMILIA **FOX**

TUESDAY 16 JANUARY, 10PM

BBC TWO PRESENTS A BBC STUDIOS PRODUCTION AN INSIDE NO. 9 FILM "ONCE REMOVED" MONICA DOLAN NICK MORAN REECE SHEARSMITH DAVID CALDER STEVE PEMBERTON EMILIA FOX RUFUS JONES MUSIC BY CHRISTIAN HENSON SPECIAL MAKE UP HELEN SPEYER DIRECTOR OF PHOTOGRAPHY JOHN SORAPURE WRITTEN BY STEVE PEMBERTON & REECE SHEARSMITH EXECUTIVE PRODUCER JON PLOWMAN PRODUCER BY ADAM TANDY DIRECTED BY JIM O'HANLON

Once Removed

- Series **4**
- Episode **3**
- Directed by **Jim O'Hanlon**

H aving tackled a 'silent' episode for series one, an episode shot entirely using CCTV cameras for series two, and an authentic period recreation for series three, Shearsmith and Pemberton were keen to push the envelope even further in terms of storytelling techniques. 'The joy with an anthology is being able to change up the way you're presenting the work,' says Steve. 'And when people think they've got the measure of what *Inside No. 9* is, it's nice to keep them on their toes.'

The pair had contemplated writing an episode told in reverse since the first series, ploughing a storytelling furrow that dates back to the first century BC and Virgil's epic poem *Aeneid*. 'We kept talking about it and it was just too hard,' admits Steve. The main issue was that neither wanted to write just any old backwards story. They wanted to craft one that was 'intact, chronologically, so if

ABOVE: The 'Once Removed' episode poster was designed by Billy Odell.

you played it the right way round it would happen in real time. And it's very hard to make the end of one scene match up with the beginning of the previous one.'

'It was,' sighs Reece, 'fucking impossible.'

Determined to crack it this time around, the boys set to work, eventually coming up with 'Once Removed', a meticulously crafted murder-mystery-cum-blood-splattered farce which, chronologically speaking, sees adulterous Charles (Rufus Jones) from number nine hiring a hitman to kill his wife May (Monica Dolan) so that he and Natasha (Emilia Fox) from number six can run away to Portugal together. May discovers the plot just in time, stabbing Viktor (Shearsmith), her would-be assassin, who has already killed Natasha, poisoned her dotty dad Percy (David Calder), and murdered desperate estate agent Hugo (Pemberton).

Like a cross between Christopher Nolan's *Memento* and an episode of *Midsomer Murders*, 'Once Removed' is a structural marvel, unfolding in real time, with a story that rewinds every ten minutes to present a different take on the matters at hand, before rewinding another ten minutes, then another, and another, constantly wrongfooting the audience as to what's what, before reaching the final reveal. 'It was like having twists every ten minutes,' reflects Reece. 'Every time we go back, we wanted you to re-evaluate everything you've seen. And how we appear at the beginning of each scene is not how we are revealed at the end, even though the end is the beginning. So our perception of these characters changes every time it reverses ten minutes, because you're learning a little more about them.'

'The reason we hadn't done it before was we couldn't find a way to make it work satisfyingly,' says Steve. 'The key to unlocking it for me, was realising that Reece's character could be a different person in every scene. It begins with him as the husband, then he becomes the son of the old guy in the bed, then the removal man. It's only towards the end that you reveal he's the assassin.'

ABOVE: Viktor (Reece Shearsmith), Natasha (Emilia Fox) and Hugo (Steve Pemberton).

WALL which they take to be
a paint swatch. PACKING CASES
which get emptied as more and
more bodies are put into them.
AT start point all cases are
full of stuff & house is empty.
As it goes back in time, bodies
are put in cases & the stuff
comes out.
WOMAN knows she's going to be killed
So borrows screw driver and
changes the 9 to a 6. The
Last thing we see.
Thats what kicks the whole action off.

4/5 chapters. Each ending
where the previous one began.
The nature of all the relationships
changes & the clues we see
around the house change.
See things in a completely different
light.

KILLER can assume different identities
We think he's an innocent at
first, who will be shockingly
killed by WOMAN. (neighbour)
___
1st scene - he's just moved in -
She's returning screwdriver.
She admires his things - knows

'Once Removed' begins/ends with Spike (Nick Moran), from Handle Me Gently removers, arriving at an isolated farmhouse to help pack the owners' belongings in advance of their selling the property. He's greeted by a jittery May and an evasive Viktor, dressed in a pink silk dressing gown and oven gloves. They present as husband and wife, but the illusion is shattered when the senile Percy staggers down the stairs and collapses, having been poisoned, a dead Natasha rolls out of a rug, and May inadvertently stabs Viktor in the back with a screwdriver, telling a shocked Spike, 'I can explain …'

'That line, which is the very last line of the whole thing, and the end of the first part, was crucial,' says Steve, 'because you're saying, "We're going to go back ten minutes and explain why there is a body in a rug and a dead man on the toilet." But five of those minutes you've already seen. We spent ages with bits of paper and cards trying to work out what the right order was, although we never wrote it in the "right" order. We wrote it in the order you would watch it, because we knew, retrospectively, it had to make sense.'

'But it couldn't only be retrospectively satisfying, even though we always enjoy the fact these things have repeatability,' says Reece. 'We wanted things in the moment that were good as well, and for you to retain them in your head long enough to think, "Oh, that's why he's covered the blood up."'

Ultimately, it's revealed that May set everything in motion, removing the top screw that affixed the number six to the wall outside Charles and Natasha's farmhouse, so it swung down to read nine

instead, thereby sending Shearsmith's assassin to the wrong address. 'It started with the removal man and ended with him, so we knew we would have this great twist – that they were in the wrong house all along,' says Steve. 'And this notion of the neighbour coming round to return the screwdriver was one of the first pieces of the puzzle.'

With the structure set, they moved on to the minutiae of the plot, as well as fleshing out the characters, with David Calder's dementia-addled Percy inspired by a chance remark Pemberton had overheard years earlier, when a businessman, trying to illustrate a point, uttered: 'I'm Andrew Lloyd Webber.' And he wasn't. 'Just that one line. This is why we're such magpies. And why it pays to keep books and books of notes,' says Steve. 'Because that line – "I'm Andrew Lloyd Webber" – I kept transferring from book to book to book, and suddenly you go, "We want a character to have some kind of dementia", and that line pops into your head. What if he thinks he's Andrew Lloyd Webber? Boom. You've got something to dig into. And we took it to the extreme.'

That meant mining 'some very particular musical theatre gags', Reece continues. '"Tell Julie Covington, I offered it to Elaine." I mean, how many people know the original Evita was Julie Covington? Not many, but it's great to be able to put in things that are not so broad that everyone

ABOVE: Emilia Fox as Natasha.

Once Removed   173

will get. Because if three people get it, we're delighted. Like Tommy says in 'Bernie Clifton': "You never say biscuit, you say Garibaldi." We learned that from Victoria Wood. It is good to be specific.'

But the appropriation didn't end there, the pair also drawing from a famous YouTube clip of a still-unidentified Australian man being arrested outside a Chinese restaurant for trying to leave without paying. 'As he's being dragged outside, he's shouting at the police in a really posh voice, "Take your hand off my penis!"' recalls Reece. 'It's a bizarre little bit that found its way into David Calder's dialogue.'

'He's an example of a character who's funny in the moment rather than retrospectively,' says Steve. 'And because he's in his own world, the time reversal doesn't impact him. Other than the fact you know he's going to die of rat poison.'

Another long-cherished idea that finally found a home in 'Once Removed' was Monica Dolan's May secretly using a Dictaphone to record her conversation with Natasha, then playing back bits of her response to dupe her husband, inspired by a similar moment in Woody Allen's *Manhattan Murder Mystery*. While Spike's 'turd in the paint pot' story was one that dated back to when Pemberton lived in Wakefield after leaving Bretton Hall. 'I moved into this house and one of my housemates wanted to decorate the bedroom. They went down to the cellar, found some paint, and prised the lid off. Inside, there was a human shit. That's something you don't forget.'

To direct 'Once Removed', Tandy approached Jim O'Hanlon, with whom he'd worked on Sky's *A Touch of Cloth*. 'He's done a lot of stuff for Marvel and I felt the action sequences in this and "Tempting Fate" would be his cup of tea. He also comes from theatre in Dublin, so has a performance-led background.'

'I was in New York when I got this script,' recalls O'Hanlon. 'I read it in twenty minutes and thought it was unbelievably funny, so tight and fiendishly clever. I knew it was going to be quite a challenge to shoot.'

'He was absolutely on top of it as far as the puzzle aspect,' says Shearsmith, who had been directed by O'Hanlon in an episode of *Chasing Shadows*. 'He's good with actors as well as the technical side of it and I remember having good discussions with him about the characters. Some directors just assume we can do all that. And that's fine. But sometimes it's nice to have new thoughts or suggestions about how to do something.'

Dolan was the suggestion of casting director Tracey Gillham and had starred in the BBC comedy

ABOVE: Spike (Nick Moran) and May (Monica Dolan)

RIGHT: Reece and Steve in costume as Viktor and Hugo.

series *W1A*, also executive produced by Plowman. 'She was part of Jon's extended acting family,' says Tandy. 'I didn't know her at all. But it was a delight to work with her. She was so professional.'

Key to that was Dolan's forensic interrogation of the script. 'She wrote pages of notes for Reece and Steve to pin down what was going through her character's head all the way through the show, and what the audience has to think, because, to begin with, she looks like she's in command, then the nice neighbour, and then she turns out to be the instigator of the whole thing,' says Tandy. 'She's selling a dummy to the audience but playing a double game with the characters in the house. Even more than the assassin, who is subject to the whims of what's going on around him, she had to have a clear line as to what her motivation was at every single point.'

'Monica and Emilia were on top of everything. Monica especially; she didn't let us off the hook with anything,' says Reece. 'We always had to have answers for her. Why does she go back? Has she planned to go back? There was lots of forensic analysing and justifying the actions.'

Dolan's performance is a masterclass of hidden tells and suppressed emotion. 'We were so lucky to have her,' says O'Hanlon. 'She has an amazing ability to be funny and real, but utterly truthful. And then can deliver a line like, "You didn't bring me anything back, not even a bratwurst" and bring the house down. There are not that many actors who can do that with the depth and emotional truth she brought, a sadness that she doesn't linger on, and an anger. Real emotions that, for me,

> Natasha: Just so you know, my father's in the
>   upstairs bathroom, so you might want to
>   warn them about the whole Andrew Lloyd
>   Webber thing.

elevated it from being a technical exercise where you marvel at the cleverness and inventiveness of it, to an understanding of why this whole crazy story happened and how it span out of control.'

Silent Witness star Emilia Fox had originally been cast in another episode of series four but had to bow out due to a scheduling conflict. 'She was genuinely gutted she couldn't do it,' recalls Steve, who, like Shearsmith, had co-starred with Fox in an episode of *Randall and Hopkirk (Deceased)*. 'By the time we came around to this, she was free, and we went, "Bingo. We'll move her into that."'

Playing Spike, the removal man with erectile dysfunction issues, was *Lock, Stock and Two Smoking Barrels* star Nick Moran. 'He was Jim's

suggestion,' says Steve. 'Sometimes you're wary of offering a smallish role, but he was great. He came in on the last day because, of course, that's the last thing that happens. We'd already done all the chaos. He came in and kicked it off.'

Shearsmith's character is, fittingly given his multiple roles, never referred to by name – the credits refer to him as Viktor – while Pemberton's estate agent Hugo, who meets a sticky end in the downstairs loo, was inspired by the late Ted Rogers, host of the classic TV quiz show *3-2-1*, 'Another way of getting humour in it was with his desperation,' says Reece. 'And that's all seeded. She says, "Try to appear not as desperate next time." And there he is being desperate. Which is fun.'

While the vast majority of movies and television shows are filmed out of order, on this occasion, given the intricacies of the plot, both O'Hanlon and Tandy recognised the need to shoot in chronological order to help both cast and crew. 'The beginning of the story is the end of the episode, and the end of the story is the beginning of our episode, so shooting it in order helped, because if we hadn't it would have been even more of a mindfuck than it already was,' laughs O'Hanlon. 'Otherwise we were going to paint ourselves in a corner. Because we needed the mop to be in the right place. And the blood. And the box. And the dressing gown that Reece puts on. We had to go through and work out where the various items are and where we were going to leave them, so they were all in the right place.'

'It was really hard to get your head round what was needed to shoot this successfully,' says Tandy. 'We tried distributing the scripts in action order, so people could understand the processes that had happened in that farmhouse. Even now, it's difficult to come up with a vocabulary to explain the causality of how you set up a prop, when you're filming it backwards. There was a lot of seeding events you hadn't seen.'

ABOVE: David Calder as Percy and Emilia Fox as Natasha.

Even more of a challenge for O'Hanlon and Dolan was keeping tabs on the emotional beats, making sure they tracked forwards and backwards. 'It had to work in both directions, emotionally *and* logistically,' O'Hanlon explains. 'It's one thing to tell a story where the narrative goes from A to Z, but this had to work from A to Z, and it also had to work from Z to A, because that's the order people were watching. And if it doesn't work from Z to A, nobody's interested in the fact it all makes sense from A to Z. And giving it an emotional climax, even though it's the beginning of the story.'

Tandy allotted an extra day to the shooting schedule, bumping it up from five to six, to allow for any narrative issues, with the production filming in a farmhouse in the Lee Valley. 'We wanted a sense of isolation,' says Steve, 'and it was nice to see *outside* number 9, because we are always inside, and we wanted a sense of the countryside around because you can see out of every window.' As with 'A Quiet Night In', the boys tweaked the script to the location. 'It was very exposed and windy and those triple aspect rooms were quite tricky,' recalls Tandy. 'John Sorapure struggled with the change of weather, because it was sunny, cloudy, sunny, cloudy, and we were relying on the daylight to match from shot to shot. Technically, it was a bit of a scramble. There were stunts, prosthetics and blood. There were fight scenes. It was packed. Having somebody like Jim, who'd been exposed to all of that with Marvel, was a good call. He wasn't fazed by the amount of coverage he had to achieve. The rest of us were going, "We're never going to make it work."'

'It was a real mindfuck of an episode,' reflects Steve. 'And what someone did straight away was recut and re-edit it and put it online. Out of all of the episodes, it must've had the highest iPlayer numbers because people immediately wanted to watch it again once they knew what it was all about. And the fact she was tricking the hitman to kill her rival all makes sense.'

Not that that stopped some people querying the logic of it all. 'There were a lot of questions afterwards,' sighs Steve, 'but you just wanted to go, "Come on. We've managed to do this thing where every scene turns what you've previously seen on its head. And that happens five times. Give us a bit of leeway." We can't say it all makes *perfect* sense …'

'But nearly,' says Reece.

TOP: Monica Dolan's make-up is touched up between takes.

ABOVE: A blood-spattered Emilia Fox and Steve smile for the camera.

NICOLA WALKER   STEVE PEMBERTON

REECE SHEARSMITH   MIRANDA HENNESSY

To Have and To Hold

To Have and To Hold

- Series **4**
- Episode **4**
- Directed by **David Kerr**

'This is where we gave up on the cheeriness,' laughs Steve of the darkest, most insidious *Inside No. 9* to date, an episode that began as Ingmar Bergman-esque drama about a marriage in decline, with the boys wondering if they could parcel out a story into five scenes based around the wedding vows. 'That was the starting point. It was a very technical thing. Each of the vows would be reflected somehow, and there were all kinds of scenarios to do with "in sickness and in health". Is someone going to die and leave some money? Is the husband going to murder the wife? Although we were a bit sick of doing murders.'

ABOVE: The episode poster was designed by Poppy Hillstead.

For the majority of its running time, 'To Have and To Hold' presents as a slice of domestic life, with wedding photographer Adrian (Pemberton) and his long-suffering wife Harriet (Nicola Walker)

preparing to renew their vows after twenty years of marriage. On the face of it, Adrian is as dull as dishwater, preferring jigsaws and tinkering in his basement darkroom to spending time with his wife. Harriet had a brief affair with a colleague but is trying very hard to make the marriage work, even engaging in a spot of sexual roleplay. But Adrian can't get it up for her, either metaphorically or literally. 'We knew they were mundane scenes from a marriage,' says Steve. 'They're not packed with jokes. They're not that funny. But it's about holding your nerve and letting it be quite boring. And you think Adrian is a bore. Even that first scene, where you see her put her head on the fridge, thinking, "Oh God, the Pot Noodles, the jigsaws." And he is bristling about her affair. We put in these mysterious phone calls to make you feel sorry for him. There was a line, where, at the end of the scene in the darkroom, he says, "I do forgive you, you know." Like he's this saintly character.'

'Often, when we're having a conversation about an idea, we hear ourselves say, "It's a slice of life" and that lets you off the hook about having some big *Inside No. 9* twist,' continues Reece. 'And then you think, that's fine, but we haven't got the other thing that's bubbling underneath. So it was like, what else is there happening in this thing?'

Quite separately, the pair had been developing an idea inspired by the horrific case of Elisabeth Fritzl, who was kept captive in the basement of the family home for twenty-four years by her father, Josef. 'I think it was Reece who said, "Let's put it in the middle of this,"' recalls Steve. 'And it was like, that's different. Because we were planning on this being very naturalistic, more like "Love's Great

ABOVE: Husband and wife Harriet (Nicola Walker) and Adrian (Steve Pemberton).

ABOVE: Hannah (Miranda Hennessy) and Max (Reece Shearsmith) are newlyweds whose wedding was photographed by Adrian. When they come to view the pictures, their happy relationship provides a stark contrast to the strain between Harriet and Adrian.

Adventure", which is the one we eventually did in that style. But then you think about it, and how everything would be turned on its head, about the marriage and how you'd been feeling sorry for him. And him being a wedding photographer gave us the basement. Once we decided to go with the hidden Fritzl idea, it just felt right. So we wrote it in that way. Very, very dark. Very disturbing.'

'The great thing about reading a Reece and Steve script is I don't get told in advance what it is,' says director David Kerr. 'So I'm approaching the script like a viewer tuning in, not quite sure what world I am in, initially. Not quite sure what the dynamics are. What the tone is. I thought it was Bergman's *Scenes from a Marriage*, or a Mike Leigh domestic drama, a very low-key, kitchen-sink drama, that literally starts in the kitchen. You're introduced to these two characters and it seems to be a slow unfolding death of a marriage, and the efforts of Nicola Walker's character to rekindle something approximating romance. But then you're thinking, "Is that all there is?"'

The answer was most definitely no. For 'To Have and To Hold' is an episode of masterful rug pulls. So while Adrian may be a bore, he's also a monster, having imprisoned the couple's cleaner Agnes (Magdalena Kurek) in a hidden room in their basement for the last nine years, and, even worse, had a son, Levi (Tom Mulheron), with her. (Adrian, clearly, has no problem getting it up where Agnes is concerned.) And the Pot Noodles he claims are easy for when he's working are food for his captives. Later, when Harriet surprises Adrian with a birthday trip to Paris – the pair haven't been away in years – he freaks, throwing himself down the basement stairs to avoid going. 'I'm sure we'd read

Fritzl used to go on holiday and would leave them food,' says Reece. 'But we thought it would be great if she springs a holiday on him, and he can't go because what will happen downstairs? That was the great catalyst for a panic station, and, in a desperate moment, he thinks, "If I fall downstairs, I won't have to go."'

After Harriet discovers a bloody Adrian at the foot of the stairs, we cut to the final onscreen vow – 'Till Death Do Us Part' – and see Harriet in her kitchen, doing a jigsaw. Max (Shearsmith) and Hannah (Miranda Hennessy), whose wedding Adrian shot, pop round with a bottle of champagne to thank him, but Harriet tells them he died, four months ago, in a fall. They leave, and we meet Agnes, now free and back cleaning, along with Levi, who carries a Pot Noodle downstairs to the basement where Adrian is chained up. 'You should have let him die,' says Agnes. 'I can't,' replies Harriet. 'He's my husband.'

While the revelation that Adrian has a woman locked up in the basement is a twist no one saw coming, the script seeds the idea of Agnes having disappeared early, and the name they've given the child is the one he and Harriet would have given theirs, if it were a boy. 'Because this was

```
Harriet:    I'd be happy doing it with just me and you
            and a ring-pull from a can of Diet Pepsi!
Adrian:     They don't do ringpulls anymore for health
            and safety reasons.
```

based on a real thing we were very conscious not to play it for laughs,' says Steve. 'That's why it was so important they triumphed at the end and that the character of Agnes had a lot of dignity, and said, "This is now my choice to stay here." And they've turned the tables on him. A bit like "Sardines", you're dealing with something horrific that people have gone through, so you don't take it lightly. But we definitely didn't want to end with him triumphing. We wanted him to get his just desserts.'

'The really dark bit is the fact the kid, Levi, is doing the feeding at the end,' says Tandy. In their original script, Levi had appeared much earlier, as a ghostly figure. 'At one point we were going to have Harriet wake up, see him and attribute it to her wanting to have a child, and not being able,' says Steve. 'You would think it was a fever dream. But he'd got out, and Adrian manages to smuggle him back in before she realises,' adds Reece.

'That was a bit of misdirection that made me think, "This is not telling the story in the best possible way,"' says Tandy. 'They got that note from me and from Jon. The early draft was more confusing and more of a puzzle box – it felt like it had supernatural elements, like a ghost or a mysterious stranger. There was a little bit of "The 12

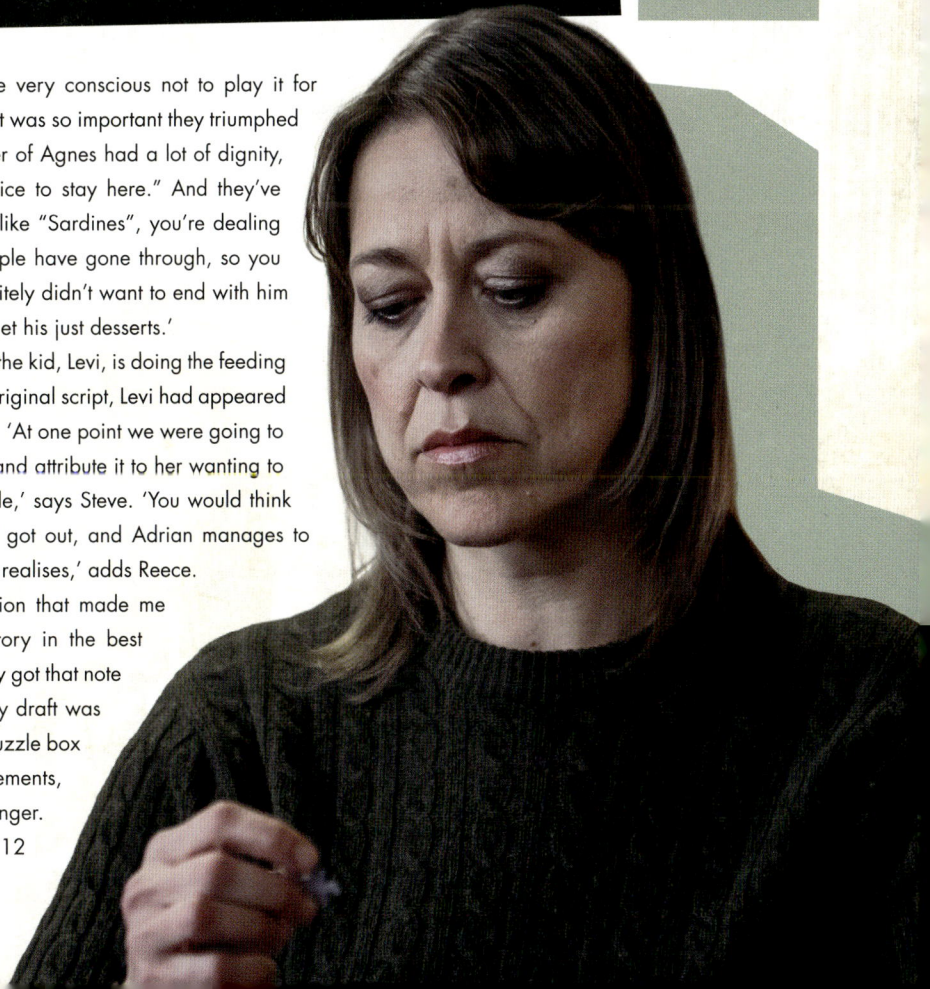

Days of Christine" about it. And I said, "Take all of that out. Make it about the marriage, explore their relationship, and try not to hint at the darker reveal until much later."' Tandy also had concerns about Adrian's profession. 'I remember Adam trying to scupper the whole wedding photographer thing, because he was like, "Everything's digital now. You wouldn't have a darkroom,"' notes Reece. 'And we were like, "Fucking allow us it. Because we need it for this story." And it was great to have all these smiling faces of these happy couples, and the absolute horrible irony of that in the wake of his life.'

For the most part, 'To Have and To Hold' is an uncomfortable two-hander between Pemberton and *Unforgotten* star Walker. 'What people forget is Nicola originally came from sketch comedy,' says Tandy. 'She just got sidelined into crime procedural, and it's comedy's loss. Nicola's sense of humour, and her wickedness, are so strong.'

'I'm sure when her agent said, "*Inside No. 9* has been in touch," she was like, "Great, a bit of a light relief from playing detectives,"' laughs Kerr. 'Instead, she gets

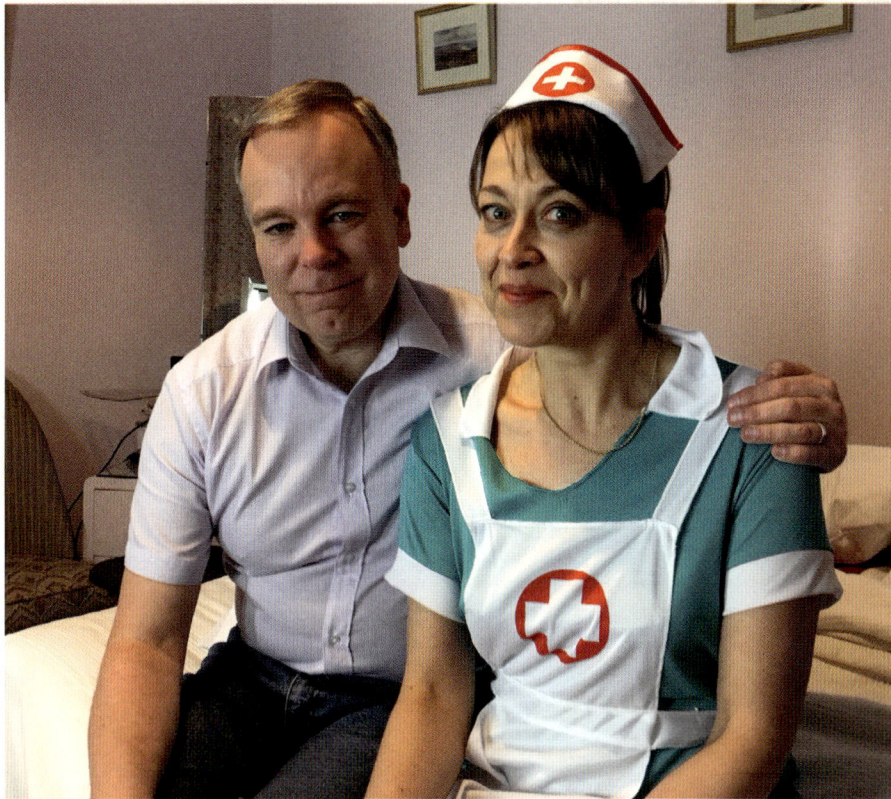

this horrendous domestic drama. But there is still comedy in it, particularly the gruesome sex scene and the moment with Reece and Miranda, and she could play the sitcom aspect of it superbly. We needed a brilliant dramatic actress, and that's what we got.'

Pemberton, too, is a revelation. 'Steve knew this was a really challenging role to pull off, because you've got a character with a very dark secret playing against that through most of the film,' says Kerr. 'Anyone who's watched Steve through *The League* and *Psychoville* will know he can play grotesque characters in glorious ways, often dialling up their eccentricities and revelling in their quirks and grim traits. But his performance in this was a yardstick of truthfulness and naturalism, and for him to be as in control as he was of the little tells, the physical details, the timing of the gaps between the lines, is the work of a consummate actor. His performance is astonishing. I could have watched those two for hours.'

The heartbreaking state of their marriage is laid bare when Harriet dresses up as 'Nurse Honeypot' and attempts to engage Adrian's 'Dick Shafter' using seductive language, baby oil, massage and masturbation, but fails dismally on all fronts. 'It's not you, it's me,' Adrian tells her. 'She, essentially, prostitutes herself to get some form of happiness out her relationship with this man who she already finds quite dull,' says Tandy. 'But she's in it for the long haul. That's what's so terrible about Nicola's character. She is trying to make it work and it's never going to happen.' The disastrous and squirm-inducing seduction is unbearable for Harriet, for Adrian, and the audience. 'It was a challenge to shoot because we all knew what we wanted it to be, which is an insight into this awful marriage, and the lengths she will go to breathe life into it,' says Kerr. 'But we wanted it to be funny as well.'

Filming the scene, Pemberton wore flesh-coloured pants and, at Shearsmith's suggestion,

ABOVE: Steve and Nicola Walker, she in her 'Nurse Honeypot' outfit.

ABOVE: The red light of the basement darkroom adds to the sense of unease.

Harriet: I thought I was living with the most boring man in the world. Turns out he was a monster.

attached a sock to them with a safety pin to give Walker's character something to 'pull on'. 'I couldn't keep a straight face,' admits Steve. 'But it gave her something physical to do rather than just miming. She was brilliant, Nicola. The hope in her face that something might happen. And then the disappointment.'

'It was awful,' says Reece. 'One of the most excruciating things was the sound. There was a lot of slapping. But it was too much. Too horrible. It was taken back in the edit, because it was more awful to be quieter. I never want to watch it again.'

'I remember someone on Twitter saying, "I'm by myself watching and I don't know where to look,"' laughs Steve. 'I thought that was perfect, because, credit to David, he let that go on and on and on. It's so sad.'

And it was a scene designed to make you feel pity for Adrian just before he's revealed to be a monster. Although Pemberton and Shearsmith wanted to present it, and him, very matter-of-factly. 'When my character is making the Pot Noodle, and he's moving everything away to reveal the secret room, we're not playing it as a horror film,' says Steve. 'This is a real house, and we wanted the mundanity of evil.'

'With the boiling of the kettle and the red light, it was all very deliberate and horrible,' continues Reece. 'And how much to show of the hand coming out, getting the Pot Noodle.'

'The horror is all suggested in this episode; it's psychological,' says Tandy. 'I loved the subterranean world of his darkroom where she bares her soul like a piece of exposed film, and he is dissembling, right the way through till the end. It's a really strong bit of writing.'

Adrian and Harriet's house was a real one in Ealing. 'The key thing it had to have was a door which could open to suggest a basement, and stairs down which Steve's character would throw himself,' says Kerr. 'And if we'd found a house that had a big basement we'd have done it all on location. But we were pretty sure we weren't going to find somewhere that had its own dungeon.' And it was Pemberton, not a stuntman, who threw himself down the stairs. 'That was done in the house and was quite scary,' he reflects. 'I mean, to fall from standing to the floor is quite scary. But to fall lower than the floor, to a thing that's going down, there's something psychologically challenging about it. I didn't really want to, even though there was a mat there.'

The darkroom was designed and built on stage at Elstree Studios by Dennis De Groot. 'The great thing about the set is you can control exactly where things are,' says Kerr, 'and the most important part was not looking at the layout and assuming there's a room you can't see. It was a way of creating atmosphere and having a really bespoke design space, where the character could be reflected. In contrast to "The Harrowing", which is Gothic Horror with a capital H, this was about the banality of evil. Here you're leaning towards the ordinary.'

Not that ordinary couldn't be sinister or scary, with Kerr and the sound department dialling up the boiling of the kettle to make it seem more ominous, coupled with the hellish, red-tinged basement. 'That was David in the mix. And we *really* pushed it,' says Tandy. 'David and I talked about making it really scary, really dark and the shot sizes that we needed to make it alarmingly scary without being exploitative in terms of what we were suggesting was going on in that room.'

Christian Henson's music is equally suggestive, starting out as a light and jolly suburban comedy score, played mostly with strings, before becoming overwhelmed by ominous dark drones, tones and the sound of the boiling kettle as the secret room is revealed. 'We toyed with taking the music out completely at that point, but ended up bringing it back in, and it is truly chilling,' says Tandy. 'It's one of my favourite episodes. It's got great performances, a really good story, it's incredibly dark, and the rug pulls, you do not see them coming.'

ABOVE: Reece and Miranda Hennessy on set, with filming in progress.

AND THE WINNER IS....

TUESDAY 30th JANUARY

BBC TWO

BBC TWO PRESENTS A BBC STUDIOS PRODUCTION AN INSIDE NO. 9 FILM "AND THE WINNER IS..." REECE SHEARSMITH STEVE PEMBERTON PHOEBE SPARROW KENNETH CRANHAM NOEL CLARKE ZOE WANAMAKER FENELLA WOOLGAR CASTING BY TRACEY GILLHAM MUSIC BY CHRISTIAN HENSON WRITTEN BY STEVE PEMBERTON & REECE SHEARSMITH COSTUME DESIGNER YVES BARRE EXECUTIVE PRODUCER JON PLOWMAN PRODUCED BY ADAM TANDY DIRECTED BY GRAEME HARPER

And the Winner Is...

- Series **4**
- Episode **5**
- Directed by **Graeme Harper**

ABOVE: The episode poster was designed by Andy Bottomley.

Three series in and *Inside No. 9* was a commercial and critical darling, racking up impressive viewing figures, endless plaudits, and countless awards, including a RTS, a Writers' Guild, and a Rose d'Or. But at the time, the show itself had yet to be nominated for a BAFTA, much to its makers' chagrin. 'Because it's not *just* a comedy, it falls between stools and, therefore, gets ignored a little bit,' laments Reece.

Not that Pemberton has any truck with awards, finding the whole idea of them ridiculous. 'You can't sit there and say, "This is a better performance than this one. This is a better show than this one. This is a better comedy than this one,"' he insists. 'It's crazy. You're not dealing in definites. You're not saying this is a race and someone's going to win. It's pot luck.'

All of this was in the boys' minds when they sat down to write 'And the Winner Is ...', which began as 'a desire to do a *Twelve Angry Men*-type scenario, with a group of disparate people, one mission, and decision to make,' explains Reece, 'and how the ins and outs of that gets swayed around the room. We had the idea to do it in various settings: train carriages, buses.'

Then, they hit upon the idea of a jury room during deliberations for a television Best Actress Award. 'We talked about it and dismissed it,' says Steve. 'It made us laugh, but we said, "It's way too *in*, and might be seen as us settling scores." We didn't want to write something about awards and for it to look like sour grapes. Because we have won a lot between us.'

'Yeah. What more do we need?' says Reece. 'But it would be nice.'

'So we thought about it some more,' continues Steve, 'and decided if the characters were good

ABOVE: Reece and Steve as struggling screenwriter Clive Carroll and committee chair Giles Grindley-Orme.

ABOVE: Kenneth Cranham as stage legend Rupert Dennis.

Giles: Jackie, let's get the view from the sofa,
            as it were. Are you a Dame Dotty fan?

Jackie: I love her. She really reminds me of my
            grandma. Apart from the wanking men off in
            car parks bit.

enough, it would be enjoyable to watch. And, to this day, it's got some of the funniest lines.'

Indeed, 'And the Winner Is …' is a pointed and blisteringly comic peek behind the curtain at how juries vote, taking satirical shots at the whole process, insisting awards are a bit of farce, with the winners and losers decided upon by a combination of contributing factors which, in this particular instance, include diversity, past wins, and even historic masturbation, rather than actual acting talent. 'It's completely accurate,' insists Reece. 'It's a world most people don't know about. Most people don't know how these things operate.'

'For those of us who have been in those rooms, the episode has extra resonance,' concurs Tandy. 'We have a funny relationship with awards bodies. There's a little bit of resentment there. And when I read the script, it was, because of all the showbiz stuff, one of the funniest things I'd read.'

'I had been a judge for the Royal Television Society for student shorts,' recalls director Graeme Harper. 'And as soon as I read the script, I remembered that meeting, because they were all there. There were only six of us, but each one was represented by all these characters. It made me laugh, and I couldn't say that they didn't behave like that, because they did. These characters do exist with hidden agendas. I've met them all.'

The jury in 'And the Winner Is …' is led by associate chair of the television committee Giles

Grindley-Orme (Pemberton) and is made up of screenwriter Clive Carroll (Shearsmith), film and TV director Gordon Norris (Noel Clarke), English stage legend Rupert Dennis (Kenneth Cranham), American star Paula (Zoë Wanamaker), *Sunday Mirror* TV critic June Bright (Fenella Woolgar), and dentist's receptionist Jackie (Phoebe Sparrow). Their job is to pick a winner for this year's Best Actress Award. The eight nominees are quickly, and cruelly, pared down to four.

Even before the deliberations begin, sycophantic Clive, who, in a lovely touch, arrives with tissue paper stuck to his chin having cut himself shaving, is trying to curry favour with Gordon in order to get him to read his latest script, constantly switching his opinion to be in line with him. 'It was a funny idea, the desperate writer down on his luck who has no integrity at all,' says Reece. 'He's so craven,' adds Steve. 'He won an award for best breakthrough in 2003. And he still hasn't broken through.'

Of the two actors, Cranham's thespian is the cantankerous old man of British theatre who abhors 'actresses who mumble', values diction above all else, and is very clearly behind the times in terms of racial and sexual politics. ('I worked with Ken on a *Boon* many years ago,' says Harper, 'and he is the most unlikely person to play that part. He's not a pompous oaf at all. He's lovely.') When asked by the chair if there are any conflicts of interest regarding any of the nominees, June insinuates, snidely, that Dennis has 'history' with the venerable Dame Dotty, dating back to their youthful days at the Royal Shakespeare Company. Dennis takes umbrage, insisting: 'I don't think a handjob in the car park of The Dirty Duck in 1976 is going to cloud my judgement.'

The Dirty Duck is a real pub in Stratford-upon-Avon, home to the RSC. Only it doesn't have a car park. 'We knew that, but the line was funnier with it,' insists Steve. 'So you make those choices, even though it's factually wrong.' As a result, says Tandy, a few people did complain.

Wanamaker's husky-voiced American in London for a West End show – who hasn't seen the

TOP LEFT: Fenella Woolgar as TV critic June Bright.

TOP MIDDLE: Zoë Wanamaker as American movie star Paula.

TOP RIGHT: Phoebe Sparrow as 'Jackie'.

ABOVE: Reece as Clive.

ABOVE: Steve poses in costume alongside the whiteboard featuring the photos of the finalists.

nominated performances and arrives with comments on crib cards secreted in her handbag – was based on a real actress. 'When we were doing "Diddle Diddle Dumpling", we were moaning about not being nominated for BAFTAs,' recalls Steve. 'And Keeley [Hawes] said, "I was on a jury once where a well-known American clearly hadn't seen any of the performances because she kept getting the names wrong," and we thought it'd be great to have a character like that, who's flown in, wants the kudos of being on the panel, but hasn't watched anything.'

During the course of the episode, Fenella Woolgar's television critic comes to the realisation that what she does is meaningless and entirely predicated on the work of more creative and talented individuals. She is, says Shearsmith, 'one of the cruellest characters we've ever created, a barnacle on a host of other people'.

'We knew critics were going to be watching it for Fenella's character because she speaks to them,' says Tandy, 'I'm glad to say most critics took it in good spirit, although, maybe, there was an element of truth in what we were saying. But it's exaggerated, of course.'

The jury also includes starry-eyed Jackie, who, we're told, has won a competition to be there and doesn't feel clever or knowledgeable enough to contribute. But Jackie isn't who she claims. In reality, she's Kelly Marsden, the ambitious former soap star and Best Actress nominee who picks up enough votes around the table to win the award. 'It was one of the episodes where, reading the script, I worked out the ending,' says Tandy. 'I think Reece was a bit put out I guessed. Because it's quite well hidden.'

For starters, they cast Phoebe Sparrow, who'd starred onstage with Shearsmith in *The Dresser*, but hadn't done much TV. Then they 'disguised' her by giving Jackie false eyebrows and long, brown hair, while the photo of Marsden shows her with short blonde hair. To help sell the illusion further, the camera never lingers on the photo, nor, in the edit, does it cut from the photo to Jackie. 'We knew it was a dangerous game to play,' admits Reece. 'We thought if you spot this, you've unravelled the ending. And some people did. Regardless, it's still twenty-eight minutes of funny characters doing funny things.'

'For everybody who guesses what's going on, they should forget what they know and enjoy the episode for what it does, and watch the manipulation of Phoebe's character as she spins the arguments round,' says Tandy. 'She does it very subtly, but it is there. Watch it a second time and you can see exactly what she's doing at every stage.'

They shot at Harefield Grove, a Grade II-listed building in Rickmansworth where Tandy had filmed a lot of *The Thick of It*. As with Morales and 'The Bill', for Harper, the biggest challenge was making it visually interesting. 'Most directors dread scenes around a table. I must have done twenty or thirty of them in thirty years of directing, so I knew how to get enough coverage, so all the eyelines were right and you knew, at any given time, who's talking to who and where they were.' Harper encouraged his cast to get up and move around, fixing themselves a cup of tea or going to the toilet, 'to keep the thing alive. And they all agreed, otherwise it would have been very dull, visually.' Initially, the idea had been to film it like a documentary, in the manner of *The Thick of It*, but, in the end, Harper opted to shoot handheld but less fly-on-the-wall. 'Graeme was giggling away in a corner, enjoying taking a rise out of the industry,' remembers Tandy. 'And what's so great about this episode is it does have an awful lot of truth. And perhaps the general audience doesn't really recognise it for its authenticity.'

Somewhat ironically, the day after the episode aired, Pemberton received an email from BAFTA asking if he was interested in being a member of the judging panel for Best Comedy Performance by a female. 'Literally, the next day,' he laughs. 'I'd never done one before, so I said yes. To see what it's like. A few people had seen the episode and were talking about it. I asked, "Is this a coincidence?" No one said, "We saw it and asked you." But it had to be.'

ABOVE: Steve's costume and make-up are adjusted between takes.

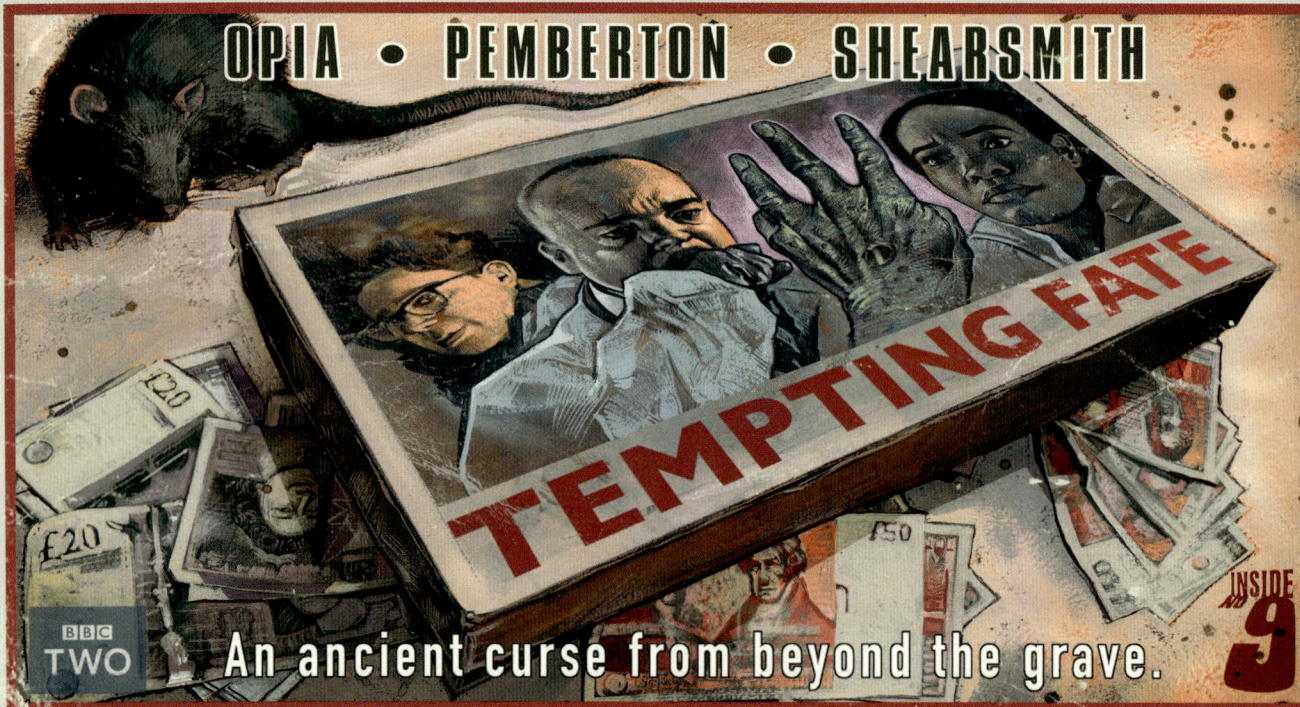

OPIA · PEMBERTON · SHEARSMITH

TEMPTING FATE

An ancient curse from beyond the grave.

BBC TWO PRESENTS A BBC STUDIOS PRODUCTION AN INSIDE NO. 9 FILM FILM "TEMPTING FATE" WERUCHE OPIA STEVE PEMBERTON REECE SHEARSMITH NIGEL PLANER RUBEN CRYER DUBBING MIXER MATTHEW BRACE SUPERVISING SOUND EDITOR CHRIS MACLEAN LINE PRODUCER FRANCES MABLE EDITED BY JOE RANDALL-CUTLER MUSIC BY CHRISTIAN HENSON PRODUCTION DESIGNER DENNIS DE GROOT DIRECTOR OF PHOTOGRAPHY JOHN SORAPURE WRITTEN BY STEVE PEMBERTON & REECE SHEARSMITH EXECUTIVE PRODUCER JON PLOWMAN PRODUCED BY ADAM TANDY DIRECTED BY JIM O'HANLON

Tempting Fate

- Series **4**
- Episode **6**
- Directed by **Jim O'Hanlon**

First published in 1902, W. W. Jacobs' supernatural classic 'The Monkey's Paw' is one of horror literature's most enduring and often-told tales. In it, Mr and Mrs White and their grown son Herbert are gifted the eponymous – and cursed – monkey's paw by an army friend recently returned from India. The object is said to grant the holder three wishes, but, as befits attempts to interfere with fate, they come with a heavy price.

The boys had explored the be-careful-what-you-wish-for conceit in a script they wrote for an abandoned reboot of *Hammer House of Horror*. 'It got quite far down the line, but didn't happen,' recalls Reece. 'It's one of the few things where we've worked very hard on the script and it didn't materialise.' Never ones to let a good idea go to waste, they reworked Jacobs' morality tale for series four's deliciously ripe finale. 'It feels right we've done it, because you see it in most horror anthologies, the famous one being [in 1972's] *Tales from the Crypt*,' notes Reece.

ABOVE: The episode poster was designed by Graham Humphreys.

'That's why we referenced "The Monkey's Paw" in the dialogue,' says Steve. 'We can't pretend we made this up. So we're playing with the awareness of that story. It was the last one we wrote. We knew what the other five were, and none were in the Gothic palette we enjoy so much.'

Still, given the abundant adaptations of 'The Monkey's Paw' that had come before, the pair felt they needed a novel hook on which to hang their story, finding it in Edmund Trebus, a compulsive hoarder who lived in Crouch End in the 1990s and who was featured in the BBC documentary series *A Life of Grime*. 'He was an extraordinary character, and it was a constant battle between him and Haringey Council to clear his house out,' says Reece. 'He was more of an anomaly then. Now it's a thing. But we thought a council house filled with stuff would be a great setting.'

They were also inspired by Carol Morley's 2011 docudrama *Dreams of a Life*, which told the tragic story of Joyce Carol Vincent, whose skeletal remains were found in her flat in Wood Green two years after she died, surrounded by wrapped Christmas gifts and with her TV still on. 'The council had to come in and investigate if anyone was related to this person who died. And so that was in our minds – and that notion, of a life left, and letters and clues, was all part and parcel of that. It's like finding the *Marie Celeste* of someone's house.'

In 'Tempting Fate', council contractors Keith (Pemberton), Nick (Shearsmith) and trainee Maz (Weruche Opia) are charged with clearing out the home of Frank Meggins (Nigel Planer), who died after falling face first into a glass-topped coffee table and bleeding out, to see if he has any living relatives. Decked out in white boilersuits and gloves, they begin sifting through Frank's gloomy flat, a maze-like warren packed full of boxes, eBay items, and, somewhat incredibly, a cheque from the National Lottery for £3.5 million. 'That setting – the darkness, the cramped flat and the investigation – was a great premise,' says Steve. 'You're eking out information. It's intriguing he's won the lottery. So why does he live like this? We started plotting it out. We spent a long time trying to work out what his backstory was and how all his wishes rebound on him. And they had to figure all that out from what they found.'

'It's a kind of domestic horror,' says Jim O'Hanlon, who directed. 'They are three pretty prosaic

ABOVE: Reece as council contractor Nick.

ABOVE: Left to right: Maz (Weruche Opia), Nick (Reece Shearsmith) and Keith (Steve Pemberton).

```
Maz:      What's a VHS?
Keith:    It's from the eighties.
```

characters whose days are normally filled by picking up rubbish in abandoned houses, and I liked the idea they suddenly find themselves in their own horror movie, completely unexpectedly. The Reece and Steve characters were more susceptible to it, whereas Maz undercuts the whole thing. She is very much Generation Z: "I'm only here until I find something better." And I liked the idea of these three slightly mismatched characters ending up in their own version of *Alien*, and so we tried to keep it as creepy as we possibly could. I wanted a creepy, haunted house-type of feel. And yet everything had to be real. That's what's great about it. All of the stuff that you think is supernatural isn't, until Nigel's character turns up.'

And it's Maz who discovers the hidden wall safe and guesses the combination to be Frank's late wife's date of birth. Inside is a videotape and a bubble-wrapped package with the words 'Danger – do not open' written on it. Ignoring the warning, Keith opens it – 'it's better to have the full picture,' he tells them – revealing a small, ornamental brass hare, the significance of which was not lost on the show's many fans. 'We thought it'd be a great moment where you build up to this mysterious thing in the safe, they unpackage it carefully, and it's the hare that we've hidden in four series, finally seen front and centre, having its moment in the sun,' says Reece. 'I don't think we ever planned it would end up being a thing. But, in some ways, it is a cursed object, because often something bad happens in the rooms it's in.'

Puzzled by the hare's significance – although Nick points out that, in folklore, hares are associated with witchcraft and trickery – the three watch the video in which Frank tells how he purchased it 'for a small fortune from a holy man in Jaipur', who told him it would grant three wishes that would transform his life. It did. But not for the better. He implores the viewer to destroy this cursed object before it ruins more lives. Keith dismisses it as nonsense; Maz sees it as an opportunity to score some quick cash; while Nick, a folklorist who, conveniently, has a PhD in Ethnology and Folklore, believes the hare is cursed, especially when a double-bagged dead rat starts wriggling again after he wishes it was alive to save on paperwork. (Listen carefully and you'll hear a little ding on the soundtrack every time a wish is made.) 'A bit like "The Harrowing", there's one character who says, "Hang on, there's a rational explanation for all of these supernatural things,"' says Steve. 'So we wanted the audience to be unsure whether the wishes thing was true or not.'

Events take a tragic turn when Maz wishes for £93,000 and winds up dead. Keith, who knows more than he's letting on, attacks Nick, wanting the money for his son Charlie, who's in a wheelchair, suffering from MS. But Keith's scheme is scuppered when a shuffling, personable and zombified Frank – he'd wished for immortality – returns home, mumbling about tinned peaches. 'We knew we wanted him to come back in that EC Comics/*Tales from the Crypt* way,' continues Steve. 'But that in itself didn't feel like an ending. So we came up with this notion that my character had been round to the flat already, having heard about the money, and was responsible for killing him. Or thought he'd killed him anyway.'

'There's this final act twist where it turns into a zombie thing,' says Tandy. 'It's weird. Weirdly supernatural. Jim did a really good job, ramping up the tension in terms of what it is you're seeing, or not seeing, at various points.'

As Frank, they cast Planer, forever remembered as Neil the hippie in eighties classic *The Young Ones*. 'I grew up with *The Young Ones* and they were my comedy heroes,' says O'Hanlon. 'So when we heard Nigel was interested that was unbelievably exciting. He'd been doing a lot of stage musicals so he was very keen to be involved.' O'Hanlon suggested they put a hole in the bottom of Frank's slippers in homage to Planer's *Young Ones* character Neil whose version of 'Hole In My Shoe' reached number two in the charts in 1984, but, in the end, they felt it might be too distracting or too meta. 'You want people to be totally drawn into the supernatural element. That's what I thought was clever about it. It all feels very real and you're going, "This isn't supernatural." Then the twist comes when Frank walks in. I wanted him to appear almost in silhouette, so you went, "Was that him?" Then we see Nigel as a zombie. And who wouldn't love that?'

'Jim really embraced the horror nature of that episode,' notes Reece, 'giving it the right level of creepiness with Frank at the end, and seeing him from quite far away at first, pottering back and forth, making a cup of tea.'

Maz was played by newcomer Weruche Opia, who later starred with Michaela Coel in her acclaimed series *I May Destroy You*. 'Tracey [Gillham], our casting director, brought her in, and I knew immediately,' says O'Hanlon. 'She was funny. A bit like Monica [Dolan, from "Once Removed"], she could land the humour, but was also very real. It's a very specific tone, Steve and Reece's stuff. Not everyone could do it. She had a totally different flavour to them, while being clearly in the same world.

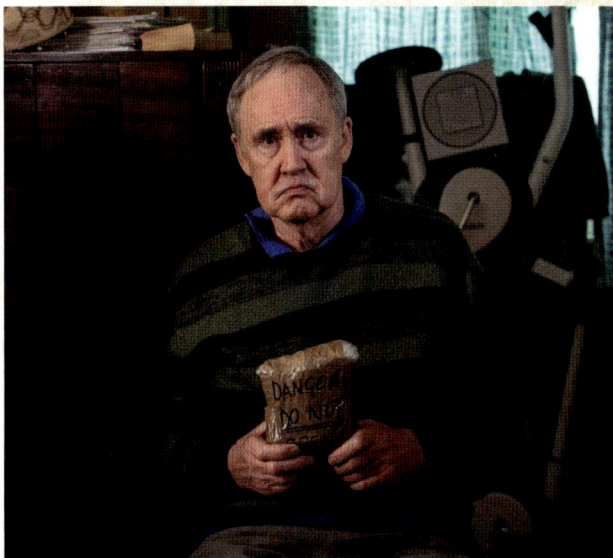

ABOVE: Nigel Planer as hoarder Frank Meggins.

TEMPTING FATE FLAT

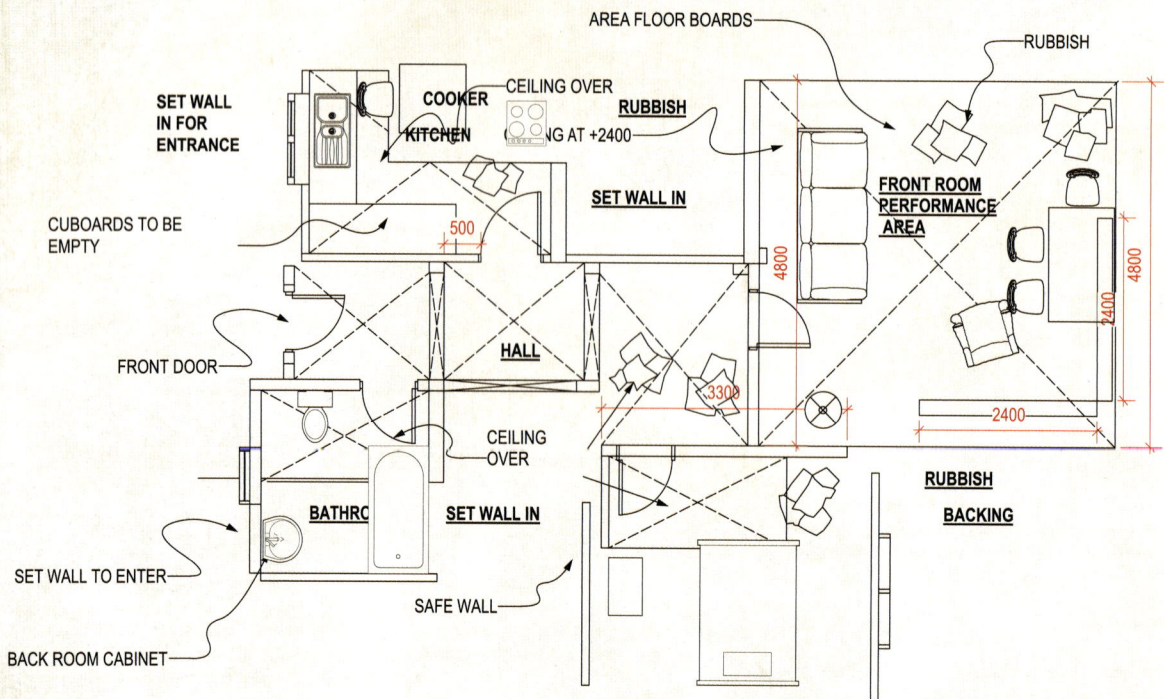

AREA FLOOR BOARDS

RUBBISH

SET WALL IN FOR ENTRANCE

COOKER

CEILING OVER

KITCHEN

RUBBISH

CEILING AT +2400

CUBOARDS TO BE EMPTY

SET WALL IN

FRONT ROOM PERFORMANCE AREA

500

4800

4800

2400

FRONT DOOR

HALL

3300

2400

CEILING OVER

SET WALL TO ENTER

BATHRO

SET WALL IN

RUBBISH

BACKING

SAFE WALL

BACK ROOM CABINET

She had to be street. But not *Top Boy* street.' In fact, Maz is a source of much humour, continually misunderstanding her two older colleagues' eighties' references. 'She was the conduit into the modern world, like a medium,' laughs Reece. 'She brought a whole new dynamic.' And knowledge of the correct footwear someone of her age would be interested in. 'We would never have known that.'

A housing estate in Acton that was due to be knocked down stood in for the exterior of Frank's flat, while the interior was a set – a dark, foreboding, shadowy place, full of nooks and crannies and piles of crap. But after having built the basement for 'To Have and To Hold' and the hotel corridor for 'Zanzibar', money was tight for production designer Dennis De Groot when it came to 'Tempting Fate'. 'I wanted to make it as cheap as possible, so it was more impressionistic, like something out of a Terry Gilliam film, where you're in a world of shit,' says Tandy. 'A lot of it is cardboard boxes stuck together in clumps, so you can lift them out in order to get the camera in. It's all very lightweight, but there was some heavy stuff for the bowling ball and iron to rest on. The idea was to make it large, complicated and unknowable, so you were in a mouse maze of clutter. The design team worked very hard to deliver that.'

The set was raised to allow for the scene where Nick lifts up the floorboards and explores underneath. 'It was claustrophobic; it felt like a warren. You did feel as if you were in a very different world in there,' says Reece. 'As soon as you went in, you felt grubby,' adds Steve. 'Even though everything was very clean.'

Among the clutter was Felicity Kendal's jacket from 'Private View' hanging up. 'There's no link,' insists Steve. 'Yves was asked to provide some clothes that they could bundle into the room.'

To navigate the flat's labyrinthine layout and towering piles of tat, O'Hanlon and John Sorapure opted to film using a MōVI Pro, a circular rig with the camera mounted in the middle on a remote head.

ABOVE: A detailed set plan for Frank's flat, created by production designer Dennis De Groot.

'It's like a poor man's Steadicam,' says O'Hanlon, 'but, for our purposes, it wasn't about the money. It's smaller, so you could get that flowing horror camera movement within the very narrow confines of the set.'

Maz's death was designed as a Rube Goldberg or Heath Robinson-style chain reaction involving an ironing board, a bowling ball, a loose floorboard and a nail. 'We wanted it to happen all the way through [the episode], the construction of the thing that will kill her,' says Steve. 'When we find the TV, I move the iron. Then when Reece is looking in the floorboards, he moves the bowling ball, and you see it constructed before your eyes. Then she knocks the iron on the bowling ball. It falls down. She steps back. And Boom!'

'That was really fun to design, and to see built across the episode,' says O'Hanlon. 'It's all about fate. If all of those things hadn't been placed into position, she would never have died. The fact they were all slightly complicit in their own fate, albeit unintentionally, felt like a rewarding thing, especially if you watch it a second time and see all the pieces put in place.'

The episode ends with an appearance by Charlie (Ruben Cryer), Keith's son, who has been wished back to health by Nick, followed by an offscreen explosion that destroys the flat, killing everybody inside – an explosion triggered by Keith tearing a gas pipe from the fireplace and zombie Frank lighting a gas ring in the kitchen to make a cup of tea. 'We went round the houses about what was going to happen with his son and was it too malicious of Nick to [make his] wish for a child, only for him to die,' says Reece. 'But Keith did try to kill him, so we thought that was fair enough.'

TOP: Steve on set, filming in progress.

ABOVE: Reece and Steve with a zombified Nigel Planer.

DEAD LINE

Steve Pemberton
Reece Shearsmith
Stephanie Cole

" ...is anybody there? "

Halloween Special 'Dead Line'

■ Directed by **Barbara Wiltshire**

'**I**t was a suggestion by Chris Sussman, then head of comedy at BBC Studios: "Would you like to do a live one?"' recalls Reece. 'And we thought, "No." Adam was always against it. He said you'll end up with a ropey version of what we normally do, so what's the point? And it's a headache. It wasn't until we thought, what if it goes wrong? That would be more fun than trying to do one that would end up looking like *EastEnders*. That was when it became worth doing. If everyone is tuning in, grimly fascinated, to see if anyone fluffs their lines, and it goes wrong, what does that lead to? That was exciting. Presenting a sacrificial episode of *No. 9* that goes wrong ten minutes in.'

ABOVE: The episode poster was designed by Andy Bottomley.

They set to work, dusting off an old idea about phone calls from the dead to use as the kicker for 'Dead Line', a Halloween special unlike any other, that starts off as a live episode of *Inside No. 9* before

descending into chaos, incorporating clips from other shows, news reports, real people and events, 'off-air' conversations in the make-up room between the boys, live Tweeting, as well as good-natured jabs at *Black Mirror* and themselves, before the show, infected by spirits of the dead, completely breaks down, culminating in their being 'killed'.

'It was a very risky enterprise on many levels,' says Steve. 'How do you structure something once you've come back to us, in the make-up room, fed up, bored, and seemingly overheard? How do you keep that narrative going? And how do you get information out without it appearing like a regular episode? Then we got the idea of using a patchwork of clips, a mosaic of weird, abrupt edits that, somehow – "the ghost in the machine" was a good phrase – the BBC had no control over, and these ghosts were spewing forth all this information. That was the key. And stumbling upon this episode of *Most Haunted* set at Granada Studios in Manchester. That really unlocked what could go wrong in our fake episode.'

In 2005, *Most Haunted* visited Granada which, it's claimed, was built on the site of a Victorian graveyard and is cursed as a result. During the tour, medium David Wells walks through the studios with *Coronation Street* actors Sue Cleaver and Simon Gregson and feels a psychic presence. 'They talk about someone in their fifties, a member of the crew who died there,' says Steve. 'So we extrapolated from that, and created this crew member called Alan Starr and a false news report about him. More than any other episode, we took from real life. And having Bobby Davro, Keith Chegwin, Lionel Blair and the *Coronation Street* cast also gave it a sense of reality. I remembered there was a fire at Granada that had destroyed *The Jewel in the Crown* sets. I had a really strong memory of it on *Granada Reports*. So the more we pulled in, the more we thought, "This is so exciting." And the audience will have to piece together what this is about.'

ABOVE: Reece and Steve play themselves as things begin to unravel.

LIVE

VOICE FROM HELL   GO PRO CAMERA?

EDDIE AT DOOR - LOOK TO CAMERA - SINISTER

CONTINUITY ANNOUNCER BEING GOT

TIGHT PHONE SHOT

HAND PEELS AWAY   CARD

within programme ? LOST

    IS GOOD LUCK STUDIO NOW AS WE GO LIVE

    TV IN THE GREENROOM

    THE PHONE LIMBS UP

    PEOPLE ON TWITTER

POSTING ABOUT   HISTORY OF STUDIO 9

REECE READS IT OUT.

With, account set up by us, with a history, going back years months maybe?

Ged out studio backstory via Twitter

PERO PHONE HAS BEEN RINGING & we see it on the screen.

We get back onto the set.

Playing things backwards?

NEWS footage?

No soup 'Newsnight will push 10 minutes early we can have that slot but whatshis your Ann

ABOVE: A page from one of Steve's notebooks shows ideas for the live episode.

Among the many pieces was a video of a 'priest' performing an exorcism at Granada. 'Big, wide shots of the empty studios. '"You must leave. We cast you out!"' says Reece. 'That turned out to be a hoax. But because we wanted to use a bit, the man had to be contacted to sign a release form. And we were terrified he would reveal what we were doing.'

Prior to reading the script for 'Dead Line', Tandy was adamant that live episodes were a bad idea. 'Do they produce anything worth watching, given how carefully we make our episodes? Then this came in and I thought, "That's good." This is fucking with the form so hugely there was every reason to do it. When it was just a live episode of *Inside No. 9*, it was a terrible idea. At the point it became meta, it was fantastic.'

In addition to several clips from *Most Haunted* and the 'exorcism' footage, the boys wanted to include an infamous and unaired clip from the game show *Public Enemy Number One*, in which the host, Bobby Davro, trussed up in a pillory, falls face first off the stage to the shock of guests Lionel Blair, Jim Bowen and Keith Chegwin. 'They'd researched it really hard,' says Tandy. 'So, early on, I got Jackie Ramsamy, a film researcher, to start clearing all this material they wanted, some of which was very difficult, almost unclearable. Things like the Bobby Davro accident have never been seen. They've snuck on to YouTube, but someone putting it up on YouTube doesn't mean it's clearable.'

'We thought we'd never get the permission,' says Steve.

'And Bobby was like, "Go on then,"' recalls Reece.

Since 'Dead Line' was a multi-camera show that would go out live, with pre-recorded elements that would need to be cued in on the night, Tandy handed the job of directing to Barbara Wiltshire, a veteran of panel shows such as *Was It Something I Said?* and who would go on to win the BAFTA for Best Director (Multicamera) for the episode. 'Barbara is a friend,' says Tandy. 'She's married to Stinky John [Marc Wootton, in "Sardines"], and I suddenly realised she was exactly the right person for this because although she'd not done an awful lot of scripted comedy or drama, as a multi-camera director she had the reflexes and skill to tell the story and keep the train on the tracks.'

The plan was to shoot at Granada, where Tandy and the boys had shot *The League of Gentlemen* specials. But a month before filming, Granada pulled out. 'They said, "We can't service your production any more. We've dug up the car park and you can't get any trucks in." And we'd written this story about being based at Granada. So not only did we not have a studio, but in theory, we didn't have a script either,' reveals Tandy, who convened an emergency telephone call with Shearsmith and Pemberton to work out what to do. Should they rewrite entirely or stick to the Manchester idea and find another multi-camera studio? They opted for the latter and quickly booked space at the TVS Studios in Maidstone, Kent. 'But, for all intents and purposes, we were in Manchester. Even Reece didn't tell his other half we were going to be in Maidstone. He let her believe they were in Manchester for three days. It got to the point where I thought we can't call it *Inside No. 9*, so we changed it to *Project Gemini*, and called it by that code name in order not to give the game away we weren't in Manchester.'

The studio switcheroo was just one part of the intricate sleight of hand involved in getting 'Dead Line' to air, where even cueing in the programme proved complex. 'Each regional part of the network was coming off a different source, so there was a different amount of time required for each announcement into the episode,' explains Tandy. 'And all of those had to coincide at the off points for our title sequence. So Becky [Rebecca Wright], the continuity announcer, recorded four different intros which we played

ABOVE: The set, ready for filming.

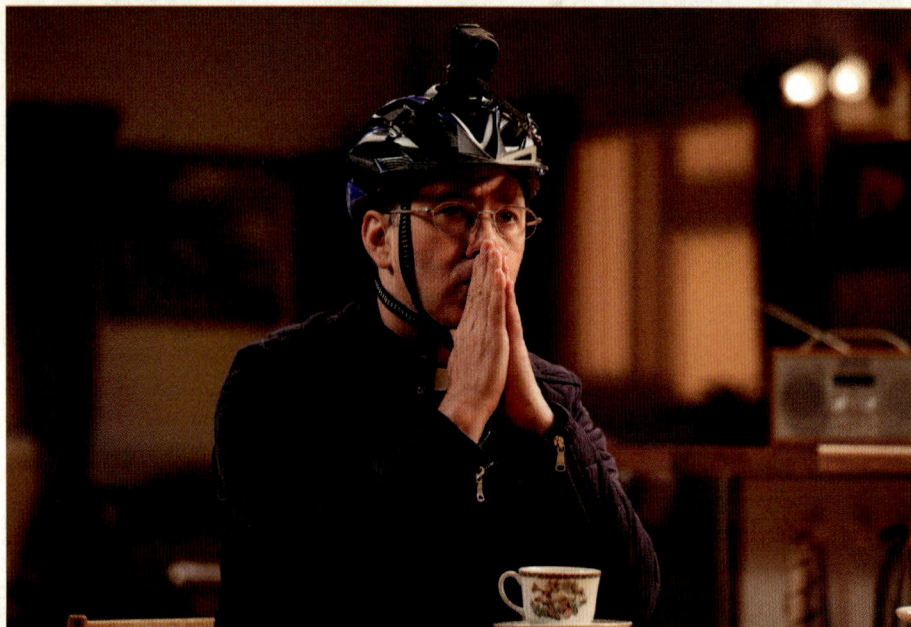

in, before we cut to the title sequence. Then we're on air, with Christian [Henson] playing his music live in the gallery.'

'Usually, you pre-prepare bits of music for someone to fire off,' says Henson. 'With horror, so much has to do with timing and anticipation. My argument was if we're ramping up to a scare as someone is walking across a room, what happens if they walk quicker or slower and we've got something pre-recorded?' The answer was for Henson to react directly to the action happening onscreen. 'I said I'd just perform it on a synth. So I had piano in my right hand and cello in my left and controlling how loud the music was against dialogue with how hard I was playing.'

The episode opens with Pemberton's elderly Arthur Flitwick walking along a short corridor, toward his front door – flat nine, of course – keying the lock, then opening it and entering his kitchen. 'It was the most terrified I've been in a long time,' he admits. 'All you're thinking is, "This is live. Everyone's watching. Don't let anything go wrong." You second guess everything. You're in a different world doing live TV.'

Pemberton wasn't the only one terrified. 'As the vicar, I had a cup of tea and I was literally shaking,' recalls Reece. 'I had to put it down. It was ridiculous.' While both men have experience of live theatre, this was 'more exposing', insists Reece. 'It's the millions watching and the scrutiny and the ghoulish fascination. That's the only reason you watch: to hope they'll fluff and to see how they will cope.'

'Plus, you've got six weeks' rehearsal in a play,' notes Steve. 'It was crucial we didn't make mistakes in that bit, because it would have undermined everything that went after. So we were determined that everything would go like clockwork.'

ABOVE: Reece as the vicar in his GoPro helmet, which later provided one of the cameras in the episode.

On entering his kitchen, Arthur puts down his shopping, turns on the radio – 'in rehearsals, I would knock it over, so I was thinking, "I've got to hold it"' – before cracking, then beating some eggs, and putting them in the microwave to cook. Arthur calls the last number dialled on a mobile he found in the local graveyard, speaking to a woman named Moira, who tells him the phone belongs to her friend Elsie. He asks her to let Elsie know he has it and says goodbye. Almost immediately a confused Moira rings back on the same mobile to tell Elsie that a nice man has found her phone. Arthur explains the mix-up, says goodbye again, then signs off and puts the phone down. Suddenly, the camera sweeps round the room, the scene changing from day to night. Arthur has a visitor, the Reverend Neil (Shearsmith), who's wearing a bicycle helmet with a GoPro on top. 'We thought that was important,' says Steve of the time jump. 'It looks like we've thought about the fact we're doing a live episode. We tried to make it as authentic as possible, even though it does look like *EastEnders*.'

Unfortunately, there's a problem with the sound. We can't hear anything the pair are saying. This goes on for a while before the picture cuts to the BBC Two logo and the continuity announcer apologises for the technical problems. 'In the script we cut very quickly to the logo and Adam said, "They wouldn't be so quick. It would have gone on for thirty seconds,"' explains Reece. 'So we had this excruciating bit where the sound's not there and everyone is thinking, "Oh no, how awful for them."'

'A bit like with "The Devil of Christmas", you needed a level of expertise and understanding of how TV works, and that's where we were very lucky to have Adam because he loves all this,' explains Steve. 'Even down to the continuity lady being the real one. So it wasn't an actor's voice coming in.'

When we cut back to Steve and Reece in the studio, the sound problems are still ongoing. The BBC Two logo then reappears, and the announcer apologises once more – 'we have a few gremlins in the system' – before informing us the episode will be rescheduled on another night and, in its place, there will be a repeat of 'A Quiet Night In'.

It was at this point that 'Dead Line' lost 20 per cent of its live audience, as viewers switched over

ABOVE: Steve as Arthur.

ABOVE: Steve and Reece in the 'dressing room' checking tweets.

Steve: Adam said that they're going to repeat
          'A Quiet Night In'.

Reece: What, now? Do we get a repeat fee?

or off, thinking the show really had gone wrong. Those who continued watching were treated to sixty-nine seconds of 'A Quiet Night In' before that also goes wrong, infected by a strange, ghostly figure of a young woman who appears dressed in a dirty shroud, her face hidden by long straggly hair and shadow. The music slows to a sluggish, unsettling drone, while the images remain at normal speed. Suddenly the woman is right up against the glass and then the picture flips upside down, before abruptly cutting. 'That was a big ask of an audience,' says Tandy of the repeated episode. 'You're expecting everybody to hang on that long before something different happens. And a lot did turn off. Some of them turned back on. Then the ones who turned off got very angry and watched it on iPlayer. And still complained about the sound.'

They weren't the only ones who were confused. 'Only a few people at BBC Two knew what was actually going on,' continues Tandy. 'There were a lot [of people] in transmission control for BBC One, looking across the corridor at BBC Two going, "What's happening? BBC Two seems to be in meltdown." Alarm bells were ringing. The show failed so spectacularly, people were watching it with horror. They were literally watching a car crash happen on screen, the way the BBC is not supposed to fall off the air.'

After the 'A Quiet Night In' breakdown, the BBC Two logo reappears and a strange voice whispers: 'Is someone there?' before cutting to a CCTV shot of Stephanie Cole, who's playing Moira, in the green room at Granada, flicking through a script. Suddenly, and incongruously, the Davro clip cuts in, with Lionel Blair singing 'Always Look on the Bright Side of Life' before Davro falls over. While the clip had been okayed for broadcast in the UK, the song wasn't cleared for the US. 'Meaning the feed going live to Brit Box in America had to have a special bit of static squeezed into it in Manchester. Because the feed was going from Maidstone to London to Manchester, then across to America,' explains Tandy. 'So Manchester was fucking up the show deliberately to cover a music copyright problem.'

From the horror of the Davro clip, we cut to Steve and Reece in the make-up room, again shot via a fixed CCTV camera high up in the corner. The pair, 'unaware' they're being filmed, discuss the problems so far and whether they'll try again with the episode after *Match of the Day 2*, moaning about Cole's 'shit' accent, namedropping both Tandy and Plowman who have gone for 'a meeting upstairs'. Steve asks Reece: 'What are they saying on Twitter?' Reece starts scrolling through his phone, reading one Tweet aloud: '"What's going on with *Inside No. 9*? Is this part of the twist?" Oh, do fuck off!' he spits, annoyed. 'We were looking at our own phones while we were being filmed,' reveals Reece, 'reading live responses of people going, "Oh my God, it's gone wrong." Derren Brown texted me: "Commiserations, mate." Ha ha tricked you. I wanted to read them, but I couldn't.'

We then cut to the first clip from *Most Haunted*, in which David Wells' medium walks through the studio with *Corrie* actors Sue Cleaver and Simon Gregson, picking up psychic echoes of a crew member who, he says, died of a heart attack or accident ten years before. In the green room, Cole hears a mobile ringing. It's the prop phone from 'Dead Line'. She answers it, telling the caller, whose name is Alan and says he works at Granada, that she's part of the cast of *Inside No. 9*. 'No, I hadn't heard of it either, but it's a BBC Two sort of comedy thing.'

Back in make-up, Steve reads out a story from his phone, telling Reece how *Coronation Street* producers were forced to perform an exorcism at Granada, and how the studios are said to be cursed, following the fire that destroyed the costumes of *The Jewel in the Crown*. He also mentions Davro's freak accident. Reece tells him that Mark Gatiss has sent them a message on the *League* WhatsApp group – 'there is one,' laughs Steve – instructing them to turn the TV in the room to BBC Two. They switch it on, get BBC One – and the *News at Ten* – then switch over to BBC Two and see themselves live on TV. Not quite believing it, Steve suggests to Reece that he Tweet: 'Are me and Steve Pemberton on BBC Two now?' He does. And Gatiss is the first to reply: 'Yes.'

'He was in on it,' admits Reece.

'There was quite a lot of pre-arranged Tweeting,' confirms Tandy. 'But Reece put that out live. We didn't really trust anybody else to do it at the right moment. The only thing we had to do was make sure the BBC social accounts were on message. We didn't want them to make jokes. Just to apologise and say, "We're looking into it."'

'My mum thought it was real when we were sat talking,' says Reece. 'We wanted to know our lines well enough to not fluff. But not to rehearse too much so that it didn't feel natural.'

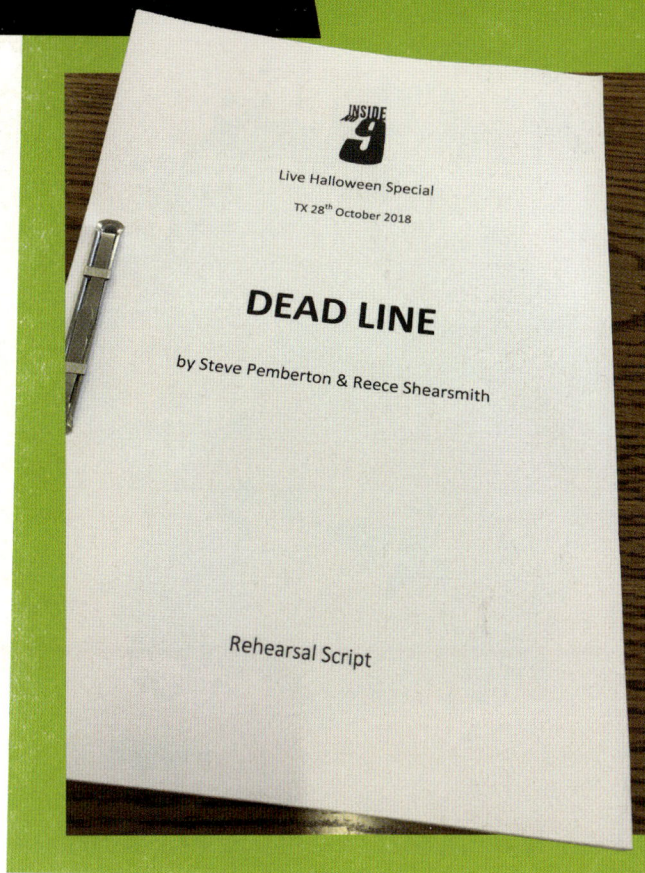

ABOVE: A rehearsal script for the episode.

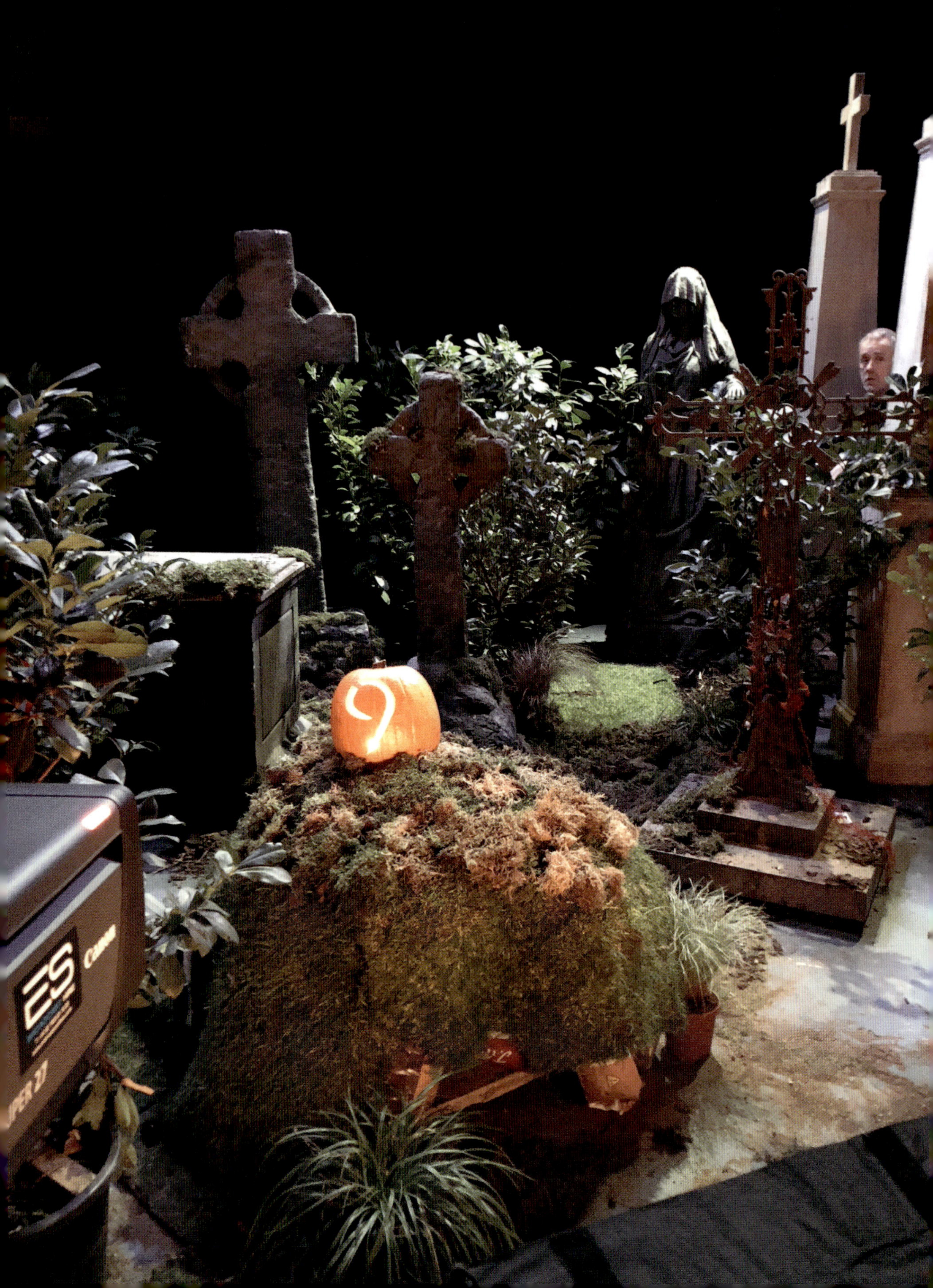
ES
Canon

And it's now that 'Dead Line' *really* goes off the rails. We see footage of Arthur in the shower, covered in blood, having killed Reverend Neil, whose severed head is revealed to be in the microwave. The doorbell rings and Arthur opens it, showing in Moira, but the scene breaks down as Cole asks a question of Pemberton, mistaking him for Shearsmith. ('That was all pre-recorded, but we made it look like rehearsal footage with a burnt in timecode,' says Tandy.) We see a quick shot of Alan Starr (Robin Berry) before cutting to a possessed Stephanie in the green room droning on about Samhain – the Gaelic version of Halloween – and spirits infecting the equipment, to which Reece replies: 'You're thinking of *Black Mirror* … This is *Inside No. 9*. It's more dark comedy and twists.'

'We were aware that we had given Stephanie a lot of lines, and experienced though she is, she had a big speech,' says Steve. 'We told her, "Do it in a measured way because you're in a trance." But because we were running slightly over, they said to her, "You've got to really speed up." But she was brilliant. After we finished, she said, "This is one of the two best things I've ever done. This and the [Alan] Bennett monologue."'

'Can't get better than that,' laughs Reece. 'But they were also running in during our gaps, when the pre-recorded footage was on, saying, "You're going too quick" or "You're going too slow". Because one of the dangers was you'd go too fast because you'd panic. But then there were bits when they were saying, "Could you tighten it up a bit? Because we're going to be overlong."'

As Reece leaves to make a cup of tea, Stephanie picks up the large knife Arthur had used to 'kill' the Reverend Neil, and we cut to Steve, on his phone, in the make-up room, as, on the TV behind him, we see Stephanie cut her throat.

Meanwhile, backstage, near a caged electrical area, a mop and bucket are tipped over by unseen forces, spilling water on the floor. 'That was live,' says Steve. 'It was on a fishing wire.'

Up in the empty studio gallery all the monitors go dead. (The crew are supposedly in the conference room 'being burnt by ghosts', says Tandy. 'There was one version where I was burnt alive, and I thought, "I'm not going to do that on the night."') Another *Most Haunted* clip plays, with historian Richard Felix talking about how Granada was built on a burial site for plague victims, and we see archival footage of the 'priest' in an empty studio trying to cast out unclean spirits.

Back in make-up, the figure of a small Victorian child can be seen standing in a doorway. Then

ABOVE: Stephanie Cole lies slumped on the sofa after cutting her own throat.

LEFT: The graveyard set.

```
Steve:      Look, BBC One. BBC Two, and BBC Four.
Reece:      Do BBC Three.
Steve:      There is no BBC Three.
```

we cut to Reece's GoPro as he makes a cup of tea. 'I remember that being a "Eureka" moment, when we thought of the GoPro,' says Steve. 'Because how do you keep filming when you're not actively filming it? And we went, "Reece could have a cycle helmet with a camera on." Suddenly, we could go into a first-person viewpoint.'

'It was tricky to get right,' says Reece of filming with the GoPro. 'You needed to look lower than you think you do to get a good angle and hope you're capturing it because you don't have a monitor.'

Hearing a noise backstage, Reece goes to investigate, walking into the electrical area, and looking around, as the door shuts behind him by itself. Walking along an aisle, he sees his own severed head on the floor in front of him. As Reece bends down to pick it up, a masked figure jumps out, making him scream. It's Steve – who takes off his mask, laughing, then walks away. As Steve tries to open the cage door, he's electrocuted. 'There's a film called *The Believers* with Martin Sheen which has the most horrible electrocution in a film I've ever seen,' says Reece. 'His wife is boiling a kettle and he comes in and the milk has spilt and she's being electrocuted, but it looks like she's just standing there. And that's what we wanted for Steve's electrocution.' It was an effect that was done live using a small electrical charge.

We cut to a (fake) TV news report about Starr and his interest in electronic voice phenomenon (EVP), then to the *Granada Reports* footage of Tony Wilson reporting on *The Jewel in the Crown* fire, then

ABOVE: Reece nervously makes his way around the seemingly abandoned set.

back to the studio where a panicked Reece comes across Stephanie lying in a pool of her own blood. Suddenly the lights go out. Reece's GoPro switches to night vision and he charges aimlessly through the studio, stumbling into a graveyard set built for 'Dead Line' where he sees several ghosts/dead people, then runs up a stairway and onto a balcony where, catching sight of another ghostly figure, he falls off, breaking his neck. All the night vision footage was pre-recorded for health and safety reasons. 'We could have done it live,' says Tandy. 'But it was the payoff to the show. There was no other way of getting that material, except from this camera, and we had to have the ghost effect at the end.'

'The placing of the ghosts in and around the episode was very carefully done,' says Reece. 'And there are some that no one has found. It was quite creepy to have Alan Starr, the crew member who killed himself, walking around. We'd seen photos of him beforehand, and then he was there on the day to flit about, and it was like, "Oh, you're that dead man."'

The final sting comes as the episode switches back to the finale of 'A Quiet Night In' as Reece and Steve's characters are shot through the head, over and over again, on a loop, before cutting to a clip of them on *The One Show*, which had gone out the previous Friday. In it, they're asked if they believe in ghosts. 'And we say, "Absolutely not,"' recalls Reece. 'Because we wanted that clip.'

'Dead Line' came off air twenty seconds later than it should have done. 'Our dress run indicated we were slightly over, so we asked for that from the channel, and they very kindly offered up a bit of extra airtime,' says Tandy. 'Everything worked like clockwork. It was the smoothest piece of live TV I have ever been involved in, yet it looked like chaos.'

'I remember punching the air at the end, which I'd never done in my life,' says Steve. 'But it was so exhilarating.'

'I think I collapsed,' laughs Reece. As the cast and crew drank a celebratory glass of champagne, someone pointed out that Reece and Steve's Wikipedia pages had been changed to reflect the date and manner of their onscreen deaths: Steve Pemberton: electrocuted; Reece Shearsmith: death by falling. 'Even Stephanie Cole. It said: "Committed suicide while possessed by demons during a live TV broadcast,"' laughs Steve.

'It lasted about an hour until some killjoy changed it back,' remembers Reece. 'But it was so funny to see how this bled into real life. We were dead for a good hour.'

For the 80 per cent of the audience who had stuck with it, 'Dead Line' was a once-in-a-lifetime event. 'What was fascinating was how the interaction with the audience became part of the narrative, with people watching it, stopping, then hearing they shouldn't have stopped by looking on Twitter,' says Steve. 'It created this thing between us and the audience that, unless you were watching it live, you wouldn't have fully appreciated. Even now I get people asking, "What happened with that live one?" As if people watching it on iPlayer don't bother to scroll past the repeat to see if it does carry on. That's testament to the fact everything we did up to that point felt really real.'

BELOW: The cast and crew celebrated with champagne after the feat of the live episode was achieved. The hare and Reece's severed head look on.

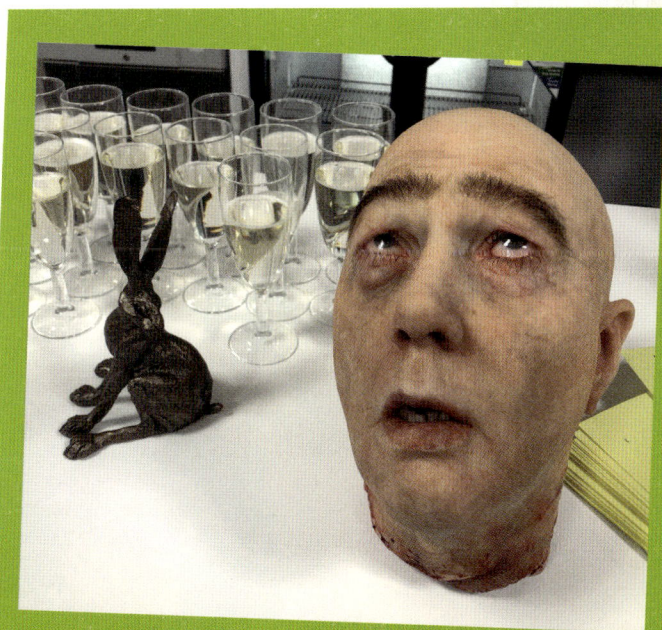

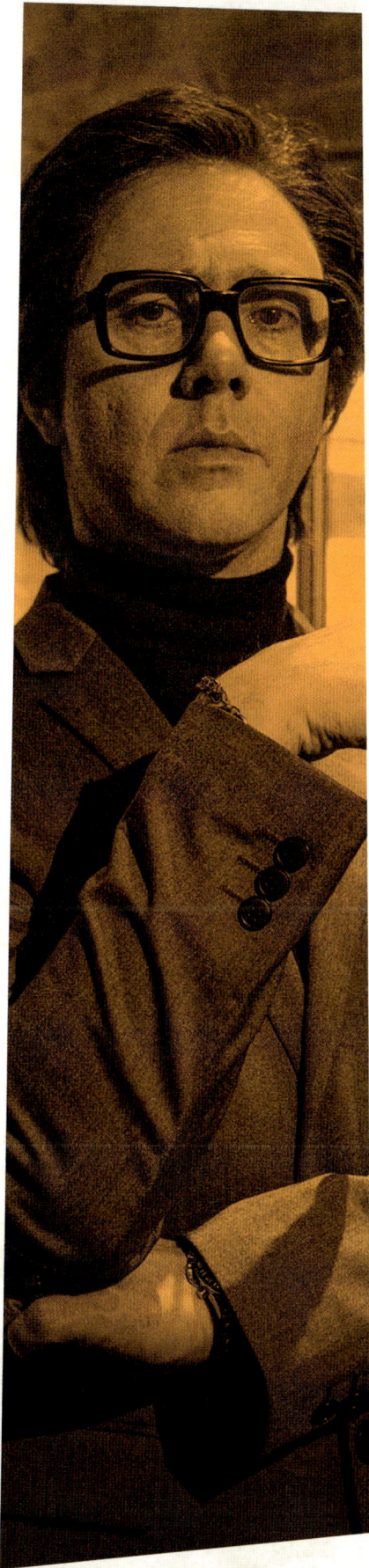

SERIES FIVE

HE'S IN CONTROL. BUT FOR HOW LONG?

THE REFEREE'S A W**ER

INSIDE NO. 9 RETURNS
MONDAY 3RD FEBRUARY AT 10PM
BBC TWO

The Referee's a W***er

- Series **5**
- Episode **1**
- Directed by **Matt Lipsey**

'The Referee's a W***er' opens with the now legendary quote from the late Liverpool manager Bill Shankly: 'Some people think football is a matter of life and death. I don't like that attitude. I can assure you it's much more serious than that.' And so it proves in series five's opener, an episode all about the love football supporters have for their team, and the lengths to which some are prepared to go for them.

Pemberton is a football fan; Shearsmith is not. 'One day I was reading a newspaper account of a manager or player who tried to get into the officials' changing room after a game, and it got me thinking,' recalls Steve, who supports Blackburn Rovers. 'No one ever sees what happens backstage at a football match, and a bit like with "The Understudy", you could be in the changing room while the drama has happened on the pitch. Equally, the structure of it appealed. It's before the match. It's

ABOVE: The episode poster was designed by Andy Bottomley.

half-time. And it's after the match. That gave you a neat three acts.'

Before sitting down to write, Pemberton genned up on all aspects of refereeing. 'It's a really interesting, little talked-about and little seen aspect of football. They carry such huge responsibilities. And are vilified. I read up a lot, listened to podcasts, to referees, getting the language, imagining what the changing room would be like, and realised it could be really tense and dramatic because there's so much at stake. That was the important thing: making it a match where the result counted. I knew it would be to do with sports betting, corruption and a decision made erroneously. But it was a real headache figuring out who was orchestrating what and why.'

'It didn't matter if you didn't know football. It was the people, the passion and the characters that drove it. Some were surprised, thinking they're not going to enjoy a football one, but it's like any other No. 9,' says Reece. 'Of course, there's lots of technical stuff. It was like Russian to me, utter gobbledygook, but I learned it phonetically, and said the lines.'

Another big influence in terms of the structure was *Clockwise*, starring John Cleese. 'You start with one character saying, "I am going to run this smoothly and perfectly, and I don't want anything to go awry." Then you enjoy, bit by bit, seeing him lose control,' says Steve. 'I thought if we get the narrative right, he looks like he's desperately trying to keep this on the straight and narrow, and it makes for a delicious ending when he is revealed to have orchestrated the whole thing.'

Taking place on the final day of the Championship, the match between United and Rovers holds great significance for both. If United win, they'll be promoted to the Premier League with all the financial rewards that come with that. If Rovers win, they escape relegation. For the referee, the officious Martin Rutherford (David Morrissey), it marks his final game, prior to retirement, and he wants his fellow officials – hapless Oggy (Pemberton), narcissist Phil (Ralf Little), and dull Brendan

ABOVE: Left to right: Brendan (Reece Shearsmith), Phil (Ralf Little), Martin (David Morrissey) and Oggy (Steve Pemberton).

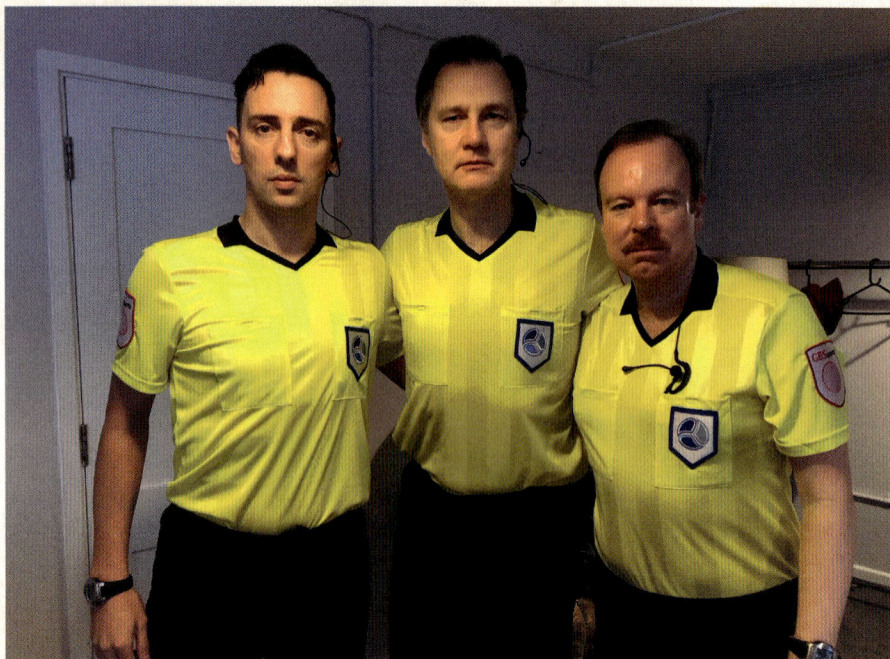

> **Brendan:** At the San Siro they had a treadmill in the officials' changing room. And someone came in every twenty minutes to replenish the towels. It's the little touches.

(Shearsmith) – to be on their best behaviour. But over the next two hours, all hell breaks loose, on the pitch and in the dressing room, after Martin's secret relationship with United captain Calvin (Dipo Ola) and allegations of match fixing by a Qatari betting syndicate come to light.

Full of ambiguity, intrigue and drama, 'The Referee's a W***er' is another episode that plays with audience perceptions right until its bombshell ending, which forces you to re-evaluate everything you've seen, even the title. Does it refer to that evergreen footballing chant, 'The Referee's a Wanker'? Or could it be that 'The Referee's a Winner'? Both are valid, although the boys won't commit one way or the other. 'Sometimes you just love a title and "The Referee's a W***er", with asterisks, we fell in love with,' says Steve.

'As soon as I read it, I realised the title could be construed as *Winner*, because that is what the referee is,' says Tandy. 'He's the one manipulating everything and the asterisks hide the story in plain sight. It's a very strange, high-concept episode and the ambiguity of the title is an extra joke.'

Similarly, there was some debate as to what the nine refers to, since the changing room doesn't have a number. Is it Calvin's position on the pitch? He wears number nine, after all. Another is more sexual in nature. 'If it had been as straightforward as a number on a changing room, we might have done it,' says Steve. 'The only way it worked was the number nine shirt. But it doesn't really fit, unless he is an inside number nine, or [Martin] has been *inside* the number nine, which is the implication.'

'It's a bit of both,' suggests Reece.

ABOVE: Ralf Little, David Morrissey and Steve in costume.

'The thing about "The Referee's a W***er" is it misleads the audience as to what you think it's about,' says Tandy. 'The corruption is seeded right the way through, yet you don't realise it's the audience that's being played, in terms of what the actual corruption is, and who's responsible for it. A lot of it is misdirection, because you're hoping the audience will assume the ref's reticence and closeted nature is to do with his sexuality, rather than the corruption story, which is at the heart of what's going on.'

Matt Lipsey, who directed all of *Psychoville*, had never been available to work on *Inside No. 9* – until now. Drafted in to helm the next episode – 'Death Be Not Proud' – he was given this too. 'We'd had a fantastic time with him on *Psychoville*,' says Steve. 'He's great with actors. Great with action. He's meticulous. *And* he's a football fan.'

'He gets funny, but he's very serious and grills you about every surreal, odd or stupid moment in the script,' adds Reece. 'He'll say, "How is that justified?" And it might be the silliest thing. But it's good. It's rigorous the way he'll want an answer.'

To play the manipulative, conniving, eponymous official, they turned to David Morrissey, star of *The Walking Dead*, who had appeared in *The League of Gentlemen* reboot. 'Even then, I could tell it wasn't enough for him,' laughs Tandy. 'He really wanted a guest role on *Inside No. 9*. So I think he was uppermost in everybody's mind when those parts were written. Reece and Steve liked being the junior officials and getting some big guys to come and do the chunkier, more athletic roles. Here they're the comic chorus.'

'Steve or I could have played [David's] part, but we thought, "Let's give it to a leading man who's got that drive,"' reflects Reece. 'And it seemed to fit with David's football credentials. He never gets to do comedy, but he's really funny. Although he's quite straight in this, ironically.'

'He has the authority, height and power,' insists Steve. 'You wouldn't mess with him. We're friends. So we sent him the script and hoped. Luckily, he loved it. I knew he would.'

There was, however, one major sticking point. At the end of the episode, when Martin removes his top, we see a massive back tattoo with the words 'City till I die' on it. Originally, it was going to say 'United'. As a lifelong Liverpool fan, Morrissey point-blank refused. 'He said, "I can't do it. I'll never be able to go home to Liverpool,"' recalls Steve. So the boys had to rename the teams to keep him happy. 'You think, wow. That transcends your natural ability and desire to shapeshift as an actor,' says Lipsey, who supports Chelsea. 'But then you go, "Okay, as a football fan, I get that."'

Ralf Little, star of *The Royle Family*, is similarly football mad; he even had trials to be a professional footballer. 'Ralf brought an authenticity to it,' says Steve, who co-starred with him on stage in *Dead Funny*. 'Originally I thought Reece would play that role, because he's northern and grumpy, and was quite surprised when Reece said, "No, I want to play Brendan." He knew that's where the laughs were.'

Brendan is the fourth official, a boring little man constantly banging on about the time he officiated at the San Siro. 'I didn't realise it's a bit of a shithole now,' laughs Steve, who plays the second assistant. 'It was just the notion of someone droning on about, "In my day …" I had been to the San Siro years ago, so that popped into my mind. It just *sounds* funny.'

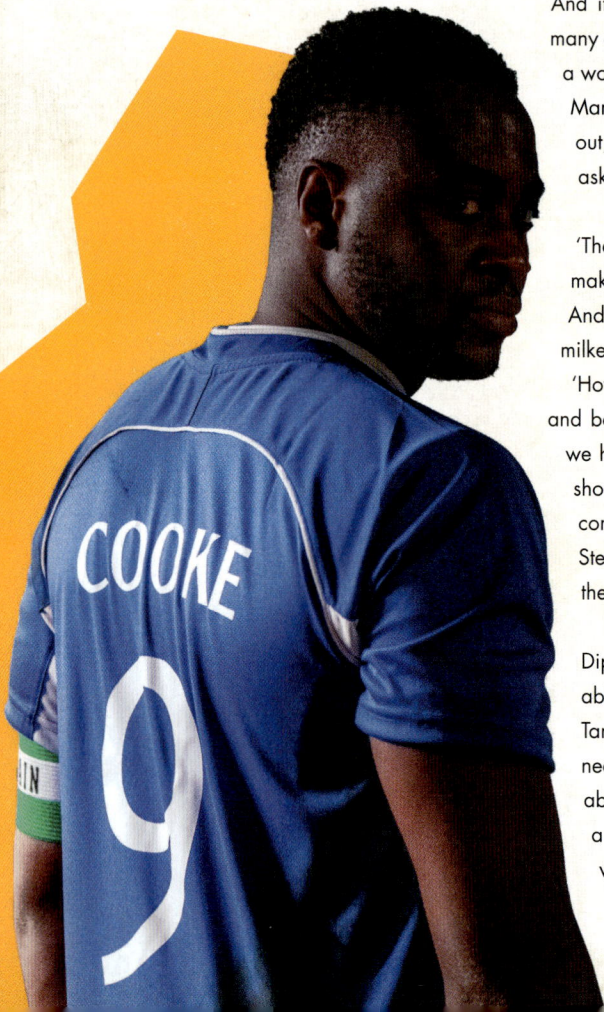

BELOW: Dipo Ola as team captain Calvin Cooke.

And it's Brendan who gets the majority of the episode's best gags, many of which involve bodily functions and pungent aromas, as well as a wonderful bit of slapstick when he's left standing, sans shorts, after Martin's relationship with Calvin comes out and the player storms out, having been red carded. At first, Brendan is speechless, then asks: 'Should I put all that in the report?'

'For me, that is the comic moment of the episode,' says Tandy. 'There was an enormous pause and I said to Reece, "Go for it, make it as long as you like. We can always shorten it in the edit." And when we did a second take, he just milked it and milked it and milked it. And we used nearly all of it.'

'How long is funny? And do you dare to let it go till it's beyond funny and becoming awkward?' muses Lipsey. 'Those were the discussions we had, and they carried on through to the cut, as to how long we should go on it. We ended up with what I would describe as a compromise. Not in a bad way. I think Reece went one way and Steve the other. But it's a great moment. Out of the bathos comes the pathos.'

Making his TV debut as Rovers' captain and Martin's lover was Dipo Ola, then fresh out of drama school. 'We needed somebody able to do the sensitive stuff, but he also had to be believable,' says Tandy. 'David is six foot two, and whoever was playing Calvin needed to be a match for him, physically. What we really liked about Dipo was not only did he have the acting chops, he's also a footballer. We didn't have to see him playing, but you felt he would inhabit that world.'

> **Oggy:** We kick off at three, quarter four it's a pie and a piss, then ten to five for Final Score and first round in; it's not rocket science.

To this day, there has only ever been one openly gay premiership footballer – Justin Fashanu – so the sight of Martin and Calvin kissing is shocking because of the context and setting, not because it's two men kissing. 'If I'm honest, I don't think I realised the impact it would have until we were doing it,' says Lipsey. 'How extraordinary it should be so affecting. It's the fact that this environment is so utterly male-driven. Of course, there are homosexual men within that world. And how ridiculous and sad they have to be closeted, still, because no one else has been prepared to do what Justin did. It's brilliantly shocking. And that was the boys' intention. In my mind, that kiss was going to be more sensual, more lingering, and what ensued was quite tame and gentle, and was better for it.'

The fifth member of the cast was Steve Speirs, who plays Mitch, the Rovers' mascot, wearing a nondescript mammal costume. 'I based it on real animals,' says costume designer Yves Barre. 'I had six or seven animals on a mood board and was literally morphing them on the computer into something very generic. The fur was a bigger problem. It had to be quite dark, but the length and type was a huge to-do.'

'You could have done a whole half hour just on the rivalry between these mascots,' says Steve. 'It's such a rich world. We wanted to cover as many aspects of football as possible, without it being a football story. Because it's a love story.'

ABOVE: Steve as the hapless Oggy.

Tandy's first instinct was to film in a real changing room, but, again, they were all too small, so production designer Amy Maguire, who was promoted from art director for series five, built it on stage at Ealing Studios. 'The set was sublime,' says Lipsey. 'The idea they're hunkered down, almost in a bunker, was hugely important. Amy did a brilliant job. The attention to detail was remarkable. The way she got the paint peeling … it's sad, it's a club that needs money.'

'As match officials are often the most vilified people on the pitch, I loved the idea of how oppressively "beneath" the stand the set could feel if we slanted the roof,' says Maguire, who also angled the walls to create more interesting shapes and divided the room into sections to facilitate movement in the blocking of the action. 'I wanted to ensure the set was designed in a way the atmosphere outside could be felt inside. The glass bricks off the corridor meant we could see the characters retreating from the scuffles happening in the tunnel, and the idea of the top windows was to generate a sense of the atmosphere, so the crowd's energy and movement at half-time could be felt in the room below.'

'Ideally, we wanted a few more extras. In the end, we had two people going backwards and forwards, but it still worked,' says Lipsey.

'They couldn't do it too much because the set was made of wood and steel and creaked,' laughs Tandy, who, one lunchtime, took twenty crew out and recorded them singing and chanting. Supervising sound editor Chris MacLean then used the recordings to replicate the noise of the crowd.

Lipsey opted to film with a mostly handheld camera. 'What was clear to me was I needed this thing to move. It had to reflect the intensity and anxiety of the central character. The fact he never really stands still was in my head from the get-go, and each act needed to use him as the pivot point.

ABOVE: Brendan holds back mascot Mitch (Steve Speirs) as things get out of hand.

As he moved, the action would move around him. The whole thing is restless.'

Morrissey brought both technical prowess and endless variety to his performance. 'He did takes where he was a little bit more arch, and others where he completely buried it,' says Reece. 'And all the way along there are slight variations to tip the wink or not. In the end we kept it all quite hidden. But you could dial it up or down accordingly.'

'If you watch it a second time, you can see the little tells David gives,' says Tandy. 'He actually gave a lot more in performance. That was brilliant for us, because that allowed us to select what we needed and to dial back the rest, to make sure his performance was truthful and authentic, but if you look at it in hindsight, you can see he is hiding something all the way through.'

'He didn't feel he had to do a comedy turn,' says Lipsey. 'He came in and did exactly what he needed to, which was to play it straight. And brought an amazing intensity. He needs to come across as this guy who plays it by the book and David absolutely got that.'

Come the ending, it's clear Martin has orchestrated events on and off the field in order to create chaos and help his team gain automatic promotion. However, it's not clear whether he is, in fact, behind the Qatar syndicate. 'That's there to be inferred,' says Steve. 'The interesting question is, did he set up this relationship with Calvin and throw this guy under the bus, or did he genuinely love him? And there isn't a definitive answer. But he's poking the hornet's nest all the way through. He knows every character's weakness. He knows Oggy is going to be the one to take the bung. But he knows he has to have Phil hear the information so it can all come out. In the end, it spirals out of control, but you see Martin has made it go like clockwork, and that felt like a satisfying through line. A bit like "The Bill", what we are watching is the version where he succeeds.'

ABOVE: Yves Barre's collage for the mascot costume. Throughout the episode, various characters disagree over which creature the mascot is supposed to be.

JENNA COLEMAN   KADIFF KIRWAN   STEVE PEMBERTON   REECE SHEARSMITH

BBC TWO PRESENTS A BBC STUDIOS PRODUCTION
AN **INSIDE NO. 9** FILM

DEATH BE NOT PROUD

THE PAST IS NEVER DEAD.

IT'S NOT EVEN PAST

BBC TWO PRESENTS A BBC STUDIOS PRODUCTION AN INSIDE NO. 9 FILM "DEATH BE NOT PROUD" JENNA COLEMAN KADIFF KIRWAN DUBBING MIXERS JOHN ROGERSON AND SIMON HILL SUPERVISING SOUND EDITOR CHRIS MACLEAN LINE PRODUCER EMILY SHAPLAND EDITED BY JOE RANDALL-CUTLER MUSIC BY CHRISTIAN HENSON COSTUME DESIGNER YVES BARRE MAKE UP DESIGNER NICOLA COLEM PRODUCTION DESIGNER AMY MAGUIRE DIRECTOR OF PHOTOGRAPHY JOHN SORAPURE WRITTEN BY STEVE PEMBERTON & REECE SHEARSMITH EXECUTIVE PRODUCER JON PLOWMAN PRODUCED BY ADAM TANDY DIRECTED BY MATT LIPSEY

Death Be Not Proud

- Series **5**
- Episode **2**
- Directed by **Matt Lipsey**

ABOVE: The episode poster was designed by Amy Maguire.

A couple moving into a murder house was an idea that had been on the cards since series one, and was inspired by the close proximity of serial killer Dennis Nilsen's property to where the boys live. 'That was a huge part of it,' says Steve. 'It made it easier to imagine because you've got one down the road. You would go past and wonder who lives there now. We didn't know if it was going to be supernatural or psychological. How does it feel? How does it affect a couple to know they've got a cheap house or a flat because a serial killer killed people there? So that was an interesting idea on its own.'

'A bit like a phone call from the dead, it just felt like a *No. 9*,' reflects Reece.

As they discussed the idea further, their thoughts turned to the possible identity of the killer/s. 'And once we start talking about murders in houses,' notes Steve, 'those characters loom large.'

'We thought, "What if it ends up being Maureen and David's flat [from *Psychoville*]?" And it's redecorated. So you wouldn't realise it was,' says Reece. 'Then we could go back in time and have some more Maureen and David. We had a lot of debate about whether or not they had ever been found out for being murderers. Therefore, could you have the house belonging to a serial killer if he got away with it? But we squared it in our minds and thought we could make it fit.'

Back when a third season of *Psychoville* was still a possibility, the boys had plotted out a storyline that involved David moving in with Emily and having a baby, but then Maureen comes back as a ghost and she's not happy with her daughter-in-law and grandchild. 'We had a whole *Psycho*/Norman Bates thing with the mother,' reveals Reece.

'Death Be Not Proud' was designed as both a sequel and prequel to *Psychoville*, meaning Maureen could be alive again, and not just appear as a ghost. 'The line that clinched it was: "Get that baby boiled,"' explains Steve. 'And as soon as we came up with this image of David being forced, almost, to boil his baby, we just thought, "We've got to do that."' Suddenly the floodgates opened. 'It allowed us to bring some of that *Psychoville* style into *Inside No. 9*, and to do jokes we would never do in *Inside No. 9*, really horrific stuff that we would never normally think of doing.'

'They're big characters, so it was great to have the reins off again. Because *No. 9* is very restrained in comparison,' says Reece. 'We were like, "Wow, this is what we used to do." And however dark it

ABOVE: This episode sees the return of *Psychoville* fan favourites Maureen (Reece) and David (Steve).

David: I met Emily at my job doing Murder Mystery evenings... We bonded over our shared passion for Jack the Ripper.

was, it was still really funny. For those that liked *Psychoville* and bemoaned its demise, we hoped it would be a great surprise if we could return with another dip into that world. Others, as I suspected, thought, "They've ran out of ideas." Quite the opposite. It was a celebration. And an enjoyment. Although some people were, "It's not *No. 9*." We just thought it would be a great, fun way of bringing them back. The new flat-owner answers the door and it's David from *Psychoville*. So this was like the point on a Venn diagram between the two shows.'

'It's what they call, in music, terms a mash-up,' says Matt Lipsey, who had directed all of *Psychoville*. 'I don't believe there is another show that's done what they've done. It's quite extraordinary. And I couldn't have been more thrilled or more excited by the opportunity to revisit. I would have moved heaven and earth to do it. It was like putting on a pair of very old, much loved, bloodstained slippers.'

'Death Be Not Proud' begins with a young couple, Beattie (Jenna Coleman) and Sam (Kadiff Kirwan), moving into a new flat, which they've managed to buy cheaply on account of its sinister past. But before you can say mango smoothie, a massive crack appears in one wall, kitchen appliances switch themselves on in the middle of the night, and ping-pong balls roll along the floor from seemingly nowhere. Concerned the property may be haunted, Beattie reaches out to former tenant and serial killer obsessive David Sowerbutts (Pemberton), who recounts a tale that involves his late mum Maureen

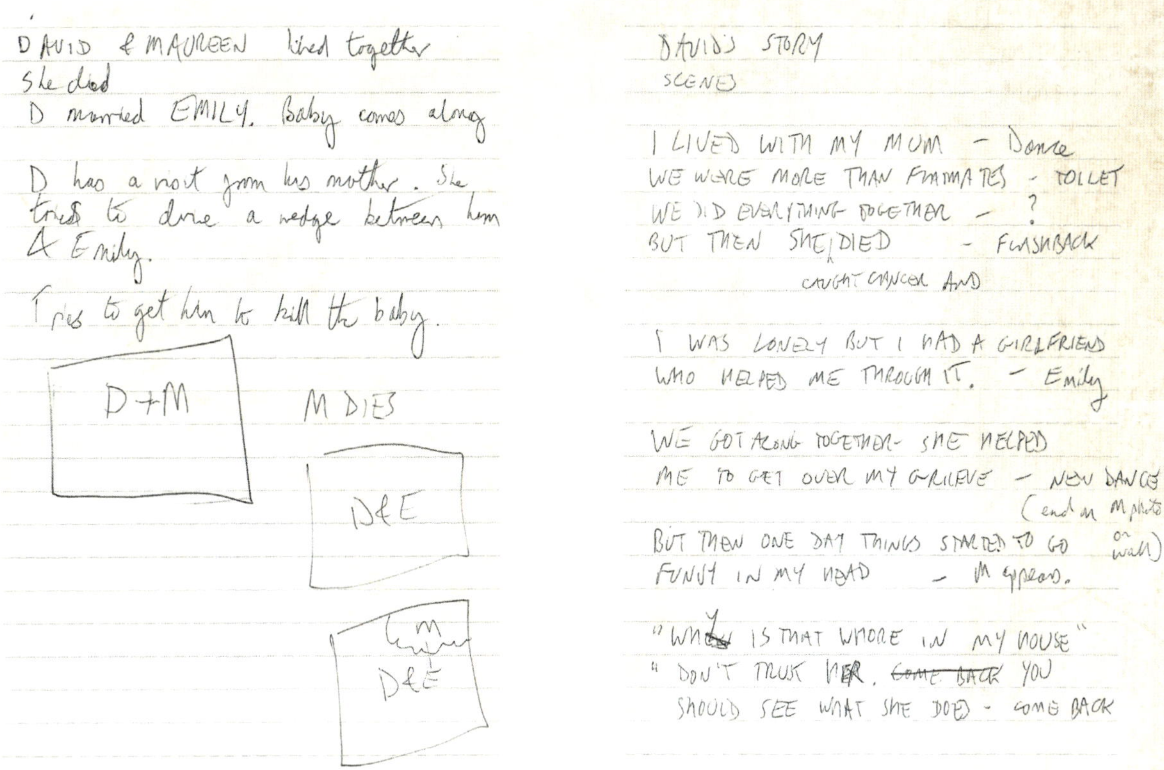

Handwritten notes (left page):

DAVID & MAUREEN lived together
She died
D married EMILY. Baby comes along

D has a visit from his mother. She tries to drive a wedge between him & Emily.

Tries to get him to kill the baby.

D+M   M DIES

D&E

D&E

Handwritten notes (right page):

DAVID'S STORY
SCENES

I LIVED WITH MY MUM   — Dance
WE WERE MORE THAN FLATMATES - TOILET
WE DID EVERYTHING TOGETHER — ?
BUT THEN SHE DIED   — FLASHBACK
                 CAUGHT CANCER AND

I WAS LONELY BUT I HAD A GIRLFRIEND
WHO HELPED ME THROUGH IT. — Emily

WE GOT ALONG TOGETHER- SHE HELPED
ME TO GET OVER MY GRIEVE — NEW DANCE
                     (end in M photo
BUT THEN ONE DAY THINGS STARTED TO GO   on
FUNNY IN MY HEAD   — M appears.   wall)

"WHO IS THAT WHORE IN MY HOUSE"
" DON'T TRUST HER. COME BACK YOU
SHOULD SEE WHAT SHE DOES - COME BACK

(Shearsmith), with whom he shared the flat and had a somewhat unhealthy relationship, her ghost, as well as his girlfriend Emily and their baby.

Shearsmith had co-starred with Coleman in *Doctor Who* and heard she was a fan. 'So we thought, "Is she free?"' he laughs. 'She's a bit of a Janet Leigh in it. You think she's going to be the thrust and is almost sidelined when our old characters come back in.' Tonally, the scenes between Beattie and David were crucial to the episode working. 'Jenna was the bridge between *Inside No. 9* and *Psychoville*,' says Steve. 'Doing my scenes with her was very different to doing scenes with Reece as Maureen. With Jenna it's a slightly older, slightly more sober David, still with the same intonations and lack of connectedness to the world. We had two days with her. And to get someone of her magnitude was fantastic, because it really sold the dummy.'

'They're so clever, Reece and Steve,' enthuses Lipsey. 'They managed to create an episode which revisits two fully formed characters from another show and bring them to this single episode where it holds together. It's properly bonkers because those two characters are so out there, but it's completely self-contained and watchable, if you know nothing about them.'

'The structure of this episode is something we hadn't done before, which is one character coming in, telling the story, with a lot of flashbacks,' continues Steve. 'So you're constantly going between me, as older David, telling the story to Jenna's character. It's a lot of short scenes. And that freed us up in a way. Normally we'd stay in the room and be with those characters. And if we'd done the story of the couple moving into the flat, we would have stayed in the present tense. It was great to once again find a different storytelling technique. And in constructing the life of David and Maureen prior to her death, we got to see Maureen in her pomp, not just as a ghost. So it felt quite natural to say, "And then she died", and play *that* scene again.'

ABOVE: A page from one of Steve's notebooks with notes and ideas for the episode.

In addition to David and Maureen, 'Death Be Not Proud' manages to bring back Mr Jelly, David Bamber's Robin, and Sarah Solemani's Emily. 'Normally you write, then cast whoever can do it,' explains Steve. 'In this instance we knew it had to be Sarah. So I sent her a message to see if she was available. Because if she wasn't, we would have had to recast or rethink. Luckily she said, "Whatever it takes, I'm going to be there."' In fact, Solemani, who lives in Los Angeles, was so keen to be part of the reunion she flew herself back to the UK.

Robin's reappearance is, perhaps, the most eye-opening of all. The phenomenon of 'adult babies' was another idea the boys had scribbled in a notebook after watching a documentary about it years earlier. 'Every time you'd look through the notebook you'd see it,' says Steve. 'You could have told that story without that scene, but it's such an unexpected thing to see. And it tickled us, the idea of Robin in a nappy and a bonnet. You want it to be as bizarre as possible. It is *Psychoville*, after all. You've got to do what it says on the tin.'

That also meant recreating Maureen and David's flat from scratch. '*Psychoville* was one of my first experiences of the art department,' says production designer Amy Maguire, 'so I had the advantage of having a very vague memory of the geography of the set from having been there making baked bean smoothies. We didn't manage to source any of the original plans, so I worked out the dimensions by seeing the ceiling height was most likely eight feet and taking an average of how far apart things looked when watching the series back.'

'They found so many of the original props,' notes Reece. 'The kitchen was in storage. They found the sofa and bed. Some things were recreated, like the wallpaper. It was a bit like going back in time, with this blue corridor and grotty carpet.'

The *Psychoville* set only stood for three days as they shot all the Maureen and David scenes first, then the art department transformed it overnight into Beattie and Sam's flat. 'It was a scramble,' says Tandy. 'They were on their knees when we turned up the following day. The paint was still wet.'

When we first see inside the flat – the front door of which is repainted blue, the number two removed and renumbered nine – there's a framed Rita Hayworth poster on one wall, a poster that drops to reveal a deep crack, through which Maureen's all-seeing eye appears. 'We wanted some notion that Beattie was being slowly possessed by Maureen, so there was a reason for David to come back and warn her,' says Steve. 'It took time to work out the plotting. We knew we had all these great set pieces and funny things we wanted to do, but it also has to do a job as a *No. 9*. It needed to tell a story that is satisfying and not just be an excuse for nostalgia.'

The poster was a nod to *The Shawshank Redemption*, which was based on Stephen King's novella

Rita Hayworth and the Shawshank Redemption, in which a jailed man digs his way out of prison with his escape tunnel hidden behind a Hayworth poster. 'It could have been any random picture that was put up, but it's a little nod for film fans. We couldn't get the actual *Shawshank* poster, but that was more cryptic.'

For the boys, stepping back into those characters after so many years was a breeze, both at the scripting stage and once they were on set. 'It's amazing how time slips away,' says Steve. 'You can remember doing it. You can remember the details of filming those scenes. We love those characters. We've always loved this twisted pair.'

'It was great to go back to that world and their obsessions,' adds Reece. 'It's such fun when she's cutting his hair, and priming him for when he'll have to do things on his own. It's that classic thing that we did, right from *League of Gentlemen*, where hopefully there's some pathos in these monsters, and it matters what happens to them. They're not just caricatures. There's some heart to it as well. And they've got a loving relationship despite the fact they're monstrous.'

They often act out the characters while writing, complete with voices. 'A turn of phrase will just come out your mouth,' says Reece. 'Whether they've pushed it forward or whether you've constructed it for them, I don't know. It's a curious osmosis.'

For Lipsey, too, it was very much more of the same. 'From camera angles to lighting we just picked up from where we left off,' he explains. 'It felt supremely important to me that it really did feel like we

TOP: The production team had to recreate David and Maureen's *Psychoville* flat from scratch.

ABOVE: Jenna Coleman as Beattie.

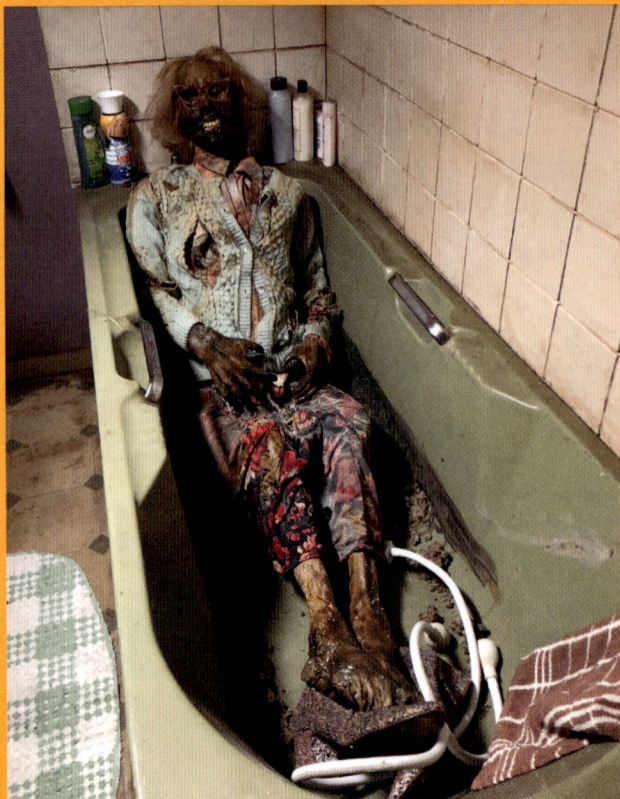

had gone back to where we were, that it had to look and feel and taste exactly the same. So a lot of it was a technical exercise, in making sure it was lovingly recreated.' He approached the Beattie and Sam storyline as a straightforward comedy-drama, using mostly long lenses, before swapping to *Psychoville* wide angles and a much closer camera for Maureen and David. 'We wanted to get that sense of claustrophobia in the flat. Except on a few occasions where we messed with that and got right back and suddenly the place seemed huge. Maureen's death being an example of that, where I wanted to suggest the emptiness and depressing nature of the situation.'

Key to the early scenes with Beattie and Sam was disguising the true nature (and history) of the flat. 'Not that anyone was going to be expecting it, but we wanted to do everything we could to not flag up where we were. The filming style was important to that. And where you allow it to start slipping. When Jenna wakes up and walks in to find the Hoover on the table, that's the point at which I allowed the camera to start going *Psychoville*. As we follow her into the room, get into the angle on the blender, and the lower angle on the balls coming towards camera, then we've gone *Psychoville*. That's where the thing starts to morph and the two worlds blend.'

Our reintroduction to Maureen comes via a flashback, in which she and David are doing the Superman dance to 'Crank That' by Soulja Boy, having famously danced to Black Lace's 'Superman' in *Psychoville*. When it came time to film the dance, Lipsey wanted to shoot it from numerous angles, but the boys said no. 'It's one of the few times we've overrode a director,' says Steve. 'We said it needs to be a hard cut from the new flat and you need to hold on it for a long time. Don't move, don't cut, don't change angle. Because we had it in our minds that you would hard cut to this ludicrous dance. It's a reintroduction to Maureen, and what you want to see is the two of them dancing. If it was up to us, we'd have the whole song. The fans loved it. They went mad for that dance.'

'I guess, I wanted to enjoy some of the detail of it,' says Lipsey of his reasoning, 'but if you hold back and give it the proscenium arch, you allow the whole performance to breathe. What we did works a treat, so hats off to them. And those sequences are so funny. There's one take where you can see the camera shaking, because the operator was laughing so much. But it's born out of character and that's what's so clever. It's about pushing the bonkers nature of it as far as you could possibly go, and still get away with it.'

As with the flat, the *Psychoville* costumes also had to be recreated from scratch. 'It was just a question of finding the right fabrics and the shops,' says Yves Barre who, at least, had the benefit of having designed them in the first place. 'Jelly's costume didn't exist any longer, so I just copied it, exactly to the letter. Obviously I didn't have the original fabrics, so I picked something that was close, but

ABOVE: The dried-out corpse of Maureen lies in the bathtub.

RIGHT, TOP: Matt Lipsey reads over the script while Maureen's corpse looks on.

RIGHT, BOTTOM: Reece as Maureen.

the construction was identical. We had to be as original as we possibly could. For Maureen, the key was her blouse and I found one in a seller who specialises in mature ladies' stock, and the cardigan was a battered green Marks and Spencer's men's one.' As for David, Barre still had all the old padding that Pemberton wore while playing him. 'Because the padding is the whole base of David. The rolls of fat, his beer gut, and so on.'

The return of Maureen and David allowed the boys to dig into the characters' obsession with serial killers, once again, both in a game of *Heads Up!*, as well as when Maureen returns from the grave, telling David she knows the identity of Jack the Ripper. It also meant another appearance of David's Jack the Ripper book, written by Pemberton's Ripporologist charactor in *Whitechapel*.

When it came to restaging Maureen's deathbed scene in 'Death Be Not Proud', the boys thought they'd just reuse the footage from *Psychoville*. 'And it was Matt who said, "I'd like to film it again, but a different angle." So we did,' says Reece, who studied the original to get Maureen's exact intonation. 'It was an important part of our story in *Inside No. 9* and contains one of my favourite jokes about "John Donne, John did",' notes Steve, in reference to the poem that gives the episode its name. 'It was a really powerful scene when we did it in *Psychoville*. And so we thought this is the one time we'll have an overlap between that story and this.'

For Lipsey, 'The question was, do we shoot it in exactly the same way? It's from a different angle, metaphorically speaking, so should it then be from a different angle, literally? And we decided it would be not a slavish recreation, but the essence of it is exactly the same. You're carrying a huge range of responsibility to the fans of the show. So we wouldn't want to do them a disservice, which sounds a bit odd, but the fans are incredibly loyal.'

After Maureen's death, Emily moves in with David. They have a baby and, for a brief time, are happy, until Maureen's ghost drives a wedge between them, even wishing harm on their baby, leading to the most horrific line in all of *Inside No. 9*: 'Get that baby boiled!' 'It's very dark,' admits Reece. 'Rarely does it happen that we're laughing doing it, but it was such a funny line, I could hardly get it out.'

'We were egging each other on,' recalls Lipsey. 'When I came up with the idea of shooting across the boiling pot, with him coming towards it with the baby, they were a bit like, "Whoa, okay." But loving it. I've no doubt Adam was looking on with a certain amount of trepidation. But you sort of go, look, if we're going there, we're *going* there. It's utterly horrific. The boys are particularly good at creating macabre characters you can still, somehow, enjoy. But there's no doubt that was as

ABOVE: Left to right: David (Steve Pemberton), Emily (Sarah Solemani), Robin (David Bamber) and Maureen (Reece Shearsmith).

extreme as I've ever gone in comedy. They don't set out to offend. That's not their modus operandi. They're about going into those very, very dark corners and seeing what they can uncover. And you want to go with them, that's the thing.' Not that the baby was ever in danger. 'Number one, no boiling water. You blow bubbles through it, bubbles and smoke. It took a while to get that looking right. So the baby is coming forward with no jeopardy at all, and the mum's always within sight lines. But once the reality around it is removed and it's just down to the artifice and you put the shots together … oh my God. But that's the joy of what we do.'

Less fun was the secrecy involved, with the entire production charged with not letting slip the fact that *Psychoville* was back. 'I kept the secret for nearly a year and a half,' recalls Tandy. 'And we were so keen not to reveal it was a *Psychoville* episode, it became almost obsessive. We gave Mr Jelly and Mr Sowerbutts code names on the call sheet, in the way of big feature films, simply to prevent spoilers getting out.' But despite their best efforts, it did leak. 'In the end, the whole thing was crippled, annoyingly, by YouKu, the Chinese YouTube,' reveals Reece. 'They did their own *Inside No. 9* trailer, not knowing we were keeping secret the Maureen and David episode, and it was full of it. The fans who must have alerts for anything *Inside No. 9* found it. And I got Tweets going, "What's this?" It was the Maureen and David dance. And I Tweeted back, saying, "Please don't tell anyone." So they kept a lid on it.'

Coleman's appearance did help throw the press off. 'Suddenly, we had a star name we could build the episode around,' says Tandy. 'All of my efforts went into promoting the couple moving into the flat. All the publicity photos were of Jenna and Kadiff. We majored on the crack in the wall, and everybody thought that's what the story was going to be about.' Reviewers were only shown the first five minutes of the programme. 'We didn't even trust journalists to watch it and not give something away. It's not for our benefit. It's for yours,' says Steve, who was following reaction to the episode via Twitter 'When that door opened to reveal David … the excitement and the thrill and the amount of open-eyed emojis and "Oh my Gods". That, to me, was what it was all about. You want to give those viewers that moment. It was worth it for the joyful reaction.'

There were also some viewers who hadn't heard of *Psychoville*. 'They thought it was a *No. 9*,' chuckles Reece. 'They thought it was bizarre, but they got it.'

'The people who knew *Psychoville* absolutely love it. They enjoyed all the references and things being tied up that were left dangling by the end of *Psychoville*,' muses Steve. 'Again, a bit like the football one, you go, "This is quite niche." But it felt exciting. By the time you're on a fifth series, you don't want to be doing more of the same. You don't want to be playing safe. You've got nothing to prove. You're free to try things. If you haven't earned the right by series five to do something like this, which is a treat episode, when can you?'

ABOVE: Reece as Mr Jelly and Steve as David.

A BBC STUDIOS Production for BBC TWO

LOVE'S GREAT ADVENTURE

An INSIDE NO. 9 FILM

BBC TWO PRESENTS A BBC STUDIOS PRODUCTION AN INSIDE NO. 9 FILM "LOVE'S GREAT ADVENTURE" STEVE PEMBERTON OLLY HUDSON-CROKER DEBBIE RUSH GABY FRENCH REECE SHEARSMITH BOBBY SCHOFIELD PRODUCTION DESIGNER SAM CASTLETON CASTING BY TRACEY GILLHAM LINE PRODUCER EMILY SHAPLAND EDITED BY JOE RANDALL-CUTLER AND CAT GREGORY MAKE-UP DESIGNER NICOLA COLEMAN PRODUCTION DESIGNER AMY MAGUIRE DIRECTOR OF PHOTOGRAPHY ALEX THOMPSON MUSIC BY CHRISTIAN HENSON EXECUTIVE PRODUCER YVES BARRE DIRECTOR OF PHOTOGRAPHY JOHN SORAPURE WRITTEN BY STEVE PEMBERTON & REECE SHEARSMITH EXECUTIVE PRODUCER JON PLOWMAN PRODUCED BY ADAM TANDY DIRECTED BY GUILLEM MORALES

Love's Great Adventure

- Series **5**
- Episode **3**
- Directed by **Guillem Morales**

Named after Ultravox's 1984 single, 'Love's Great Adventure' was the episode 'To Have and To Hold' was originally meant to be: a gritty, naturalistic, social drama in the vein of Ken Loach's classic TV drama *Cathy Come Home*. 'We'd just written "Misdirection", which was very elaborately plotted and took a long time to get right. And we wanted to exercise a different part of our brains,' says Steve.

'As creators, it was getting to be hard,' explains Reece. 'It felt like we were treading water; the same again but wrapped in a different way. What would change that tonally, artistically? It was a rail against feeling staid, and the formula of these half hours.'

'We're in series five. Why can't we do something that throws you? That's the joy of this anthology

ABOVE: The episode poster was designed by Amy Maguire.

series,' adds Steve. 'And for us, as actors, you've got to change. Imagine being David and Maureen, then the next week you're in this world? We have to write all these different styles and bring them to life. It's a challenge, but it's what keeps us interested and excited.'

Using the advent calendar to parcel the episode into twenty-four scenes, 'Love's Great Adventure' centres on a northern family – Trevor (Pemberton), Julia (Debbie Rush), daughter Mia (Gaby French), grandson Connor (Olly Hudson-Croker), and Trevor's brother Alex (Shearsmith) – in the run up to Christmas, scraping by as a family, dealing with low pay, disappointment, as well as their estranged son (and Connor's dad) Patrick (Bobby Schofield), an addict and mostly absent father. 'It's a lovely framing device,' says Tandy, 'but would have been a whole lot easier as a feature film. We've got twenty-nine minutes.'

'You could have told the same story without using that device, but it's useful for us to hook something on it, and to be able to miss out day nine,' offers Steve. 'You come back and Trevor's got his arm in a sling and a black eye. Shit, what's happened? We've missed something here and it's not made much of for a long time. And then you get that really sickening scene where you see what did happen. So we were using No. 9 storytelling techniques, and it made the advent calendar essential, rather than just a gimmick. It was about this countdown and about skipping this day. Once we hit on that, it didn't feel it was an indulgence. This was about love. About support. It's not about killing somebody or having revenge or serial killers. It's about the love families give to each other and overcoming difficult times. It was very, very low key.'

And for once, the twist happens off screen. 'It's quite oblique, the way that comes out, because

ABOVE: Left to right: Connor (Olly Hudson-Croker), Patrick (Bobby Schofield), Julia (Debbie Rush), Trevor (Steve Pemberton) and Mia (Gaby French).

ABOVE: Steve as Trevor.

you've got to piece it together for yourself,' says Reece. 'And it was so slight, people were like, "That can't be it." But it's mostly the ups and downs of life. It was almost going to be called "Plodding On". The purer version of it was an idea that had been floated for a few years, of doing an improv version of *Inside No. 9*, where we don't know what we're going to do, we just film scenes.'

'I don't think Adam would ever allow us to do that,' Steve notes. 'This took on some improvisation, but we did write a full script.'

'They wanted it to be loose,' reflects Tandy. 'But I warned them that if they did improvise everything, they would find it very, very hard to distil what they needed out of the material, and it would look a mess. And we didn't want that.' For Tandy, the biggest worry was that it might come across like *EastEnders*. 'If it started feeling like a soap, we'd lost our way. But if you feel these people are real and they love each other, then you've done a huge part of the work you need to get to the conclusion. Which is, if you love each other, you'll do anything – even grievous bodily harm using a motor car. So it was not going to be soap acting. It had to be film acting.'

Unusually, they auditioned for all the roles. 'We cast them to be a family,' says Tandy. Debbie Rush, whose daughter Poppy starred in 'The Harrowing', had just finished a stint on *Coronation Street*.

'We don't watch *Corrie*, so we didn't know her at all,' admits Steve. 'Normally we go, "We need a big name …" She *is* a big name. But not to us. We never met her until she was cast. But we'd seen her tape and knew she would do a good job.' Gaby French had co-starred with Shearsmith in Martin McDonagh's *Hangmen*. 'She's Welsh and did a brilliant northern accent,' notes Reece. Bobby Schofield comes from a family of actors. His father, Andrew, had appeared in Alan Bleasdale's *G.B.H.* 'He had an intensity and an honesty about him that stood out,' says Steve.

To find their Connor, casting assistant Michelle Cavanagh visited several schools and youth groups in Yorkshire and Lancashire. 'We weren't looking for stage school kids,' says Steve. 'They videoed several. Showed us the best. They asked them all to tell a story about what happened at school that day. And we picked Olly. He had a lovely quality.'

Tasked with directing 'Love's Great Adventure' was Guillem Morales. 'I remember not being sure he was the right guy for it,' says Steve. 'And it was Adam who said, "I think he'll do a good job."' Even Morales wasn't convinced and turned Tandy down. 'I said, "Get another director. I don't like that kind of cinema. I'm not interested in filming in a Ken Loach style." They wanted to see me out of my comfort zone.'

Eventually, Morales signed on. But given the story's naturalistic style, neither he nor Tandy felt it would be beneficial to rehearse the cast. Instead, they invited them to come for Sunday lunch, so they could get to know each other and bond as a family. 'That was crucial,' says Steve. 'If you're going to be improvising and acting naturally as a family, you have to build those relationships. You spend time with Olly, especially, so he feels completely comfortable, playing games, and so he feels excited to come on to set. We never gave him a script or told him what to say. And you can see, he was absolutely in it. There's no acting going on.'

'During lunch, Schofield sat on his own, mimicking Patrick's estrangement from the family. 'He was very withdrawn,' says Tandy. 'He was trying to find a naturalism and, of course, his character is the one that's most troubled and internalised. The fact he doesn't talk much is what makes the narrative motor really work, because he is a slightly unknown, slightly capricious force of nature. Finally, he breaks down, and you realise everyone will pull together for him, despite all the stealing, using and fighting. He's lost his partner, he barely sees his kid, he's in trouble and he owes money. That's pretty fucked up. It's an odd family. You think, initially, Connor is their son, and it comes as a revelation it's a much more complicated situation, and Connor is the grandson, and what's happened to his mother is a tragedy in itself.'

When it came to the shoot, Morales eschewed his usual storyboards, precise camera and formal set-ups for a looser

approach, working with cinematographer John Sorapure to capture the performances and action in a manner that felt real and unrehearsed. 'John did all of this series apart from "Stakeout" and is very good at a handheld, observational camera that moves around and feels natural,' says Steve. 'That was important. Guillem did a brilliant job. It's not his milieu at all. He kept going, "I'm being lazy, you're just doing it." But that's what it's about: observing.'

'For the first time in my life I had the feeling I was not doing anything as a director,' bemoans Morales. 'It was awful. You can direct the actors, but you don't have your main tool, which is the camera.' Even so, after the first day, Tandy took him aside and said what he was doing was still too elaborate. 'The blocking was nothing, but it didn't feel quite right, so we had to do it again, more like Ken Loach,' remembers Morales. 'So I told myself, I'm not going to do anything. I'm just going to record them, and that's it. But I didn't enjoy it at all. I felt very lazy.'

Because of the confined nature of the location, a house on an estate in Hemel Hempstead, the camera could never be too far from the actors, so Morales and Sorapure shot with wide-angle lenses, which meant there was a lot of ceiling and floor visible in the frame. As a result, Tandy suggested they letterbox the episode. 'Along with "The Devil of Christmas", it's the only one that has a different aspect ratio,' he explains. 'Hilariously, we all forgot about it in post-production. I was looking at the image thinking it looked really loosely framed and couldn't work out why. Then it clicked: we hadn't cropped it.'

Once again, the boys' choice of music – the Ultravox song that gives the episode its name – proved contentious. 'That was a fight,' remembers Reece. 'Adam was, "It's totally wrong. It's a Christmas thing. We should have a carol." And we were like, "No."'

'There's no relevance to the song, but what a great title, "Love's Great Adventure". Because what is life, other than love's great adventure?' says Steve.

In his audition, Hudson-Croker had been asked about his day at school, and told a story about slimy aliens which they asked him to repeat for the episode. 'He goes on about space aliens quite a lot, because he was improvising and that was the thing he wanted to improvise,' says Tandy, who was worried the audience would think that's what the episode was actually about. 'I kept going, "Some people are going to think that's the twist."'

Entirely coincidentally, when the episode aired, the BBC Red Button appeared onscreen near the end, inviting viewers to press to access its digital interactive services. 'On this occasion it said: "Do you believe in aliens? Red button",' recalls Steve. Needless to say, a large number of viewers pressed red.

'Connor was babbling on about aliens, and people thought, "There's another bit to this," and missed the end. They thought it was linked,' says Reece.

'A lot of people got taken to some random podcast series they were trailing,' says Steve.

Even without the confusion, 'Love's Great Adventure' proved to be divisive with viewers and critics alike. 'It got the most glittering reviews, all the way to "That was utter shit. It's just an episode of

ABOVE: Clockwise from bottom left: Trevor (Steve Pemberton), Mia (Gaby French), Patrick (Bobby Schofield), Alex (Reece Shearsmith), Connor (Olly Hudson-Croker) and Julia (Debbie Rush).

EastEnders where nothing happens,"' recalls Steve. 'In a way that's good, because you're not resting on your laurels. You're not doing what is expected. And there was huge debate afterwards: "Where was the twist?" There were those who'd spotted what happened, and others who hadn't.'

'Fundamentally, you don't need to be able to work out that Debbie's done a bad thing with a car a week earlier, because the moral heart of the story should be enough,' insists Tandy.

And for most viewers it was. 'You feel you know that family and those characters, and what was really pleasing reading the reaction to it was that people were tense all the way through, because they knew something, probably, was going to happen. And that tension, even though we were doing very little, was because it's *Inside No. 9*.'

'There is real drama and tension when they're having Christmas together,' says Reece. 'There is the dread of the knock on the door, and the panic in the dad's eyes when he knows it's, potentially, this horrible man his son has brought into the household. In my mind, it was a bit like that scene in *The Night of the Hunter* when Lillian Gish is sat outside on the porch with the gun, waiting for Robert Mitchum to turn up.'

'I absolutely love this episode. It's one of my very favourites. And it was a real joy to do,' says Steve. 'It was so freeing to be able to improvise. Normally, our scripts are very, very structured. This had a structure, but we were free within it, because some of the scenes have very little of the dialogue we wrote and some are word for word.'

'It says something about the world. It says something about society. It's exciting. There are moments of tension. There's great heart,' muses Tandy. 'I think it means something personally to Steve. He comes from that part of the world, so it feels like it's from his roots rather than his imagination or his love of horror films. It's a huge achievement.'

ABOVE: Debbie Rush as Julia.

Misdirection

■ Series **5**
■ Episode **4**
■ Directed by **Guillem Morales**

ABOVE: The episode poster was created by Amy Tyler.

Having ticked off witch trials from his bucket list with 'The Trial of Elizabeth Gadge', Shearsmith turned to another of his obsessions with 'Misdirection'. 'I've been a massive fan of magic since I was little. In my attic at home I have a bookcase that, at the press of a button, opens up to reveal the room where I keep all my magic,' he explains. 'I've got lots of old books, cabinets full of tricks, even a Zig-Zag Lady. Jeremy Dyson and I are big fans. I used to do tricks. Now I mainly collect old stuff. So we'd wanted to do something in that world for a while. Rival magicians was one possible idea, but we didn't want to redo that Mitchell and Webb film *Magicians*. But exploring the different types of magic was a jumping-off point, the idea of two magicians and the secrecy that abounds with magic and how they're all so mean to each other as far as never revealing anything.'

'Misdirection' begins with Neville Griffin (Shearsmith), an up-and-coming practitioner of the magic arts, being shown an astounding trick – 'a chair-raising experience' – by seasoned magician Willy Wando (Pemberton). Knowing a game changer when he sees one, Griffin offers to buy the trick from him. But Wando, who's content to use it for kids' parties and as his entrée on to the cruise ship circuit, refuses to sell. So Griffin kills him using a prop guillotine, then steals his book of tricks.

Fast-forward nine years and Griffin is world-famous, thanks to Wando's chair-raising illusion. After running through the Zig-Zag Lady trick with his wife and assistant Jennie (Jill Halfpenny), she leaves for a business trip, spending the night in a hotel. Meanwhile, Griffin is visited in his workshop/ storage facility by Gabriel (Fionn Whitehead), who's there, ostensibly, to interview him for a student newspaper. But Gabriel has a few tricks of his own, one he's eager to show Griffin, who doesn't see what's coming until it's too late.

Magic tricks rely on concealment, sleight of hand and misdirection, much like *Inside No. 9*, in fact. 'The key to unlocking it for me was the title,' says Steve. '"Misdirection". It's perfect, because this is exactly what we do, we *misdirect*. And we wanted to put that upfront and say, "This is about misdirection," and to have Griffin be an expert magician and know all about it. Yet the joy is he has been suckered in, with the ring switch that happened right at the beginning. He immediately

ABOVE: Steve as seasoned magician Willy Wando and Reece as Neville Griffin, an up-and-coming practitioner of magic.

MAGIC / MISDIRECTION

RING / WATCH DEVICE WHICH CAN COPY
THE HAND MOVEMENTS & THATS HOW THE
COPY DRAWING TRICK IS DONE?
ALSO USED TO COPY THE MOVEMENT OF HAND
TO OPEN A SAFE, GET THE CODE

IT'S NOT BEEN ABOUT THE TRICKS, RATHER
THAN GETTING INTO THE SAFE / GETTING
SOME INFORMATION etc. — THE MISDIRECTION
WAS THE MISDIRECTION.

WOMAN CALLED MISS NORTH iE MISDIRECTION —
I SPOTTED YOUR LITTLE TRICK

OLDER MAGICIAN TESTS YOUNGER ONE

DOES HE HAVE a challenge — trick me
& win the shop / win my fortune

Does he have a priceless document — Houdini
letter describing his trick?

YOU'VE caught breaking into the safe. OLD says

notices his ring has been stolen, but from that moment, he is in Gabriel's hands. And the trick Gabriel brings to him, that Griffin takes apart and rubbishes and says, "I know how you did all of those things," he's falling into this trap. So the misdirection is the misdirection. That's such a great hook for an episode. And you've started with this murder; you know Griffin's guilty. So seeing Gabriel plot this guy's downfall, and use his arrogance against him, makes for such a satisfying ending.'

Coupled with the magic of misdirection was the cunning of *Columbo*. Most famously played by Peter Falk in the long-running US TV series, Columbo was a homicide detective who always got his man. Or woman. 'The very first idea we had was, "Could we do a *Columbo*, where you know who's done it, then you see how they get caught?" That was something we hadn't done before,' says Reece. 'I've always wanted to be the murderer in a *Columbo*. It was nice to know he'd done it and got away with it. Then this boy turns up. And it's not really a surprise that Fionn has something to do with Wando.'

'Revenge is a great motivator for our kind of tales,' agrees Steve. 'But here the reveal isn't that Gabriel is Wando's grandson, it's how he gets him. That's what makes *Columbo* still stand out as one of the very best detective shows. It's not a whodunnit. It's how is he going to get him? I think that's why people loved this episode. It was one of the strongest.'

'There is no twist. There's no grand revelation, really, apart from the final reveal of the safe,' says Tandy. 'It's as much a revenge piece as "The Riddle of the Sphinx" is. But whereas "The Riddle of the Sphinx" is played out through a crossword, this is played out using magic.'

To fill Griffin's magic workshop – in actuality, a former garage in Dalston – with tricks and paraphernalia, as well as create Griffin's chair-raising stunt, the production turned to brothers Gary and Paul Hardy-Brown, whose company The Twins FX provides magic and special effects for stage and screen. 'They were able to build exactly what we needed,' says Tandy, 'or had it in one of their barns. They were able to lend us a lorry-load of props for set dressing. Everything either came from them, or from Reece's collection.'

'I loved that set,' says Reece. 'I wanted to live there. I've now got them building things for me. They had two massive buzz saws, one of which they got cheap from a travelling circus because an escapologist had both his hands cut off with it.'

When it came to creating a trick that would be worth killing for, Pemberton and Shearsmith wanted something simple but clearly impossible. Wando sits down in a fold-up chair, covers himself with a sheet, stamps both feet, then both he and the chair float into the air. 'The twins were charged with

making this trick come to life, for real, and Guillem wanted to see it in one shot. And you didn't know how it was done,' says Steve.

'You have to believe magic is happening. If you cut away, then you know it's a trick,' insists Morales. 'I wanted to tell the audience to see the trick and to believe it. And lingering without cutting is what makes you believe there's something magic there.'

In reality, Pemberton places the chair on to a crane, which lifts him into the air. The crane is then digitally removed in post-production using visual effects. 'Because of health and safety, in case anything went wrong, I had to put a seatbelt on under the sheet, which was a real faff,' reveals Steve. 'But it adds a bit to the mystery, I suppose, of what's going on under there. I didn't feel scared. I felt more scared going in the guillotine.'

Inspired by an episode of *Columbo* in which an egocentric psychic kills a magician with a guillotine, Wando's death was originally written to be a swift decapitation until Morales pointed out that the guillotine was a prop and therefore not fit for purpose. 'I was worried,' he explains. 'We have to believe Steve is dead. But because it's *Inside No. 9*, maybe he's going to come back. So we had to be very clear and show he's dead. Because it's a prop, it's going to be harder than expected.'

ABOVE: Jill Halfpenny as Jennie and Reece as Neville.

'The murder is grim,' says Reece. 'We thought he would just cut his head off. But Guillem said he should have to finish him off, pushing it through, which was really nasty. And we're like, "Oh yeah, that's horrible. Let's have that."'

To start with, Griffin bashes Wando around the head, but the magician doesn't stay down, leaving Griffin to improvise with whatever's at hand, picking up a rope to strangle him. But the rope is another prop, and completely useless. 'That was my idea as well, because I don't only have nasty ones, I have comedy ideas too,' laughs Morales. 'There was another moment where Reece picks up a sword, which became a bunch of flowers. But we had to cut it because the episode was too long.'

Only then does Griffin manoeuvre Wando into the guillotine, forcing the blade down and decapitating him. 'That was a big taste call for me as to how we could shoot that without crossing the line,' says Tandy. 'You don't see a lot of blood, or hear very much distress, and the prop is an illusion, so there's always a doubt that what you're watching isn't real. And we are never on Willy's head in close-up for long, or see the blade go in. The grade is quite dark. And we concentrate on the comedy of Reece making a hash of it, rather than his unfortunate victim.'

When we first meet Griffin, he's desperate and dishevelled. 'There's a little bit of Jonathan Creek in the early version of that character, with the long hair and the duffle coat,' says Tandy. Once he's

TOP: Filming in progress.

ABOVE: Director Guillem Morales talks to Reece.

stolen Wando's act and made his fortune, he transforms himself, and looks less like Jonathan Creek and more like actor and magician Andy Nyman with his big glasses and jewellery. 'Andy said, "That was me, wasn't it?"' recalls Reece. 'And I said, "A little bit." But not in manner or personality.'

Fionn Whitehead broke out playing a British soldier in Christopher Nolan's *Dunkirk* and had recently appeared in the 'Bandersnatch' episode of *Black Mirror*. 'We needed somebody to be a young foil for Reece, so it felt like we needed a young, upcoming star, and Fionn was very high up on our list, might even have been top,' says Tandy. 'He was great,' notes Reece. 'He said yes straight away and was so natural and intense when we wanted him to be.'

Much like 'The Riddle of the Sphinx', 'Misdirection' is mostly a two-hander, in this case a duel between Griffin and Gabriel, as they battle and spar, using, variously, packs of cards, bananas, straight razors, mind games and misdirection, in an attempt to gain the upper hand. 'It was incredibly detailed in terms of all of the objects we needed to shoot,' says Morales. 'It was very wordy, and you needed to do long, complicated tracking shots to get through all the explanations and all of that patter.'

'Misdirection' is an episode in which tricks are replayed to reveal different outcomes, beginning with the ring gag when Griffin and Gabriel first shake hands. 'That's something Guillem brought, because it wasn't in the script,' says Reece. 'He realised that, at the end, a lot of information was going to be explained in flashback, so if we did it from the start, you knew that was the world we were in, and it would be there as a stylistic conceit that played throughout.'

'With *Inside No. 9*, you're often looking for looks and moments where the tells are,' says Tandy. 'We shoot them and then use the ones that help the storytelling. For this, we had all of that, but we also had the detail of the tricks, and we needed to be able to see the detail of all of that happening, partly because some of it is misdirection. And if you don't have it, you're not doing your job as a storyteller.'

ABOVE: Steve on set.

'Misdirection' features another incredible score, with Wando's theme, played during his chair-raising trick, inspired by Mike Oldfield's 'Tubular Bells'. 'That was Christian again, wanting to come up with something playful and mischievous that would underpin the mind games going on,' says Reece. 'It's a piece of music Christian had lying around that he thought would be good for us. And it does have that slightly rubbish stage magic quality to it. But the rest of it is quite lush and deep and textured and has to serve a lot of different styles: mystery, creeping tension and out-and-out horror.'

'It's got drive, especially that ending, which is a series of visual reveals and flashbacks, and a dawning on Griffin's face,' adds Steve, 'so you needed the music to do a big job there. And I think it's one of the best. It gives the end a lift, because ultimately what he's doing is unlocking a safe, looking inside, and going, "Oh shit, he's got me ..."'

The episode ends with Tom Goodman-Hill's mac-wearing policeman arresting Griffin for his wife's murder, and, in flashback, we see how he's been framed. With Gabriel using misdirection, a tracking device, and Griffin's own hubris against him, to place the murder weapon – the straight razor he used in his trick, which Griffin so arrogantly handed back to him – inside the safe to which only Griffin has the combination. 'We did have a conversation that her head could be inside,' says Reece, 'but it was on the heels of mine in the microwave in "Dead Line", so we thought, "We've done that already."'

Once again, the episode ran long. Not only did Morales' flowers gag have to go, so did some of Gabriel's interview with Neville. 'There was more about Ali Bongo, who was another magician who got namechecked,' laments Reece. There was also more with Wando and his backstory. 'It was a very dense episode, and you don't want to sacrifice the great moments to get everything in, so a lot of it was nipping out lines, which we don't normally do,' says Steve. 'We like to take a chunk out. But it was seamless. You would never know.'

'I wanted to treat magic seriously,' insists Shearsmith, 'and I got a lovely letter from the president of the Magic Circle saying he was so pleased we gave it respect. And I know a lot of magicians who loved it. They all liked the fact it was authentic and was done from a love of the craft. It was enjoyable, too, to mention Derren Brown. And Wayne Dobson got in touch to say he was pleased to get a namecheck.'

ABOVE: A short section from Christian Henson's score for the episode.

RIGHT: Steve and Reece as Willy Wando and Neville.

THINKING OUT LOUD

BBC TWO PRESENTS A BBC STUDIOS PRODUCTION AN INSIDE NO. 9 FILM "THINKING OUT LOUD" PHIL DAVIS · MAXINE PEAKE · SARA KESTELMAN · STEVE PEMBERTON · IOANNA KIMBOOK
REECE SHEARSMITH · SANDRA GAYER DUBBING MIXER SAM CASTLETON CASTING BY TRACEY GILLHAM LINE PRODUCER EMILY SHAPLAND EDITED BY CAT GREGORY MUSIC BY CHRISTIAN HENSON COSTUME DESIGNER YVES BARRE
MAKE UP DESIGNER NICOLA COLEMAN PRODUCTION DESIGNER AMY MAGUIRE DIRECTOR OF PHOTOGRAPHY JOHN SORAPURE WRITTEN BY STEVE PEMBERTON & REECE SHEARSMITH EXECUTIVE PRODUCER JON PLOWMAN PRODUCED BY ADAM TANDY DIRECTED BY STEVE PEMBERTON

Thinking Out Loud

- Series **5**
- Episode **5**
- Directed by **Steve Pemberton**

ABOVE: The episode poster was designed by Andy Bottomley.

Given it's an episode that deals with split personalities, it's fitting that the impetus behind 'Thinking Out Loud' came from a variety of sources. The main one being the boys' desire to do a series of monologues à la Alan Bennett's *Talking Heads*, 'but in which the characters had a genuine reason to be talking to the camera rather than just "monologuing" in an artificial way,' says Steve. 'We wrote down a list of situations – dating video, vlog, police interview, therapy session – then thought, there's got to be something binding these together. It was a great lightbulb moment when we went: they can be all be one person.'

Not that split personalities was a particularly novel idea – 'It's an old chestnut,' admits Steve, 'from *Psycho* onwards' – and the boys had toyed with it before. What made it different this time was the treatment. Here, Nadia (Maxine Peake), who we meet talking to an unseen therapist (Sara Kestelman) via her computer, is an ANP, or apparently normal person. Everyone else in the episode, bar Phil Davis's Bill, are part of Nadia's fractured psyche and exist only in her head, brought on by suppressed childhood trauma. 'We didn't want to do a glib version of multiple personalities, or dissociative identity disorder [DID], to give it its medical name,' continues Steve. 'She is suffering from DID but isn't really aware of it. That meant you could seed things throughout.' Each of the personalities had to be fully formed and contrasting but, equally, were all part of her imagination. 'I remember getting quite tied up with questions like how does she know about YouTubers? Which is why we put in the line about her daughter. Similarly, with the prisoner in the Deep South, it's a clichéd film version of a serial killer with mother issues. But there were lots of things which, thematically, really worked, and we felt that this was a perfect symbiosis of these two ideas.'

They also managed to smuggle in several more besides, plundering the notebook for the story about the 'smugs' as well as the gag about porn star names. 'This was a real magpie episode, picking up stuff from all over, just different, odd ideas and bringing them together,' says Steve.

Maxine Peake had long been on the list of actors they wanted to work with. 'She's obviously very in demand,' says Steve, 'so we asked, crossed our fingers, and she really liked it. She was terrific. I think that final sequence, where you see her become all these different characters, with the subtle differences in her face, was brilliant.'

The first personality to manifest is the 'Persecutor' who represents self-hatred and negativity and who takes the guise of Pemberton's backwoods serial killer Galen. 'It could have been anything, as long as it was someone talking about a crime. But because it's coming from her imagination, it can be a filmic portrayal of a killer, someone who's in the cell across from Hannibal Lecter in *The Silence of the Lambs*,' says Steve. 'So we Googled redneck sayings and language and enjoyed plunging into all that.'

'A huge performance from Steve,' says Tandy. 'We got him a dialect coach so he could be authentic. It's actually a very small part of the show in terms of screen time, but he's such a "big" character and so important in terms of the action.'

Galen is followed by social media star Angel (Ioanna Kimbook), one of Nadia's 'Protectors', who exist to try to influence the system to fight back against the abuser. 'We had talked about doing a YouTube character before,' says Reece. 'This idea of influencers, who are, quite literally, powerful. And their word and approval on things matters.'

'It's such an alien world to us but we enjoyed dipping a toe into it,' notes Steve. 'That came from a newspaper article about this girl who'd tried to blag a hotel room in Ireland and the owner said, "No. Who do you think is going to pay the wages of the people tidying up and cleaning up after you?" And her response. Angel grew out of that.'

ABOVE: Maxine Peake as Nadia.

ABOVE: A noticeboard that briefly features in the episode, showing the names of the different characters.

Kimbook was fresh out of drama school when she auditioned. 'We saw a lot of people,' says Steve. 'What was good was you could say to them, "Send in your version of it." And Ioanna edited a version that was almost like the finished thing, and we thought, "You get it." It's a painfully funny three minutes you spend watching her. She bludgeons you into submission.'

Aidan (Shearsmith), who is dying of cancer and recording a series of video messages to his unborn daughter, represents the 'Caretaker', a source of love and reassurance. 'He's the caring, parental figure who, like Angel, is a force for good within the system,' says Steve. 'He's fiercely protective of his "angel" and we wanted the emotion to be genuine, in contrast to Galen, who was more caricatured. There are probably elements of Nadia's husband in Aidan, a real person as opposed to the characters she's made up.'

And finally, there's blind gospel singer Diana (Sandra Gayer), who represents the side of Nadia who 'sings to herself to drown out her mother's screams'. The character was a late addition to the script. 'Knowing that would be difficult to cast, we Googled singers who were blind and came across Sandra's website,' says Steve. 'One of the clips was her singing "Amazing Grace". Watching her sing that, we thought, "This is perfect," and we added it. When she came in, she said, "I'd love to do more." And so we had a little chat, looked back at her website and there was "O Mio Babbino Caro" from Puccini's *Gianni Schicchi*. And, because of what happens at the end, it was also perfect.'

Bill, who we see recording a dating video, right at the start, is the only other real character in the entire episode. 'We used two cameras to film him because it is not in her head,' says Steve. 'It's meant to be a genuine dating video, if such things exist any more. We watched a lot of funny ones from back in the day, and how people make themselves look so unappealing.' Appearing awkward and mild-mannered, Bill's true colours are only revealed at the end, but his video gives you all the clues you need, not least his offhand remark, 'I've had quite enough of male company, thank you very much,' meaning he's spent time in jail. 'It is definitely one you can rewatch and pick different things up,' continues Steve. 'There are a lot of lines about stuff going on inside the head. All the characters are talking about this process that she is working out herself.'

Structurally, the episode owes a debt to David Mitchell's novel *Cloud Atlas*. 'It's a series of different stories told in different styles, but begins and ends with the same one,' says Steve. 'Then the second and the penultimate are the same, so you're moving towards the centre. I thought that was a handy way to help structure this, starting with Phil's character and ending with him turning up at the house. And the second character you meet is Maxine, and she's the penultimate.'

Davis and Pemberton had, of course, starred together in the hit ITV show *Whitechapel*. 'I think we started *Inside No. 9* when I was still doing *Whitechapel*, and he was such a fan,' notes Steve. 'And I could see him as this rough and ready, befuddled character. Phil often plays really snarling, horrible characters, so, at the beginning, it was nice to see him playing against type.'

While Pemberton and Shearsmith co-directed two episodes in series two, this time Shearsmith didn't feel the need or desire. 'Just didn't want to do it. I enjoyed it before. But, ironically, talking about this episode, I didn't want to split my mind into two.'

> **Nadia:** We had some good news this week. Kelly's best friend Sophie who she goes to school with, well her parents are both really well-educated, really attractive, really sociable... and they're getting divorced!

'Similar to "Cold Comfort", this was about directing performances rather than thinking of shots and lenses, which is not my forte,' says Steve. 'Also, similar to "Cold Comfort", we didn't want to water down the aesthetic. We wanted to do it without moving a camera, and I think a lot of directors would have struggled with that. It turned out to be quite a tough assignment in the end, because it was very technical. But I'm really glad I did.'

Unlike the vast majority of episodes, 'Thinking Out Loud' takes place in multiple locations. 'We looked hard to find a house where we could get many different looks,' says Tandy. 'Then we had to build a set for the cell and go to a church.' They picked a house near Ealing Studios, which stood in for Nadia's home, Aidan's bedroom and Angel's room, before moving into a church, also in Ealing, to record Diana singing, and using its adjoining hall for Davis' dating video. 'We shot with a smaller unit because we were using non-professional cameras.'

Pemberton wanted all the monologues, apart from Angel's, to play without any cuts. 'I spoke to everyone beforehand and said it is important they are continuous, the camera will never move, and you have to keep going. So you have to know the whole thing. That's quite a big ask. But once it was set up, you could do take after take.'

'Everybody turned up knowing their lines,' says Tandy. 'That was huge, given how long Maxine's

ABOVE: Left to right: Bill (Phil Davis), Angel (Ioanna Kimbook), Galen (Steve Pemberton), Nadia (Maxine Peake), Diana (Sandra Gayer) and Aidan (Reece Shearsmith).

contribution was. But she was able to do each scene without a prompt. She knew it all. She was performance perfect. She understood where the jokes were, where she had to be confused, when it all started falling apart, how that had to affect her performance and her thought process on screen.'

They began with the final scene, in which the various elements of Nadia's fractured psyche appear together and Nadia/Galen stabs Bill, who she, and we, learn is Nadia's father, recently released from prison for killing her mother. 'It's seemingly one shot from when she learns the truth talking to the therapist, then moves the camera when he comes in. But there's an invisible cut when she covers the lens,' explains Steve. 'We did that first because it was the trickiest, then Maxine, Ioanna and Reece, over two days. Then myself, Phil and Sandra at the church.' As the scenes couldn't be cut, timing was crucial. 'Maxine was never the same and really playful. I kept going in, not only giving her notes, but saying, "Can we cut this bit and that bit?" Because if it was spreading, it would have a knock-on effect. And as we ticked on, it became increasingly fraught.'

'Even more than on "Cold Comfort", we were looking at our watches, thinking, "Can we get them to do it with more emotion but faster?"' says Tandy. 'We had that with Reece's performance, which is beautiful, but he had too many words to say, so we had to shorten it. But it's crafted so carefully, every line is there for a reason, and if it's a joke, it informs the character.'

'If we were a Netflix show, we could have gone to thirty-seven minutes. We are stuck with our twenty-nine and a half,' reflects Steve. 'Reece had such an emotional story you didn't want to be rattling through it. The funniest thing was Adam at the monitor turning to me, "See if you can make Reece cry." And I thought, I'll just ask him to do it again. Quicker.'

'You would sit slack-jawed at how brilliant these people were on camera,' says Tandy. 'I don't just mean Maxine, but Reece and Steve. You watch Reece pouring out his heart to the daughter he will never see, and think, we literally plonked him in front of the camera and said, "We've got half an hour to get this." And he did it. That's pretty special. They are properly good actors.'

The videos were all shot differently, from Aidan's bleak confessionals to the micro-edit frenzy of Angel's YouTube clips. For the latter, Pemberton had Kimbook do the entire monologue, then broke it down into individual lines. 'I'd say, "Give me three awesomes" or three of that line and she'd do them in a row. It was really fun and an unusual way to do it.'

Visually, the story's fractured nature was represented in the stained-glass mosaic that housed the nine above Nadia's front door, as well as throughout the episode. 'I thought it would be great to have a sense of fragmentation in every sequence,' says Steve. 'The only one we didn't manage was Galen's, because that would have stood out too much. With Aidan's character, you'll see moonlight reflected on the wall behind him that looks like stained glass. Nadia has a lamp which is made up of fragments. And with Angel we put some mosaic on her shelves. You're not expecting anyone to pick it up. Although one or two people did, amazingly. It's just layering.'

The hare, too, is a fractured presence in this. 'You only ever see bits of it in the domestic settings,' says Tandy. 'The ears, tail or a paw.'

There are also deliberate echoes of the other lives and the other personalities, in each of the monologues, that both unsettle and hint at a deeper, hidden meaning, with repeated names and phrases. Galen's mother is called Doreen. So, too, is Aidan's unborn child and Bill's dead wife. Nadia, Aidan and Diana are all anagrams. As are Angel and Galen. 'That idea arrived quite late but seemed, thematically, to work,' says Steve. 'We were looking for five-way anagrams, but that would have tipped the wink too much.' But when Galen pops up in Angel's bedroom, all bets are off. 'That's a real rug pull for the audience,' says Tandy. 'It's a moment of, Arrrrrgh, I really don't know what's going on now. I need to pay a lot more attention.'

The underlying connection between the characters is finally revealed by Kestelman's therapist in Nadia's second video when she explains that Nadia is suffering from DID, brought on by her father's release from jail. Although the therapist is also another facet of her imagination. 'She is the gatekeeper,' explains Steve. 'All these types of characters are often present in a personality system. You will have someone who represents the young girl, the victim, the innocent. You will have a more evil presence, who represents the abuser. And you will have someone who is as an influencer, trying to keep you positive. It was amazing how well they all fitted with the characters we'd created, because a lot of our research was done after having written the monologues and coming up with the characters.'

Initially, the boys wanted the ending to be less explanatory than it wound up being, bowing to pressure from executive producer Jon Plowman to 'explain it more'. 'I think it's over-explained,' says Reece. 'Our audience are clever; they would have got it.'

'What Jon was concerned about was what he calls "the hard of thinking",' says Steve. 'But if Nadia knew she had this condition, there wouldn't be any explanation. The fact is, she's confused, so the therapist is explaining it to her. There were people who said, "Why does it always have to end with these people being dangerous?" But it wasn't like we turned her into a crazed killer. It was a revenge story.'

'It's *Inside No. 9*, and it's a great idea, right back to *Psycho*,' insists Reece. 'A lot of people loved it. As well as those who thought there was too much explanation at the end. But that's just taste. The "hard of thinking" would have enjoyed it being explained to them.'

ABOVE: Steve and Reece on set.

STEVE PEMBERTON   **REECE SHEARSMITH**

THE STAKEOUT

3 NIGHTS. 2 COPS. 1 MURDER.

BBC TWO PRESENTS A BBC STUDIOS PRODUCTION AN INSIDE NO. 9 FILM "THE STAKEOUT" STEVE PEMBERTON   REECE SHEARSMITH   REBECCA CALLARD   MALIK IBHEIS
DUBBING MIXER SAM CASTLETON   SOUND RECORDIST ALEX THOMPSON   LINE PRODUCER EMILY SHAPLAND   EDITED BY JOE RANDALL-CUTLER   MUSIC BY CHRISTIAN HENSON   COSTUME DESIGNER YVES BARRE   MAKE-UP DESIGNER NICOLA COLEMAN
PRODUCTION DESIGNER AMY MAGUIRE   DIRECTOR OF PHOTOGRAPHY MATTIAS NYBERG   WRITTEN BY STEVE PEMBERTON & REECE SHEARSMITH   EXECUTIVE PRODUCER JON PLOWMAN   PRODUCED BY ADAM TANDY   DIRECTED BY GUILLEM MORALES

The Stakeout

- Series **5**
- Episode **6**
- Directed by **Guillem Morales**

For the final episode of series five, the boys initially wrote a musical. Problem was, it was too expensive. 'It was huge. We just don't have the resources for music and recording orchestras that you need,' says Tandy, who asked if they wouldn't mind writing something else. Something cheaper.

'It was a week before the Christmas holidays,' recalls Reece. '"Can we have another one?"'

'But it has to be cheap. And very, very contained,' adds Steve.

'As the creators, we try to write not worrying about constraints,' notes Reece. 'Although we always have half a mind on those things you know will be cut or changed anyway. We came back to the office and thought, "Me and you in a car. Talking. Policemen on a stakeout. Doing nothing."'

ABOVE: The episode poster was designed by Polly Stevens.

It was one step up from a radio play.'

Written in just five days, 'The Stakeout' fused the cheap conceit of two men in a car with their long-held idea of doing a hidden vampire story. 'Normally you know when something is about vampires,' says Steve. 'This was a different take on it. This was, let the end be: "Oh my God, he's a vampire." That's your reveal.'

'The Stakeout' opens with the gruesome sight of PC Varney (Shearsmith) in the back seat of a police car, appearing to be the victim of a horrific attack. 'He's covered in blood, and it looks like Steve's character has killed me,' says Reece. 'And he's going to explain to us how he got there. Although, of course, when you get there, it's not what you thought.'

The story flashbacks three nights as Special Constable Varney joins Constable Thompson on a stakeout at the local cemetery. The grave of Thompson's recently deceased partner DC Dobson (Malik Ibheis) has been disturbed and he wants to catch whoever's responsible. And over the next three nights, as the two men talk, play games and keep watch, we uncover the truth of the situation. That Varney is a vampire and it's Thompson who's the victim, while Dobson has been turned.

Writing a hidden vampire that misdirects the audience, while, at the same time, seeding obscene amounts of vampire lore into the dialogue, is no easy feat, but the boys pull it off masterfully. 'You need to present an alternative truth to the audience, so they think they're watching something else,' says Steve. 'So the story around the story has to be really intriguing, enough for you to think that you're watching something about these two guys who maybe don't trust each other. One of them is a new partner. We know he ends up dead. So you tell the audience the story you want them to think they're watching, while, at the same time, telling them another story they don't know they're watching.'

'We thought it was so obvious, writing it – every time I mentioned "bat" or "long in the tooth" or "sleeping dead to the world". It's all there. Blaring like a bell at a railway crossing,' says Reece. In

ABOVE: Steve as DC Thompson and Reece as SPC Varney.

Left diagram labels:

2-The whole action, reframing, jib up

14-On Thompson, from the roof banging to Varney getting out.

12-On Varney, from the roof banging to him getting out

3-On Thompson, alone at the beginning of the scene, until Varney tapping on the window.

8-Close up of Varney's vest

6-Dolly in on Thompson, from 'anything to report' to the end.

7-On Varney from "anything to report?" to Varney getting out.

5-On Thompson, from the beginning to "are you wearing a wire?"

4-The whole scene on Varney

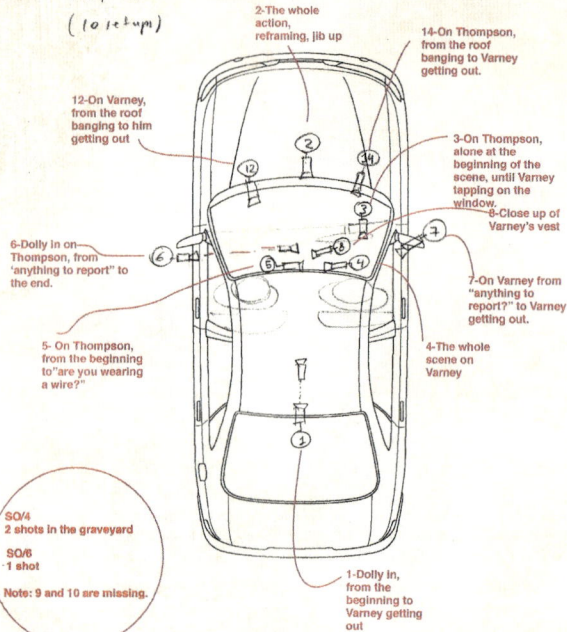

SO/4
2 shots in the graveyard

SO/6
1 shot

Note: 9 and 10 are missing.

1-Dolly in, from the beginning to Varney getting out

26
DAY 26
SO/9 pt2
and
SO/11
(6 setups)

STATIC (MODULAR) CAR IN GRAVEYARD

Right diagram labels:

33-Close up of Thompson

18-Close up of the wipers

14-On Thompson from getting the dagger until turning on the wipers

31-Dobby coming in.

32-On Varney from Dobson scratching on the window then becomes Thompson's

15-Dolly in to the car door.

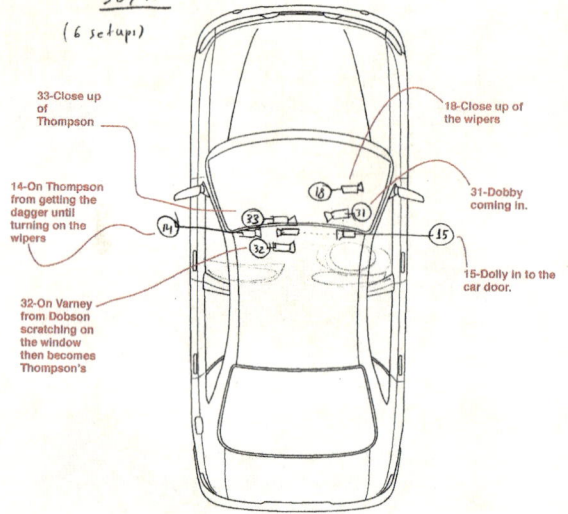

Thompson: You're a special constable, which basically means you're the Bez to my Shaun Ryder.

ABOVE: Detailed shooting plans drawn up by production designer Amy Maguire and director Guillem Morales show the different angles for filming in and around the car.

another bold move, Reece's character is named after the first fictional vampire who, predating Bram Stoker's *Dracula*, appeared in a series of Victorian-era serialised horror stories known as Penny Dreadfuls. 'You've just got to hold your nerve and hope no one's mind is in *that* zone. And we're in a graveyard. It's going to be spooky. But we thought that the audience will think it's more to do with the mystery of digging up the body. It's quite an oblique thing that's happened to his partner. He's taken it that some people have desecrated his grave. But it's not that. He's come back and crept out.'

'The thing we were really nervous about is Reece's line, "Can you let me in?"' recalls Steve. 'Because that's quite well-known vampire lore. You've got to be invited in. But he's holding two coffees and it's, "Can you open the door, please?"'

Somewhat annoyingly, their old pal Mark Gatiss had co-written a three-part version of *Dracula* which had aired on the BBC just before series five went out. 'And so everyone was up to speed with all the tropes,' suggests Reece. 'Despite the fact we filmed this a year before that. But we were hopeful people's minds wouldn't run to it.'

In fact, 'The Stakeout' is chock-full of vampire lore. In addition to the 'may I come in' gag and Varney's name, at one point they drive away from the cemetery towards the docks, and Varney redirects the car so they don't travel across running water. Varney also throws out Thompson's Indian takeaway, because garlic is an ingredient of chicken tikka. 'If it was garlic bread, it might have tipped the wink,' says Reece. 'It's hiding that stuff in things you think we put in because it's funny. Like Bill Oddie and bats. You laugh, and don't realise we've smuggled information in.' And then there's the title which, of course, has two very different meanings, one of which is vampire-related. 'The brilliant thing about vampires is the rules are all conflicting and different,' says Steve. 'Some can walk among hallowed ground, some of them can't, some can turn into bats, some can't, some use telepathy, some can't. So we thought we can pick and choose whichever we want.'

Some people questioned why Varney spends three nights in the car with Thompson before he kills. 'We explain that he's bored, he's been alive for centuries. He's literally playing with his food. He could kill him on the first night, but then you haven't got an episode,' says Reece.

'Plus, he knows he has to wait until the resurrected Dobson is ready to feed,' says Steve.

The episode unfolds at a deliberately slow pace, with the pair engaging in a series of word games to give the sense of boredom you have on a stakeout. 'We played long takes and took our time, but we ended up having to cut a lot out,' says Steve. It also answers that age-old question of how do people use the loo while on a stakeout? The answer being an empty tube of Pringles. 'That's not based on anecdotal evidence or anything, but it would be, I imagine, pretty watertight.'

League devotees might have recognised a familiar refrain, spoken by Thompson, when he's discussing the graveyard vandalism. 'Probably just Goths. They come over from Leeds.'

'We were thinking about the Gothic nature of what we were doing and that line pinged into our heads,' says Steve. 'A few people spotted it. Little crossovers like that are really there for the fans.'

When it came to picking a director for 'The Stakeout', there was really one choice: Guillem Morales. 'Originally, we'd been looking for someone to do the musical episode, but when it became "The Stakeout", it was his,' says Tandy. 'He might've had to have his arm twisted, but once he'd read the script, he was in.'

The script originally had the police car outside the graveyard. Morales suggested it would be better if it was inside. 'They're on a stakeout, so that means they don't have any lights in the car,' explains Morales. 'We could have a light, but it would be wrong. So the light has to come from outside. Which means the episode is going to be richer if we see through the windows into the cemetery. And I wanted a very nice cemetery.'

'It was a great decision,' says Steve, 'because Guillem's vision is filmic. I think the TV version would have been us two, sitting in there, playing a game, squabbling. He added a rich, visual dimension which we hadn't imagined at all.'

"THE STAKEOUT" latest draft (16/01/19)   22.

VARNEY
Trope number five, tick.

They stare out of the window.

VARNEY (CONT'D)
So, anything to report?

THOMPSON shakes his head.

VARNEY (CONT'D)
I thought I saw someone by the car as I came round the corner?

THOMPSON
I didn't see anyone.

VARNEY
Probably just a trick of the light. I hope you don't mind but I looked at your case notes. You were the last person to see Dobby alive?

THOMPSON
Yeah. I was only gone a few minutes.

VARNEY
How awful. He must have thought the world of you.

THOMPSON
I don't know. We never talked about our feelings, the way you do. It was just banter you know. I did love him though.

VARNEY
You said his grave was vandalised?

THOMPSON
Yeah. They dug it up, took the lid off. It was horrible.

VARNEY
Do you think whoever did it was looking for something?

THOMPSON
God knows. It doesn't make sense.

VARNEY
I believe the murder weapon went missing from Forensics?

THOMPSON
Did it?

ABOVE: A script for the episode annotated by producer Adam Tandy.

Alas, the downside of seeing outside the car was cost. And so an episode that had been written to be cheap ended up requiring a massive lighting set-up. 'That became a very expensive proposition for the lighting department,' says Reece. 'Suddenly they had this big expense we'd never considered. I don't think we thought about how it would be lit.'

'It was a huge undertaking,' says Tandy. 'It took us a day and a half just to get the cables into position together with the cherry pickers and these big light panels which you stick up in the air. But we couldn't get everything we wanted – they were in such demand – so we ended up with a lot of standing lights with a lot of electricians behind them.'

'The challenge with this was I wanted to do the darkest episode ever,' says Morales. And so he and director of photography Mattias Nyberg (*Detectorists*) used the Sony Venice camera, which has a special night-time sensor. 'Mattias did wonderful, wonderful work. And it's *really* dark. I mean, you can't go darker in TV than that.'

Adding to the cost of the episode was the fact Morales needed more than one police car to get all the angles he was after, including the opening and closing overhead shots, looking down on Varney. 'The design department and Guillem worked out they needed three cars in the same way we needed two tables for "The Bill". One that moved, two that didn't, and could be taken apart,' says Tandy. 'I couldn't afford three. We ended up with two, and then, last of all, we sent one to have its roof cut off so we could get the shot of Varney in the back seat. We had some scenes in a moving car, but most of the time we are in a carcass which we cut open, took off the doors, and popped out the windscreen.'

Varney starts the episode with pale skin, and his complexion gets lighter and lighter as the nights go by, until he's ready to feed on Thompson. The effect needed to be subtle, so as not to be obvious, and was achieved by a combination of make-up and tweaking the grade in post-production. When Varney was ready to finally feed, Morales was determined it be memorable, with the camera lingering on the bloodsucking which we see both directly and via the rearview mirror (with Shearsmith absent, as vampires don't cast reflections). 'Guillem said, "We'll go, via the mirror, to him feeding and he's not there, but we see the pulsing chewing of the neck happening." I thought, brilliant. I've never seen that before. And he wanted that shot of me feeding on his neck to last longer than you would normally expect. It seemed to go on and on,' recalls Reece, who had blood in his mouth which he spewed on cue. 'And I was like, "Can we cut?"'

Come the editing, Shearsmith was still unsure how long the shot should last. 'He was like, "Is this too long or is it just me?"' laughs Morales. 'That was quite an achievement, to make Reece uncomfortable.' Pemberton was less concerned. 'Because you withheld all your vampirism, you want to make the most of it when it comes in,' says Steve.

To play the undead Dobson, Morales insisted on casting creature performer and mime artist Malik Ibheis. 'The line producer said, "Let's get an extra in." And I said, "No. He's a vampire. We need someone special." He doesn't have a line, but that doesn't mean he doesn't have to act. He is a creature, coming from the grave, and is starving.'

'The Stakeout' is that rare episode where the

location moves. 'It was exciting to do the bit when we drive around,' says Reece, 'it was a *No. 9* where the world was going by, not just in some bloody house.'

In the end, it proved to be another fine vehicle for the boys' talents and the only episode in series five that was, more or less, just the two of them. 'I think we underestimate that people like seeing us interacting, so it was good to have another one of those,' says Reece.

'We didn't rehearse it as such,' says Steve, 'but we know each other so well, obviously, there's an unspoken comfort. And I think that comes across, even in the car. You feel at ease with these characters.'

In fact, Tandy liked 'The Stakeout' so much he wanted to kick off the series with it, but the boys disagreed. 'We felt it was quite low key. Whereas something like "The Referee's a W***er" has real pace and energy and more overt humour. And you've got a bigger cast,' says Steve.

As it was, 'The Stakeout' continued the tradition of finishing each series with a horror episode.

'That was never by design,' says Reece.

'But it does feel like a good ending,' muses Steve. 'And it got a great response.'

Ever since series one, the boys and Tandy have previewed two episodes at the BFI in London, followed by a Q&A. For series five they opted to show 'The Referee's a W***er' and 'The Stakeout'. Rather pleasingly, when it came to Varney's vampiric reveal, the audience hadn't guessed the twist. 'Everyone was slightly open-jawed,' notes Tandy. 'And they were all going, "How did we not see it?" At the Q&A afterwards I said, "It's even there in the title." And there was this groan from the audience that this thing had been in plain view since they bought the tickets, and they still hadn't guessed it was a vampire thing. So I think we covered our tracks pretty well.'

'It was fantastic,' recalls Steve. 'There was a big gasp. It was really satisfying.'

ABOVE: The vampiric DC Dobson (Malik Ibheis).

Acknowledgements

First and foremost, I would like to thank Reece Shearsmith and Steve Pemberton, for not only creating one of the greatest TV shows ever made, but for entrusting me with the telling of its many secrets. For two hugely creative, super talented people, you're remarkably humble and down to earth, and so getting to spend time in your delightful company, talking about a TV show I love, was a pleasure that could hardly be called work.

To Caroline Chigwell, aka the incomparable Chiggy, who was instrumental in helping put this book together, who found it a home, and who behaved like a mensch throughout – I will be forever in your debt.

To the fabulous team at Hodder Studio, Myfanwy Moore, Izzy Everington and Tara O'Sullivan, and to the wider *Inside No. 9* team, Alice Morley, Steven Cooper, Sarah Clay, Aaron Munday, Will Speed and Claudette Morris. Your enthusiasm and belief in this project from day one has been both infectious and greatly appreciated.

To Martin Stiff of Amazing15 who, once again, has taken my words and set them in a wondrous piece of design, you rock.

To Adam Tandy, producer extraordinaire, who went above and beyond to help this book be as good as it possibly could be, I salute you.

Massive thanks to everyone else who contributed their time, stories and memories to this book. You're listed at the front, but your names are worth repeating here: David Kerr, Guillem Morales, Dan Zeff, Jim O'Hanlon, Matt Lipsey, Graeme Harper, Yves Barre, Simon Rogers, Christian Henson and Amy Maguire.

And finally, my heartfelt appreciation to Laura, Milo and my mum, for their endless love, support and understanding, without which this book wouldn't be what it is. Nor, indeed, would I.

£20

£20

Couchette #9

9A	9D
9B	9E
9C	9F

35°C